Colored Threads ...

(Memoir of an Adoptee)

Forward

This is my story. I don't know who my target audience is, a cardinal sin for any writer. At first, I thought it would be good for my children to have this as a reference, but then I considered other adoptees of a similar age might also relate to my story in any number of very personal ways. Shortly thereafter it occurred to me perhaps even law makers or elected officials might gain some insight which could prove beneficial to their adopted constituents. Staff at some adoption agencies need a better appreciation for the information they guard, so might they learn something from this as well? I know many laws are in the process of changing. Many have already changed, but some are retroactive only to a specific or often arbitrary date. If we realize the need for open records, why do we only do this for some and not all adoptees? Who is it that grants rights to a specific group, and excludes the rest? And for what reason? What is the justification? Are we not all equal?

My target audience may yet to be defined, but my guess is it is larger than I first envisioned. I hope you read this with an open mind and heart. This is about a human being who came into this world the same way you did. I was born. How I came to be is likely different than you and what happened next is certainly not the norm, but I know numbers of others who have followed the same or a similar path. There are many emotional stories thoroughly documented that rip at your heart or fuel anger and outrage. The film documentary **Three Identical Strangers** comes to mind as does the **Hicks Babies**. How much callous experimentation, theft, and abuse existed by highly accredited agencies, respected people of lofty social stature, and unscrupulous doctors, will never fully be known. This is not one of those stories. It is more in the vein of **Long, Lost Family**, a television show sponsored by Ancestry, where they help reunite families separated by adoption or abandonment. It might involve an adult child looking for parents or a parent looking for a child. There were siblings looking for a long-lost brother or sister too. I could never watch that show for more than a few minutes before I'd have to leave the room. My wife would always ask me to stay, but I knew the nervous and shaking adoptee reuniting with his or her mom or dad or a sibling would *never* be me. Now I watch and the tears freely flow as I empathize knowing firsthand what they are feeling at their core. You have to live it, to fully appreciate this powerfully emotional feeling.

My journey has taught me a lot about myself. I suppressed feelings and emotions for most of my life and was pretty good at it. I compartmentalized anything that caused me emotional discomfort or made me feel insecure. I used comedy to neatly deflect conversations I found the slightest bit uncomfortable. I also realized the ability to engage others in laughter gave me an enormous sense of satisfaction. It provided me a place and a space to be someone other than me. I didn't talk to others much about being adopted because there was no common ground to be shared, and there would be no answers to their most basic and obvious of questions. What is your nationality? I was clueless. Family medical history? How many times over the years did I shrug my shoulders and say, "I don't know; I was adopted." There were times when an innocent observation would simply hit me in a way that caused me stress.... "Gee, you look like your mother." They obviously don't know my situation ... and are obviously not looking hard enough, or are they just making casual conversation, or I don't know… I wasn't related in any way to who they were comparing me with.

Before I get too far ahead of myself, I need to establish a starting point. Looking back at a beginning seventy years after the fact, can be an arduous task. To even contemplate what came *before* my beginning lays bare countless possibilities and speculation (which I have fully entertained all of my life). When we couple those possibilities with logic and whatever "facts" are available, a picture, fuzzy as it may be, emerges in subtle tones and shades. The gaps in the timeline, voids of content or evidence, can keep you awake at night. Speculation, unlike fact, opens the door to endless second guessing. Everybody has a story. We are all different, thus by definition, unique. Each story has a beginning, a middle and an end. Mine has multiple "beginnings," a middle, and an end that has yet to be written. This is my attempt to assemble what I know into a cohesive string of events.

A timeline is a constant, and this chronology is a mix of research and recollection (I saved calendars from 1971 on). Hopefully, any speculation will be obvious. There are also omissions that may never come to light. I have some answers, but those gaps are what keeps me hungrily looking for more. As DNA technology improves exponentially, we also lose the most valuable of resources, human resources. People get old and pass away taking their knowledge of the now distant past and their unique perspective along with them. Documentation, if any, they possess is often meaningless to anyone other than the author or keeper and can easily be discarded as mere trash. Have you ever cleaned out a lifetime of memories for a deceased person? If it was a loved one, you may recall the significance of a photo or a letter. Other items may surprise you with some obscure reference to an event or place or person you didn't know about. Others may seem out of place entirely. This personal collection tells a life story if you are clever enough to decipher the clues and connect the dots. Items saved were cherished for a reason and had meaning.

This book is about a timeline. My timeline, intertwined with others as I reconstruct my origin to answer that very essential question, "Who am I?" It is the pursuit of my identity, my *self* … where did I come from? The time of my birth represents a different world and culture to what we have today. Times have certainly changed.

Setting

1953:

- Dwight D. Eisenhower was our president.
- Joseph Stalin ended his leadership of the Soviet Union.
- Unemployment was at 3.0%.
- Dark Star won the Kentucky Derby.
- TV guide and Playboy hit the newsstands for the first time.
- The War of the Worlds appeared in theaters across the country.
- The Chevrolet Corvette was introduced to the masses.
- Edmund Hillary reached the summit of Everest.
- Dr. Jonas Salk went on CBS radio to announce his vaccine for polio.
- Crick and Watson declared their discovery of the DNA structure.
- The world population was well under 3 billion and the USA fraction came in at a mere 160 million.
- Approximately 4 million babies were born in the USA that year, almost double the population of Connecticut.

It was a far simpler time with far fewer distractions. No cellphones or computers vying for or demanding your attention. Broadcast television consisted of three major networks plus an "educational" channel, and none of those aired around the clock (remember black and white test patterns and the sound of static?). AM radio was where you listened to music. Vinyl records played at 33, 45, or 78 rpm on your record player (or "vic" as my dad would say. Short for "Victrola" as in RCA Victor … the dog listening in front of a megaphone with his head cocked to one side). Jukeboxes, pinball machines, soda fountains were ever present. Baseball cards were attached to bike frames enabling them to loudly slap against the spokes to imitate the sound of a motor. Penny candy cost a penny back then. In a real way it was akin to Normal Rockwell's take on life in America.

Problems back then were hidden rather than discussed openly as they are today. For a teenage girl or young woman who found herself "in trouble," it was especially difficult. There was shame associated with pregnancy outside of marriage. These girls were looked down upon by society. They often moved away from home before they began "showing," and their obvious absence in the neighborhood became the source of nasty gossip and unsubstantiated rumor. They were not merely embarrassed, they were stigmatized.

BIRTH AND ADOPTION

Hartford, Connecticut, Friday February 27, 1953. It was unseasonably mild and had been so for several days. For most people it was an ordinary day, the end of a long work week. But for one unwed twenty-one-year-old woman, it marked the conclusion of her lonely pregnancy. Her parents may have been present in the hospital with her on this day, but there is no record of this anywhere. Maybe they arrived after she gave birth or as soon as they got out of work… I hope she was not completely alone at this critical time. I wonder what was going through her mind in the final days leading up to my birth.

Her decision to place me for adoption had already been made, but were there any regrets? Did she ponder what the future might be like if she kept me? Did she consider the feelings of my father? Was she sure exactly who the father was? Did she recall the moment of conception? Was it all worth it? Maybe these thoughts flooded her mind between contractions, or maybe she simply blocked everything out… I'll never know the answer. All I do know is **Dr. Robert Bunce delivered an infant boy, smallish in size at 6 pounds/15 ounces, but otherwise unremarkable** on this day at an unknown time in Hartford Hospital. The name on the medical chart and ID tag read "Martin Clarke Decker." This would later be altered in such a way as to safeguard any connection between my biological mother and me. This collusion was in motion long before I took my first tiny breath on my own. My mother was "protected" from others learning the secret that she brought a child into this world by the laws of the state of Connecticut. Like everyone else who was adopted, I had no legal recourse … no rights under the law to learn what others take for granted.

The only clue I would cling to so many years later was my birth name.

Married couples spend hours discussing the name for each child before he or she is born. I have always wondered what the significance of my birth name is. To me it was an inkling or a map as to my origin. I sincerely believe my mother spoke to me in some way with that name. Martin... Clarke...Decker. "Decker" is the easy part to decipher, my mother's surname. I am a "Decker" for certain, but which Decker family was I a part of? Decker is a common name.

"Martin" on the other hand is tougher to figure out. Why "Martin"? Who in her life was worth naming a child after? By all accounts my mother, Joyce Louise Decker had an active social life. She was an honor roll student all through school and contributed to the high school paper. She made contributions to the school yearbook too. The local newspaper in Dalton provides a wealth of articles referencing her activities in dances, sports, and various church affairs. The musical director for the church was named Margaret R. Martin. She lived on Central Ave in Dalton, MA just a block away from the Decker residence. It doesn't seem much of a stretch to say my mother and Margaret saw each other often. There is a good chance I was named after Margaret Martin. There is another theory based on my mother's love for the written word. Among others, Joyce had a penchant for Charles Dickens. The Life and Adventures of Martin Chuzzlewit may hold sway as to why I was named "Martin." I have not read the story yet but from what I have gathered, Martin was cast out of his grandfather's home because he fell in love with the orphaned girl who was living with his grandfather as his companion. Was I cast out of my grandfather's home too? Was my mother subtly telling me something with my name? Maybe my mother wanted to keep me, and it was my grandfather who actually made the decision to have me placed for adoption.

"Clarke" is a real pickle. There was a "Steven Clarke" who lived a few blocks from my mother in Dalton. He was older and worked with my grandfather at Crane in town. Did she babysit for his kids? Did she admire him? Did she wish he was my father? Did they have an affair? Did she believe he was in fact my father? There is no way to answer that. "Clarke" spelled with an "e" at the end, sure looks like a last name to me as does everyone else who has ever puzzled through this.

My original birth certificate (which took *decades* to obtain) listed my mother's address as 319 Barbour Street in Hartford, CT (only a twelve-minute drive to the hospital). This was a home for unwed mothers run by the Woman's Aid Society, and the only Protestant Home for "girls in trouble" in the state. I don't know how long she lived there or what friends she may have made. I can only imagine how difficult it must have been for her. She left her home and family for a shelter of like women and girls. She had very little personal time and minimal opportunities for visitors, though the idea of visitors other than her parents seems farfetched. Such a lonely environment for someone literally full of unborn life with the intent on giving it away the moment the time came.

Though there was no plan for her to keep me, my life obviously meant something, and I am grateful an abortion, illegal at this time, was not considered a viable option. I was not simply a "thing" to be discarded. I can only imagine the emotional toll she paid bringing a child to term and then letting him go without ever learning of his fate. Was it her decision to make or her parents? Would this new life truly be better than the one she could offer? Did my mother ever hold me? After all that time in the womb, did she even see me, or was that too emotionally painful? I'll never know the answers to these questions either.

The March 3rd edition of the Hartford Courant listed the local births for February 27th…. I was not there. There was no listing in the local Massachusetts paper (the Berkshire Eagle) covering my mother's hometown either. Only a very few people knew about me, and they all pledged to keep the matter a secret...forever. My birth certificate was filed away at the Bureau of Vital Statistics and would require amending at some point. Ultimately, I was turned over to the adoption agency and placed in a foster home. Baby Martin was separated from his mother, had no identity and all of this was by careful design. A legal conspiracy of deception was entered into with no regard for the questions likely to come years later. This "necessary" action was based on "protecting" the identity of my mother and by extension, her family. My right to know anything was not a consideration.

The agency now became my guardian, my temporary protector, until such time as a suitable couple could be scrutinized and ultimately granted legal custody of me. What was that process like? My mother needed no unusual screening to have me and if she chose to keep me, there was no one there to say she was unsuitable, unless she did something wrong that drew the attention of the law or some other organization. I suppose I was added to a list and compared to others by prospective couples looking for that "special child" they could love and call theirs. How many deserving couples got a look at me I wonder? How many said, "No, not that one." Was it like the vegetable or fruit aisle at a grocery store or perhaps the local animal shelter for selection of a stray?

*And the **babies** lie there in a pile*

*And the **adults** they come **after awhile***

*And they **always** pass by*

*All the **babies** that cry*

*And take only **babies** that smile-smile*

*They take only **babies** that smile...*

*Even **triplets** and **twins** if they'll smile*

.... Paul Kantner

Unnamed foster parents, in an unidentified foster home, raised me for several months knowing they would give me up when suitable adoptive parents were found. Who were these wonderful people who took guardianship of me after I was born? They have my sincere thanks for caring about me when no one else did.

Eventually in mid-June, a young couple married two years prior, who could not conceive on their own, was given the nod to be my adoptive parents. Dad (Monty) was 26 years old and Mom (Nancy), 22. A house with a child is a happier place and this new family bonded. A short time later in July the adoption was finalized; Daniel Reed Stedfast was now ."born," and that original birth certificate was then amended and refiled where no one was likely to ever see it again. A new birth certificate was made public for Daniel and would be readily available with a simple request.

My dad was a salesman for the family business located in Boston, and my mother, a nurse. Good professions, stable and secure. Just the kind of credentials you would want for a worthy couple looking to raise an infant child. We lived in Avon, not far from where I was born.

I've seen a few Polaroids from when I was a baby and by all accounts I was in a good home with loving parents, and I wanted for absolutely nothing. I was well dressed in clean new clothes, with my hair combed and I always appeared smiling. I remember the sound of my mother's voice reading me a bedtime story. I vaguely recall turning the pages... a very normal memory, not unlike millions of other adoptees who share something similar. I remember a little of one of the stories ... something about a baby ... a special baby... chosen

... adopted... loved. I didn't know anyone else who was read that story. I thought it was about me. I was special, chosen, adopted, and loved. The story was "The Chosen Baby" by Valentina P. Wasson. I really was different but didn't realize it quite yet.

We had a family dog too. Brandy was a boxer, and she had a litter of puppies in my playpen after I outgrew it. I loved that dog; she was my buddy. In 1955 my parents adopted twin girls; their birthday was exactly one week after mine. The family was growing. The fact that I and my sisters were adopted, was never kept from any of us.

AVON

My earliest memories were from our first home in Avon, CT. I think it was a ranch style, but I could be wrong. We had a front yard and a short driveway with a garage. My dad had a boat on a trailer alongside the house. I recall a flood where we piled into his boat then floated about our neighborhood. How much of this is actual memory or simply "remembering" what I'd heard, can't be separated. I do vividly recall losing a game of "king of the mountain" to a little neighbor girl who clocked me good with the corner of a metal snow shovel as I approached the "summit" of the dirt hill in the back of our house. It left a small gash close to my left eye requiring a few stitches to close.

I also remember a picnic table in our backyard with the benches flipped upside down on the tabletop, probably in preparation for winter. I was walking the center line between the bench legs when my foot found its way into a knothole on one of the bench seats. I lost my balance and fell to the ground with the bench coming down on top of me, knocking the wind from my lungs.

The twins brought an interesting dynamic to the family. They communicated with each other using a language all their own. They seemed to understand what *we* said, but responded with sounds that made no sense to anyone else except me. Somehow I knew what they were saying and was able to translate for my parents. I didn't speak their language, but I could figure it out.

Once I felt sure a bee was after me. I ran into the house screaming, "Bee! Bee!." My dad tried to convince me there was no bee as I ran around in a circle in our living room. He rolled up a newspaper or magazine then smacked it against his other palm. Crack! "I got it!" he said, and I stopped running. Psychology in action!

These are just random memory bits like everyone else has. They have no special meaning or purpose, they just are, and loosely bind you to a place and point in time. My earliest memories.

WAYLAND

The family moved north to the neighboring state of Massachusetts where we had a new home in the small town of Wayland. This would be an easier commute for my father to his office in Boston located on Deerfield Street under the iconic Citco sign in Kenmore Square. This house was bigger, having a second floor, and bordered on a network of wide bridal paths stretching for miles into the abutting dense woods. So much more room for me to explore.

The neighborhood had several kids my age. We rode bikes in the street and went sledding down a hill on that same street when winter came. There wasn't a lot of traffic. I remember Dad tying a rope to the frame of my flexible flier, the other end secured to the bumper of the family station wagon, then towing me around behind. Great fun! I always loved being outside in the winter.

Christmas time meant decorations and my dad took a back seat to no one. He made a huge star out of a sheet of plywood, wired it with lamp sockets and white light bulbs, then attached it to the top of our chimney. I remember it gave off a lot of heat. Guywires descended from the lofty star above the house to the stonewall marking the front border of our yard nearest the street. These were strung with more lights to look like bright rays. It was beautiful and lit up the darkest of winter nights.

It was in this house I recall celebrating a second birthday in July, commemorating my adoption. I don't know how many second birthdays we celebrated there, but I thought they were pretty cool. I didn't know anyone else who had a second birthday. I felt special yet different at the same time. I don't recall a second birthday for the twins and eventually mine was no longer celebrated.

My bedroom was on the top floor of the house and overlooked our backyard. Through my room was the entrance to the attic. I think there was a squirrel living there as sometimes I heard strange noises at night from the other side of the door. These are the sounds that stir the imagination of any young boy. I would lay there listening for the slightest sound and wondered what creature might be lurking just on the other side of the door only a few feet from my bed.

I had a Kenner Girder and Panel building set- actually two sets (a neighbor moved, and they gave us/me the second set). The floor in my bedroom was transformed into a city, with many city blocks clearly defined by the "roads" in between. I had to be reminded to leave a path to my bed and the attic door. I just loved to build things and would keep going until I ran out of materials. Often, I would improvise by stacking books to make additional "buildings."

I remember a night so bright with moonlight I could see the entire backyard from my window…swings and jungle gym … tables and chairs, stone wall, trees etc. I told my dad the next morning the sun was out all night. He tried to explain it was just moonlight I saw; I was disappointed he didn't believe my version.

We had our share of drama at that house too. My sister Jenny fell off her tricycle onto a piece of jagged glass lying on the sandy shoulder of the road near the end of our driveway …. Blood poured out of her face from between her eyes with each pulse of her heart. I rode my bike as fast as I could to summon help. It took 40 plus stitches to close the gash. What a bloody mess!

Our parents planned an outdoor party. Sister Judy drank most of a pitcher of Manhattans just before we all sat down at the table. She flopped forward and passed out. It took a moment before anyone realized what she had done. She was rushed to the hospital and had her stomach pumped. Did they really taste *that* good?

Was I really so different than other kids? We all loved to play the same games. We all ran around the yard or rode bikes in the street. We built forts and played in the stream. We went to school and sat in the same rooms, listened to the teacher, and played outside at recess ... kickball! I loved kickball. We were all the same... well, except for one kid. His skin was dark and his hair, curly ... I think his name was Skippy. Some of the kids called him names and even threw stones at him, just because he was different. I remember telling them to stop and suddenly they were yelling things at me, and a couple of stones were tossed in my direction. I don't remember that happening again and I don't recall seeing Skippy after that either. I was totally confused by the whole thing. I had no concept of race, but it seemed my peers did.

There was a morning unlike any other in my young life. I woke but knew something was wrong with me. I couldn't put weight on my leg (don't recall which one). I struggled down the stairs keeping my weight off it but knew at the bottom it was as far as I could go. I couldn't cross the kitchen to the breakfast table. My adopted mother wanted me to hurry up and I explained my dilemma to deaf ears. She told me to stop fooling around and eat my breakfast. I took one step away from the supporting wall and instantly fell to the floor in a heap.

I ended up in traction at Boston's Children's Hospital for weeks. I didn't like it there. I saw a kid come in on a gurney, burned from head to toe. I saw his blackened and raw flesh with bits of gauze stuck to it. He screamed from his room, and it terrified me, then he stopped, and I have no idea why. Another kid would come up to my bed (which had bars like a crib) and teased me when no one else was around. I was tied down with straps and couldn't do much. I told my dad I wanted to poke him in the face, and he said if I saw an opportunity to go ahead and let him have it! I held a cup by the handle under my covers and waited until the next time he put his face up to the bars. I popped him with the mug, a clean hard shot to his nose. He cried but left me alone after that.

After weeks in traction, I returned home to my yard and friends. We played in the woods, collected tadpoles from the pond and played in the brook that snaked its way between the houses and under the road. Things returned to normal. My dad uncovered a nest of snakes living in a stone wall in the backyard (he hated snakes). It was the first time I ever saw him afraid of anything.

I heard my mother (Nancy) used to have a snake as a pet and would take it with her while performing tricks on a plywood disk towed behind a powerboat. It always sounded like a circus act to me, and I've never seen a picture to validate the story, but I did see her ride the disk without the snake. It was white with a large blue star in the center and either small red or blue diamonds or stars around the outer edge. My dad was a great water-skier, slalom. He had a Correct-Craft for our family's boat, and we used it on Sebago Lake in Maine and Winnipesaukee in New Hampshire. He loved that boat and so did I.

My toddler cousin Michael Covin got lost in the woods behind our house with his little beagle named Sally. We, along with our neighbors, went out looking for him without any sign. We were out of ideas and about to call the police when suddenly Michael appeared in the backyard safe and sound. We have no idea where he went or how he found his way back.

FAMILY VACATIONS

Our family camping trip on Lake Winnipesaukee was an adventure and probably the reason we never did much of it again. My dog and best buddy Brandy had passed away. We now had two large German Shepherds, three kids, and a huge pile of camping gear. Our campsite was on an island – two trips in the boat were required to get our stuff out there. After we were all set up and had dinner, my mother wanted to cool off with a moonlight swim in the lake. She was just off our little beach in knee deep water when she cut her rear end on a sharp piece of glass. We tied the dogs up to a tree, piled into the boat then headed back to shore.

My mom's dad (Bumpo) was a doctor (druggist), and he stitched her buttock up at the local hospital or clinic. We stayed at his house in one of the cottages he rented out that night. In the morning, Dad and I returned to check on the dogs and load everything back in the boat. I think we stayed with Nana and Bumpo for the rest of that vacation, so much for camping.

I was close to my mother's adopted brother Donny. He had recently moved out of the house but had not shared where he was living with the family. He took me to his apartment though. He was the coolest guy I knew. He played guitar and read Mad Magazine. I enjoyed every minute with him. He was an artist and loved to sketch. Sometime later, he joined the Air Force as an MP and gave me a military cap decorated with his artwork and a letter explaining why he joined. I kept that letter with me for years in my wallet until it was stolen (but that's another story). My uncle Donny was eventually killed by a drunk driver shortly after the birth of his daughter. I never met his wife or my cousin.

Bumpo loved the game of golf and decided to teach me how to swing a club in the backyard while we visited. He went over the grip and the stance and the point of contact, etc. before he let me have my first crack at it. He told me to aim for an aluminum pole that was at the center of a revolving clothesline. I loudly rang the ball squarely off the pole on my first swing... Bumpo was delighted beyond belief and told his golf buddies to meet us the next day on the course; he just had to show me off.....different day, different outcome. I couldn't hit the ball to save my life. He was so embarrassed, we left very early. I still see him in my mind's eye, sitting in a green leather chair watching golf on television.... Boring.

My dad's parents were very different than my mom's. Their house in Maine was huge. A total of seven buildings were spread out over their property. A short walk outside brought you to what the previous owners called the "servants' quarters" and a laundry. There were no servants living there while my grandparents owned it. A little farther down the gently sloped gravel driveway was the garage. There were several stalls inside and in one was an old woody-wagon. I heard stories of my dad driving it from the back seat while poking the gas pedal with the end of a broomstick. My Grandmother drove a Cadillac usually, but once in a while she would take me into town in the woody. A really cool old car.

At the bottom of the driveway was a workshop heated by a potbellied stove when it was cold out. It was full of tools and lumber stored under long wooden workbenches. Much of the scrap from various projects was used as firewood for the stove. I loved playing with the odd shapes of scrap wood and would build things like "bug traps" or mazes.

Attached to the far end of the shop was "Honeymoon Cottage." I don't know how it got its name, but when we had a large enough family get together, someone would usually occupy it. Across from the grass tennis courts and flower garden was the "Folly." It was a concrete foundation right on the lake with changing rooms for swimmers. There was a small beach at the bottom of the stairs. We had a wooden dock attached to the Folly, making it easy to pick up or drop off passengers and gear. The boat was stored in a separate covered building down past Honeymoon Cottage. The boathouse was very interesting to me as a child … kind of dark and cool on a hot day. The waves made a strange echo sound inside.

Sebago was a very clean lake with lots of sandy bottom. My dad loved to run the boat or waterski behind it. When he was younger, he had an amphibious plane, and from what I've heard from my aunt and others, he used to shear the tops of pine trees off with the crossbar connecting the pontoons. The first fish I ever caught (a trout) was on that lake, with my grandfather. I learned to skip flat stones there and was pretty good at it too.

In anticipation of an upcoming trip to the lake I spent a month building a battery-operated plastic submarine. This thing was awesome. The fins were adjustable and could be programmed to allow the sub to dive for a period then swivel to allow it to return to the surface. I couldn't wait to try it out on the lake! When the day came for the maiden voyage, I was very excited. It was a beautiful day. If I wore a life jacket, I was allowed to swim far away from the dock on my own. I set the fins to cycle and switched on the motor and watched my sub cruise along the surface with me swimming alongside. It went into its first dive, and I watched it with open eyes underwater. It rose to the surface again before initiating another dive. It was so cool watching it go through these maneuvers. What I failed to notice was the sub was spending less time on the surface each time it rose. Eventually it wouldn't reach the surface before the fins shifted back into dive mode. By then it was too late for me to do anything. I couldn't dive for it myself because of the lifejacket I had on. I watched it slowly drift away and out of sight into the depths of the lake. I was one sad little guy!

I loved the house in Sebago. All the neighbors had pointed wooden signs like arrows nailed to trees with their surnames painted on. There was a network of intersecting gravel roads where these signs steered you to where everyone lived. The grounds around the house had apple trees and blueberries (pies and pancakes to me) and blackberry bushes. I used to pick blackberries for my grandfather. He would eat them by the bowlful with cream and sugar.

A path through the woods took me to Mrs. Spaulding's house... Dorothy Spaulding was a good friend of my grandmother. She had suffered a stroke which left her partially paralyzed. I would visit her in this magnificent house, which seemed more of a museum than a place to live. She had an eclectic collection of unusual things from around the world everywhere you looked. My imagination would soar with each visit. There was a suit of armor, an elephant's foot hollowed out and stuffed with umbrellas and canes, a large black bird in a cage, rugs and paintings, and all kinds of mementos and memorabilia. I felt so sad for Mrs. Spaulding as she was always in bed whenever I saw her. She couldn't speak well and certainly couldn't appreciate her wondrous collection of things anymore. The people who took care of her always seemed happy when I showed up for a visit.

My grandmother loved flowers and had a huge garden that ran parallel to the lake and tennis court. She loved to tend and cut gladiolus (glads) to bring in the house and set on tables. Outside the porch were other flowers and tiny hummingbird feeders mixed in between. My grandmother told me to keep my finger close to the feeder and if I was patient enough, a hummingbird would eventually land on it. She was right! I would lay down for what seemed an eternity, then watch in amazement when a tiny bird perched on my finger to feed from the small tubular feeder. The porch was enormous and wrapped around two sides of the house facing the lake, and was completely screened in. My grandfather had electric awnings on the outside to keep the dew and rain off the furniture. I loved watching them rise one after the other in the morning. We often ate breakfast out there.

The main room of the house was huge and paneled with natural wood. A massive bull moose head adorned the wall above my grandfather's desk. There was a grand fireplace and mantle on the opposite side of the room with wooden sitting benches to each side. These benches held all kinds of treasures in the storage areas under the seats. Board games, puzzles, paddleball sets, balsa wood planes, yoyos, gyroscopes, tops, a wooden labyrinth game, decks of cards and several other toys and items I've surely forgotten. I loved every minute of my time at that house and always looked forward to going there.

A LITTLE MORE DRAMA PLEASE...

My childhood was good with vivid memories of happy family times. Sprinkle in a little drama for spice and you have what I think of as normal family life. I mentioned drama, right? In a case of history repeating, there was another morning where I couldn't walk ...this time the other leg (actually it was the hip giving me these problems). I didn't want to go back to the hospital, so my dad rigged up a traction system for me at home using pulleys, rope, and bags of nails for weights. The doctor had specific instructions for my dad to follow and was quite impressed with the result. Nancy Wells was an older girl who lived down the street from us. Her family had the pond where we (my friends and I) collected tadpoles from. She came to visit me every day to keep me company. I always enjoyed having her there. Our paths would cross again many decades later as she was a friend of my brother Dick's mother-in-law... small world.

Somehow, I made an appearance on the Big Brother Bob Emery television show in a wheelchair. I remember doing the toast to the president of the United States with my glass of milk. My dad was in the small audience just below the stage. I survived the traction and was fortunate not to develop a limp according to the doctors. This odd illness never bothered me again for the rest of my life.

Table manners were a big deal at home and with both sets of grandparents. We were all taught how to set a table, when to use which fork or spoon, and how to hold these wondrous utensils too. No slurping soup or drinks, lean over your plate when eating, tip your bowl away from you, sit up straight and no elbows on the table! We had to ask to be excused and there was no dessert if you didn't at least try everything on your plate. I was taught how to fit in at the table... anyone's table. It seems these lessons are lost on the youth of today.

With all this attention and family interaction, everything seemed good. We were taken care of, well fed, educated, loved, experienced adventure, and thrived. If the agency that placed me for adoption did a follow-up, they would surely have been impressed. Another successful adoption... next! "All things are destined to change with time" as the saying goes ....

THEN IT WENT OFF THE RAILS

I don't know exactly when my parents' marriage began to sour, but stress crept in slowly and steady. I remember my parents arguing loudly and often, but I don't know what about. I desperately wanted them to stop but they wouldn't. It seemed like they didn't even know I was right there watching their ugly exchanges. Finally, I had had enough. With tears in my eyes, I screamed at them both to stop or I would call the police. The phone was off the hook and in my left hand, my right index finger positioned above the "0" hole on the dial. They both stopped in unison and just stared at me. They assured me everything was okay and that I could put the phone back on the hook; they were done.

Mom and Dad were more careful when they argued after that and took precautions to hide their verbal salvos from me. They really tried to be quiet, but I knew it was still going on. One day my dad had a talk with me... a serious talk. He asked me if I had to make a choice between living with my mother or him, which would I choose. I had no idea how serious his question was. An eight-year-old boy was asked to make a decision that would shape the direction of his life forever. My dad was my hero. In my mind, he could do no wrong and there was nothing he couldn't do. He was a builder, a boater, a skier, he could fly a plane, he played sports, he was everything to me. My mother could sing, she was a great cook, but I never felt as close to her as my dad. This was my path; I chose my father. A divorce ensued shortly thereafter. My adopted twin sisters went with their mother. In a rare move, the Massachusetts court system awarded my father custody of me. Dad's first marriage ended and caused a break in the family structure – we became dysfunctional as a direct result. Details had to be worked out on visitation schedules. Who drives where and when etc. My world was spinning at this point. I didn't know anyone whose parents were divorced. There was one family in the neighborhood where the parents had been married to another spouse and each had children. I think the spouses had passed away and then they married, combining their kids into a very big family. That was odd, but not divorce.

My dad and I took a trip to visit my Aunt Joyce in California. This was my first time on a plane, and I was very excited. We had a scheduled stop in Chicago and the instant the wheels touched down, I was sick. The stewardess cleaned me up and made sure I was okay. She gave me a pin to wear (and keep), wings, I think. When we took off again, they made a point of keeping me distracted by inviting me into the cockpit with the pilot and crew! That was a dream for any kid. Dials and buttons everywhere, and a phone! They said I could pick it up and listen. I heard weather reports and wind speeds, and other info pilots would want to know about. They had me push buttons for them, when necessary, but I just loved watching the world through the windshield. The plane went through the clouds! I was thrilled and hated to return to my seat before we descended. Of course, they were worried about me getting sick again before we landed and had an airsick bag at the ready. I didn't need it and have never felt sick in a plane since.

Seeing my aunt, uncle, and cousins was great. We went to some amusement park and/or zoo where I wondered off and managed to exit the park through a revolving, one-way metal gate. When I couldn't get back in my dad was pissed and directed me to the car parked close by, where I had to sit alone until the rest of the family was ready to leave. I never wandered off again. I listened to all the good things my cousins saw or did inside and was sad, but I learned my lesson.

Back home in Wayland, we took in a married couple (Marilyn and Kent?) to watch me and take care of the house while my dad was at work. She became pregnant ... he was selling cars out of our driveway and my dad wasn't too pleased. Dad was dating... I remember pretty women, stewardesses I think ... and then a secretary from a local TV station in Boston. Wedding bells sounded, followed by selling our home and moving away from all my friends to a new town called Magnolia.

MAGNOLIA

Marriage to me meant a new beginning and a new home in a new town called Magnolia. We watched our new house being built from a rental property directly across a field from where we would soon live. The small house was a converted stable belonging to a building that was once a German embassy back in the 1930s? The field between the "barn" and our new house was once a four-hole golf course. I remember digging up the occasional old golf ball every so often in the strangest of places. My room was in what used to be the silo, so it was very round! Funky and unusual. Perfect! I was feeling funky and unusual too.

Despite missing my old friends from Wayland, I really was happy in Magnolia... There would be run ins with bullies, but that was true everywhere. I wasn't any different than any other new kid in a new town.

Our newly built home was set out high on a ledge, with no power or water and barely a road, without a name I might add. Our address was simply "off Hesperus Ave." My dad had to bring everything in as no one had ever lived on that rock before us. He brought in loam by the truck load and fenced in the back yard so no one (like me) would wander off to the chasm just a few yards toward the water from the backdoor. It was a sixty-foot drop straight down between sheer rock walls. At the bottom, the rocks were roundish from the sea turning them in the numerous storm surges over the years. The far end of the chasm was open to the ocean and the swells would roar toward the rock cliff before their powerful momentum would divert the waves into the crevice, filling it with several feet of frothing white water. As each wave retreated, the rocks rotated and rumbled like thunder, echoing up and out of the chasm. It was an awesome place no one seemed to know existed. I would love to know the story of how my dad found this piece of property.

I vividly remember my best friend Nick standing on a large rock near the ocean entrance to the chasm when an enormous wave hit the cliff in front of him. The wave engulfed him and swept him off the rock as it raced up the chasm toward me. I ran as fast as I could until I found a place where I could climb the wall to let the wave move by under me... I didn't see Nick until the spent wave retreated. He was directly in front of me, soaked from head to toe and as I saw more of him, he laughed saying he never hit the walls! The wave shot him twenty yards up the chasm but kept him centered the whole way. He didn't have a scratch on him!

As kids, we had to sneak over to the edge of this massive crack in the earth so no one we knew would see us. We weren't supposed to go anywhere near it for obvious reasons. We found our way down a narrow rocky path to the bottom where we would play... it was always cooler down there on a hot summer's day. In the winter there were towering icicles adhering to and pulling away from the rock wall. We tossed rocks at them and on occasion one of these monsters would break free causing us to flee for our lives. The width of these was measured in feet rather than inches.

Our playground was the ocean.... Rocks, waves, boats, beach, pier, islands. It was paradise for a young boy. I could see the Eastern Point lighthouse at the far end of the breakwater in Gloucester out the family room window. Any boat going in or out of the harbor was visible from our house. In the opposite direction was Kettle Island with a sandbar just below the breaking waves, which once was dry land connecting the island to the shore. It was grazing land for sheep and cattle way back when, until a severe storm turned the pasture into the island we see today. Far off in the distance beyond the island was the Boston skyline. My dad always referred to our property as a view with a home rather than the other way around. There was so much to see from that vantage point!

In the summer of 1963, I was ten years old when I had my first boat. It was just a small fiberglass dingy with an air bubble at the bow that formed the front seat. The bubble was designed to keep the boat afloat if it swamped or capsized. There was a set of oars and oarlocks, a couple of cushions and a short line at the bow. Very basic. Before I could use it, my dad wanted to teach me safety and lifesaving skills. We went next door to a neighbor who had a pool. Lesson number one: What happens when you tip over in the ocean? You need to be able to float! Your clothes can weigh you down and sap your strength, so you need to remove anything bulky.

I was fully dressed in a sweatshirt and sneakers when Dad pushed me in the pool. I sank like a stone to the bottom while struggling to pull an arm out of my sleeve, looking up through the water at my dad standing by the edge. I could hold my breath a long time, but the frustration of not making any progress was taking its toll. Suddenly I was scared I might not make it to the surface and was wondering when my dad was going to come to my rescue. There was a splash and a neighbor's kid who was older than me jumped in and pulled me up and out. Gasping for air and staring at my dad I could see he was disappointed, but he did manage to put the fear of God in me which, in retrospect was probably what he was after anyway. He tried to convince me a wet sweatshirt with some work could be made into a bubble... I didn't believe him then and I would love to talk to him about now. From there he gave me the speech about always wearing a lifejacket. After what just happened in the pool, there was no way I wouldn't be wearing a life jacket! Which got me thinking, why didn't that "test" allow me to have a life jacket on? I think that was all part of his master plan, but I didn't say anything. As if I wasn't scared enough already, he went on about getting tangled in ropes. I feared what the next "test" might involve! This, it turned out, wasn't so bad. He wanted me to have a knife. "You always have to carry a knife, and it needs to be on you, not near you... and it has to be kept sharp. If you get tangled in a rope, you may need to cut your way free." A knife sounded pretty good to me! To this day I always carry a pocketknife with me. He showed me how to use a whetstone and of course my knife wasn't sharp unless it cut the hair off your arm when gently slid across your skin.

I knew I would only be allowed to row around the harbor, but listening to him, it seemed he was preparing me for an overseas voyage. I learned a few basic knots and then came the day when we dropped a mooring close to the pier and ran a loop line from it to a cleat near one of the many ladders running the length of the pier to the low tide level. We launched the dinghy from the beach, and I received more lessons on balance, how to move slowly and with purpose in a boat (things he had gone over with me years ago on the lake). He taught me to row and tie up to the float connected to the pier by a ramp. We exited and reentered several times, rowed to the ladder to clip the boat on the loop, then pulled it out to its mooring making sure it wouldn't brush up against any rocks. He showed me how to secure the rope to the cleat near the top of the ladder. I thought that was the end of it, but no! He wanted to watch me do it all by myself. I went through all the steps with him coaching constantly. I did okay and it felt like I had conquered the world! My dad was proud, I think. He was tough to read sometimes.

Many kids in Magnolia had boats and they started young. When I think of my kids, having a boat at ten years old would have been out of the question. Funny how your perspective changes with time. I learned quickly though and appreciated the power of the ocean and the importance of detail and planning. My dad was thorough. Dad loved the area and the water. He spent a lot of time in boats on fresh water when he was younger. Before too long he had a small sloop and moored it in Kettle Cove. The dinghy ("my" boat) was tied to the pier. Other kids had boats with motors, but I was just glad to be on my own and I learned to row. It was cool. I loved it.

I collected baseball cards. I was constantly buying bubblegum at the corner drug store to expand my collection and have fresh rigid cards for playing games of skill to collect even more cards. I would go through my cards looking for doubles or triples. These would be the cards I would use later when I needed to knock over that last leaner to gather the pile of cards which accumulated during the game. I was good at it and always made a point of not winning too early. Another game was distance and I excelled at that too, but you couldn't win as many cards that way. Closest card to a wall was another game I'd play. Anything to grow my collection. After the games were over, I'd go through my winnings to see what new players I could add to the collection of cards I never gambled with.

As part of the custody agreement set up during my parents' divorce, I had to visit with my mother every third weekend and for an entire month in the summer. Interesting to note, my sisters never visited with my dad. This was something that made me different than all my friends. It might not seem like such a big deal to many of you but think about what that does to a kid trying to forge relationships with new friends. You wouldn't be around on a lot of weekends, while your friends would get together for good times without you. They had adventures I wasn't a part of. Adventures became memories to exaggerate upon as time went by and I wasn't part of them. It created holes where they shouldn't exist.

Sports were another problem. I wanted to play baseball, but a Little League team wouldn't have me, knowing I was going to miss an entire month in the summer. When I played in lower-level ball, it was tolerated. Same with football. I was a defensive guard for the Magnolia Lions and really loved it though I would miss an occasional game.

As I got older I graduated to having a larger boat. I don't remember if the Old Town or the Amesbury skiff came first. They were both 14' long wooden boats. I learned how to perform routine maintenance on them, like stripping paint and barnacles, recaulking the hull with cotton, repairing floorboards, touching up brightwork etc. I had a few lobster traps which put a few bucks in my pocket and was spent primarily on gas. My boat would stay at mooring and my few lobster traps would go untended when I visited my mother. My world came to a standstill at regular intervals.

I hated the drop off and pick-up point. Usually at a Howard Johnson's parking lot somewhere halfway between "homes." As soon as the hellos were out of the way, the questions would start, especially from my mother. I always felt I was being pumped for information about my father. My dad did this too but to a much lesser degree. I didn't know anyone else who had to go through that. In a word, it sucked. I felt manipulated, more of a thing or a tool rather than a person. Eventually I asked them to stop asking me about their respective ex's. What kid should ever have to make a request like that?

Nancy was an odd duck. To her credit she was excellent with our dogs. Heidi was a smallish German Shepherd and trained to be a show dog. There were many framed ribbons displayed in the home. Nancy made extra money by breeding shepherds. As kids we took turns changing the newspaper in the puppy pen every day. We all loved having the puppies climbing all over us and hated it when they were sold off. We quickly bonded with the clumsy little furballs, and it was hard to see them go. Nancy was a great cook. She had a recipe for an oatmeal molasses bread that is the best I've ever tasted to this day. She would only make it if I agreed to mix it as the dough was too tough for her to handle. The recipe is lost now but not forgotten. She performed in local musical theater productions and loved to sing. I believe she met her third husband, Ivan there. She loved to watch Jeopardy and the Flintstones on TV. The news was always on during dinner, and we were not allowed to talk while it was on. Nancy was not a good mother. She drank to excess. She had regular deliveries of alcohol to the house. She would berate my twin sisters when they had grades lower than mine. "Why can't you be more like your brother?" was tossed in their faces often. I hated it when she made those comparisons. One of the girls wet her bed and Nancy's idea to solve the problem was to parade her around the neighborhood on a dog leash while she wore a diaper. It was massively humiliating, but that's the way her warped mind worked. She had more than a single screw loose!

The friends I made in Saxonville (where my sisters lived) were casual. I didn't see them often and we didn't stay in touch when I wasn't around. I was split between two very different worlds and often felt like I didn't belong in either one. I learned to adapt, but I never learned to like it.

Life seemed good with Dad's second wife, Marie (Mother #3 --- that doesn't include Marylin). Starting my life over with another woman playing the role of mother to me was something I tried to get used to. She tried, but it was going to take me a while to warm up to her. It seemed to me she wanted to appear to be my mother rather than be a mother to me. The clothes she bought me were usually something I didn't want to wear and were way different than what my friends wore. Her culinary skills were meager (I'm being kind) compared to Nancy's. There was something fundamentally missing in our relationship from the very beginning. Nancy, despite her antics and actions, was still my mother though this was gradually fading. The sense of missing something was growing inside me.

I knew I was adopted, and, in my mind, this equated to not being wanted by my real mother. My adopted mother didn't want me either as was evident by the terms of the divorce. I was getting used to Marylin as a mother figure before Dad married Marie. It seemed mothers were temporary people to me. I wanted one but didn't trust Marie was it. I knew it was best to keep that kind of thinking to myself. The only stable people in my life were my dad and grandmother. I felt the love when I was with them. I bottled up what I had to and just tried to go with the flow.

As I grew up, I became more aware of my surroundings and the people that moved through my days. The feeling no one really got me, I'm sure, is common among most young people at some point in their lives. For me I *knew* I was different. I didn't know anyone remotely like me. No one I knew was adopted. I used to describe my existence as living in a bubble. I felt detached from normal family and social life, and would seek it out at a friend's house, wishing I had a mother like theirs. I felt more at ease and comfortable at a kitchen table with a family that didn't include my stepmother. At home I practiced avoidance, the less contact with my dad's wife, the better. In the summer I would leave home at the crack of dawn and return before it got dark for dinner, unless I was invited to dine at a friend's house!

My presence often felt more ephemeral than anything else... temporary in some odd way. It was kind of like when you toss a stone into a pond and watch the ripples radiate away from the center. They are real, you can clearly see them as they move but if you were in the pond when the ripples finally met your skin, there was no sensation. They were too small and insignificant to register with your senses. I felt like I was a tiny ripple. I felt like an actor, like I was playing the role of a normal kid. No one asked me about it, so I guess I played the part pretty well.

Acceptance was an elusive thing, which admittedly, I have chased most of my life. The flip side of course is rejection, something I don't handle too well. Being funny was a way to connect with people. You can't fake genuine laughter. If I could get that smile of understanding from a well-placed joke or a real belly laugh, it meant I connected on some level. I fed on the slightest success and would always attempt to build additional momentum then maybe go too far. Losing the moment meant rejection, failure.... crash and burn, but I knew I had something for a while. It was always about acceptance with me. I wasn't a big kid, not a tough kid. I wasn't charismatic but I wanted to be noticed somehow.

I started smoking cigarettes at age 8 (didn't inhale until I was 10). I wanted to be cool like the older kids seemed to be. I was in a new town with people who all grew up together and I didn't have a shared past with any of them. I wanted to fit in like I had with my friends back in Wayland. I wanted to be part of the group. The first kid I met was the son of the contractor (also the Mayor of Gloucester) who built our house. I spent a lot of time with him that first summer in Magnolia. How things change! It turns out he was the town bully for our age group, and everyone was afraid of him. Once school started and there was an audience around, I became his new target. I couldn't believe how he changed, like flicking a light switch. He called me names and we fought on the bus or at the bus stop. This would continue off and on for years. One on one he was fine. He would even come to my house, and we would get along for short periods. He knew I would stand up to him if others were around, so the actual fighting eventually ended between us. By accident I learned he was afraid of the dark when I turned the light off prematurely while he was still downstairs in our basement. He emerged crying his eyes out. He didn't bother me much afterward out of fear I would expose that side of him I suppose. He still picked on other kids though. Mostly smaller or younger than he was.

Another new kid showed up in town. His name was Nick, and he lived a short distance from my house just off of Hesperus Avenue. There was a short path through the woods that took me past his house on the way to the bus stop. We became best friends. Our bus stop was in front of a large rock, which sixty years later, is still there. We would arrive there early and climb all over it. Sometimes we would jump off the top and latch onto to some sapling trees and slowly drift down to the ground. There was a small field across the street and once, following a heavy frost, I found dozens of bees "frozen" on the wildflowers growing there. I was amazed I could get so close to see the detail of the bees. I cut a handful of flowers and brought them on the bus to show everyone. I planned on showing my teachers when I got them to school. The bees however had other ideas. Slowly they thawed out and one by one took flight, causing some major chaos on the bus. The driver pulled over and had me throw the flowers out while he opened all the windows. It was a chilly ride to school.

When winter came, Nick and I would build walls out of snowballs or chunks pushed to the side of the road from the plows. We set them out on the edge of the road for the bus to crush when it picked us up. We kept making the walls bigger until the bus driver told us to knock it off. Sometimes cars would have to swerve out of the way to avoid hitting our snow walls... they were not pleased. We were just killing time, waiting for the bus!

Once we lit some gasoline in a small metal can behind the bus stop nearly setting the woods on fire. We were lucky to put it out on our own. Nick and I had a lot of fun adventures while waiting for the bus!

I always found ways to use my imagination. Snowpack could be turned into a maze of paths. We would walk sideways with each footfall overlapping the previous one. This packed the snow down and created a narrow path in the fresh snow. We would keep at this until we constructed a significant maze of connecting paths. Once we were satisfied with the network, we played tag. You had to stay on the path as you ran and if you left it, you were "it" whether tagged or not. If you argued about leaving the path, the snow would reveal if you went out of bounds or not. Self-policing! If the snow was crusted over from a rain shower or partial melting, we would cut the crust into rectangular slabs and stack them into walls. We would build snow forts and have snowball fights. Our creativity and drive were noteworthy.

In 1964 my hair was longish, especially in the front. I was always flipping my head up and my hair away, to get it out of my eyes. When the Beatles arrived in the US for their first appearance on the Ed Sullivan Show, my dad's eyeballs grew a few sizes when he saw pictures of them and their haircuts in the paper. Theirs were far too similar to mine, and he immediately informed me it was time for a much shorter haircut. I didn't understand what the fuss was about but was also powerless to change his mind. Hello whiffle…. He didn't *get* their music, and he *hated* the hair.

For Christmas in '64 or '65 my dad bought me a record player and a few albums: The Rolling Stones, Animals, Petula Clark, Herman's Hermits, and The Beach Boys. I've often wondered how he came to select those specific albums. They represented a diverse mix. I wore those records out and couldn't wait to buy more. I had my first transistor radio in 1965 or '66, followed by an 8-track in 1967 or '68. Music was an escape for me. I knew every word to every song and somehow projected their meaning into my life any way I could. Lyrics resonated and I let the emotion move me no matter the topic. It was all safe in my head. My own private world where nothing bothered me. Music became a constant for the rest of my life. I listened to everything, rock, pop, country, soul, jazz, show tunes, it didn't matter. Music gave profound meaning to my life, and I was always on the hunt for something new.

I loved climbing trees to see how high I could get and what kind of view of the world I'd have when I got there. There were a few trees in Magnolia by the town landing that were very old and leafy. They weren't that tall, but they offered a view of the street, which put you very close to people without them realizing you were there. You could hear conversations. I could sit up there for hours and watch events unfold below. I was alone and separate but comfortable. No one ever looked up, so no one knew I was there. I was invisible, just like I felt sometimes when my feet were on the ground.

I enjoyed sitting on the rocks and watching the sea roll. Spray, splash, wind, gulls, boats ... I was connected somehow. Everything was in motion and evolving and in sync. I was comfortable though alone. My imagination was free to roam. Was I on that fishing boat or the sailboat? What could the seagull see as he glided on those strong breezes? How far had that swell rolled? Where did it start from? How long did it take to get here? How much salt is in a drop of water? I loved the power of the waves when they exploded against the rocky coast! I would walk the rocks for hours to see what had washed ashore, you never knew what might turn up or what story brought it to this spot.

Running the rocks was something I excelled at ... sure footed, quickly shifting weight to maintain my balance ... I would love to race anyone. Those who could beat me on flat land couldn't keep up with me on uneven rocks. I was in my element.

At night, lighthouse flashes through my bedroom window made a rhythmic pattern on the walls... I could predict when they would all flash at the same time and then watch as the angles favorably illuminated this wall or that as the sequencing changed. It was comforting and familiar to me, just like the sound of the house creaking as the temperature changed was also a soothing sound.... it too was predictable. The creaking and groaning sounds of the wood coming faster and faster before eventually slowing down to nothing.

One fall I developed a severe case of bronchitis. I was driving everyone in the house crazy with this deep throaty cough that started way down in my chest and went on for weeks. I had to go to the doctor and there were lots of questions being asked about my medical history that my dad couldn't answer because I was adopted. An understanding nod from the doctor and the questions stopped. Bronchitis would stay with me for the rest of my life. The only thing that helped was codeine. I remember having many small bottles of cough medicine around the house and would take doses often to settle my hurting lungs and chest. That medicine allowed me to sleep. It worked wonders for the entire house!

On the opposite side of Old Salem Path leading up to our driveway I discovered several grey-aged, thick boards flat on the ground. There was a distinct gap between them, and one showed some obvious decay. Curiosity took hold as it usually did, and I started digging around them. I suspected there had to be something underneath. Eventually I pried one up and found nothing but empty space. Whatever it was seemed pretty cool so with added energy I continued until I got the other board to lift. It was obviously dark inside with just a little light coming through the new opening. My eyes adjusted and I saw the floor was dirt and only about three or four feet down. Excitement flowed as I thought about showing my friend Nick what I had literally unearthed!

Later that day we got a couple of small candles and dropped down into the hole. Once the first candle was lit, we saw the room was round and made of stacked stones. We set short candles in the walls and wondered what exactly it was we were in. How long had it been there, and no one knew about it? We heard a car on the road and peered out to see who it was. The mailman. He dropped the mail off at the end of the driveway, turned around and left. A few minutes later, my stepmother walked out to collect whatever was in the mailbox. We had ourselves a spyhole! No one could see us, but we could see them! We thought it was pretty cool, but over time the novelty wore off. I told my dad what we found, and he was stunned. He thought it was an old, abandoned cistern or cesspool and told us it wasn't safe to play in. He covered it over to keep us out and make sure no one could accidently fall in.

Our house sat alone and high on a solid granite ledge giving us an incredible view. Dad set up a powerful flood light that would illuminate the night all the way from our fence post to the rocks at the ocean's edge. During the more powerful storms, the spray would ride the wind and the light made for a spectacular show. Storms at our house were breathtaking to watch. We had a front row seat to appreciate the awesome force of nature. Your eyes could pick out the largest waves from a distance and follow them to the point of impact against the rocks. I spent hours at a time watching the ocean.

The sea spoke a unique language and provided visuals that captured my eyes every day and in all kinds of weather. Sounds of bell buoys and fog horns.... cargo ships hauling anchor and always the waves breaking on the shore..... Wind, gulls, lobster boats, trawlers, fishing boats, party boats, deep sea fishing boats, pleasure boats, every kind of sailing vessel you could think of. Skiffs, dories, dinghies, scuba divers, row boats, prams. ... I was happy, very happy living in Magnolia.

I loved looking in tidal pools to see what was alive in them. You never knew what you'd find. The ocean filled my imagination with mystery. I knew when the stripers were running by the clamor of the gulls. The bass would chase smaller fish, like mackerel, into the cove in front of our house. Once they had them trapped, it would be easier for them to feed. This in turn attracted the seagulls who were always eager for an easy meal. They would swarm the cove and steal whatever they could. It was a free for all!

There was always something to see on the water. Ships from around the world came and went. The Coast Guard also had a strong presence in Gloucester. They had amazing rescue craft and crew, as well as larger vessels patrolling the New England shores. There were also rare sightings of submarines in the local waters not too far offshore. Later in life the whale watching industry would be a prominent attraction for summer visitors to the area. I had no idea how close I was as a kid to the whale habitat just a few miles off the coast. Had I known, I would have found a way to get out there. It was probably for the best I was unaware.

Around this time Marie became pregnant and soon thereafter I had a sister, and my dad had his first natural born child. Susan was like nothing I had ever seen; this cute little person had sparkling eyes and would smile at you and laugh. I loved spending time with her and watching her grow and she liked the attention too. This was probably the beginning of the transition initiated by Marie.... I was now the "non-blood" in the house. The change was subtle at first but steadily grew as time passed. I was the outsider.....The ugly face of rejection had arrived yet again. The fact Susan and I bonded was bothersome for Marie.

Susan would listen intently to me and watch my every move. She couldn't pronounce her name yet, so it came out as "Boopa" and to this day it remains her pet name known to only a few people. I loved watching her play and figure things out for herself. Learning became a kind of game... she was inquisitive and so smart. I created an imaginary friend named Herman that would only talk to me, which fascinated Susan. She always wanted to know what Herman was saying. I would hold something up to my ear and pretend to listen then pass on what Herman said. Herman might suggest she draw a picture or clean up her toys or ask her if she wanted me to read her a story. Susan thought Herman was quite cool and never seemed sad she couldn't see or hear him. Herman lived through me. We spent a lot of quality and fun time together.

I could entertain myself for hours as a kid. I had a vivid

imagination (I might have mentioned that a time or two already). I would get lost in a daydream that would become a story, with characters and a plot and I was involved and important. I would see this through to some improbable or impossible conclusion, only to start down a new path to an even better ending. These daydreams could be so detailed I might cry as though they were real rather than fantasy. I could fly. I was strong. I was relentless, unstoppable. Honest, and pure of heart. I helped people. I fought evil and embraced all that was good. I was my own superhero. I loved comic books. Every month I went to the local drugstore to see what had arrived so I could continue where the last book left off. Cliffhangers got me every time. I had a large collection of comics well into my teen years. My dad felt I should have outgrown them and eventually he made me get rid of the entire collection. Looking back at what I had, they would be worth tens of thousands of dollars today! That's probably a conservative estimate. Between my baseball cards and comics, I had a valuable collection of unrealized wealth.

I remember the ads in the comics and on the back of cereal boxes. My dad explained how they were false advertising hoping kids like me would order an aquarium of sea monkeys or some pill that grew into a monster when placed in water. I read every word on every box of cereal. I loved to read. Books were everywhere... encyclopedias, dictionaries, magazines, the newspaper... anything. But I really loved comics. Most of my friends who read comics preferred DC; Superman, Batman, the Flash, Green Lantern etc.... these were "okay" to me, but the Marvel comics were my favorite. The artwork was great, the characters seemed real and looking back, I think it was because they were all flawed in some way. They were troubled by something, they had a secret to keep, they were vulnerable … Kind of like me. Marvel Comics were well written and forced me to the dictionary repeatedly to learn the meaning of the words being used.... My vocabulary grew as a result.

I read the series of Tom Swift Jr books, Tom Corbett Space Cadet, H. G. Wells and Jules Verne, Edgar Allan Poe, H. P. Lovecraft, J. R. R. Tolkien anything that stretched my imagination. I read Tom Swift (the senior) also. These were old books I believe came from my grandparents. These too were science fiction but from a different age. The so called "wonders" of that time were reality in today's world. Airplanes, motorized bicycles etc. These were interesting and taught me perspective as it related to time.

On 11/9/1965 we experienced a huge power outage, which affected New England, the neighboring states, and parts of Canada.... I was twelve years old and alone at home reading my comics until it was so dark I couldn't make out the words anymore. I checked with neighbors and knew we were all affected. I don't recall where the rest of my family was or how long before they came home. I wasn't scared, I just wanted to keep reading. The electrical grid was configured differently after that event to ensure there was never a repeat. I believe there was a spike in new births nine months later.

Being so much older than Susan I did enjoy getting out and exploring new things on my own. A bike meant freedom to travel far in a relatively short time. I rode into Gloucester or Manchester (now known as Manchester by the Sea). I'd go as far as I dared. I just had to be home before dark. That was the rule. There were times I rode hard to make home before curfew. I put a lot of miles on those tires.

Somewhere along the line I acquired a BB gun. I had no real place to go to target shoot, so I improvised. I used to go in the backyard or on the porch when no one was home and take aim at the seagulls flying by. I don't think I ever hit one. One day a neighbor came to the door. He was upset and wanted to talk with my dad about something. He handed him several BBs and said they came flying into his patio while he was out there! No doubt it was me who was responsible, who else could it be? I was dumbfounded. Never did I aim anywhere near his house. I always aimed out to sea. What I never factored in was my elevation and the onshore winds. The BBs would head out so far then make a u turn in the wind as they descended. They changed direction by more than 90 degrees! The BB gun was taken away immediately.

I wanted a boat with a motor and my dad agreed. Nothing big, just a fourteen-foot Oldtown wooden skiff with a paltry 7 hp used Johnson outboard motor. It wasn't fast but it was something. Soon thereafter I had half a dozen lobster traps. Not many, but the sale of a few lobsters would keep gas in my boat. I had friends with twenty-five or fifty traps … some more than that. The boat gave me even more independence and freedom. In the summer I would spend all day on the water (and away from Marie). A boat made travel that much better… I could go to McDonalds in Beverly (the only one around) where they had a dock! I could go under the cut bridge, up the Annisquam River, and on to Rockport. The river kept me close to shore, but there was still so much to see. Beautiful homes, a railroad bridge, boats of all types and people making a living from the sea. Exploring Gloucester harbor was a blast. There were different languages spoken and enormous boats unloading fish or picking up supplies. Wealthy yacht owners with sleek sail or powerboats tied up or under power. People waved to each other. The magic of the sea cast a spell on everyone it seemed. I would head south to cruise the beaches in Manchester and Beverly too.

When I first had a boat with an outboard motor, I was told I couldn't leave Kettle Cove (Magnolia Harbor). Heading south, away from Magnolia was easy but going north into Gloucester meant driving past my house where I could be seen. If I went north, I would head far out to sea first before crossing in front of my house hoping my little skiff would go unnoticed. I don't recall ever getting caught. I loved the freedom I found. It was an escape. I always imagined I was on an adventure wherever I went.

Marie was pregnant for the second time and gave birth to my brother Dick, at last I had a brother. He was a kid who got into everything. Like Susan, he and I bonded…. and once again Marie didn't like it. My dad called Dick "The Holy Terror" which suited him to a tee. He rode his tricycle in the house up on two wheels leaving rubber on the floor. He was also responsible for filling our oil tank with 50 gallons of water while playing oilman using the garden hose. The list goes on and on. My dad would get mad at the things he did but also had to stifle his laughter. Dick was unpredictable and an absolute riot. I'm pretty sure Dick's antics reminded my dad of some of his own escapades when he was younger. I loved my little brother!

UNRAVELLING 2.0

Marie and my dad began arguing and it was all too reminiscent of those days with Nancy. I didn't have the attachment with Marie I had with Nancy when I was small, so I indifferently turned a blind eye to what was going on. I didn't care if they fought. Marie was cruel, at least to me, and I was selfishly glad she was in trouble with my dad. Marie would let Susan into my room when she was a toddler and what do you think toddlers do? She made a mess of everything in there. I had a flip lock on the door well out of reach from Susan but somehow, she "managed" to get in. Susan actually told me her mother opened my door for her. This happened more than once. I couldn't get mad at my adorable little sister as I surely knew who was really at fault. My resentment toward Marie hit new heights a few years later when Susan told me I wasn't really her brother! There was only one person malevolent enough to put a thought like that in her head!

My dad enjoyed alcohol (with good reason in my opinion) … Canadian Club Whiskey and Carling Black Label Beer. As the arguing with Marie grew, so did his daily consumption. At some point in every useless argument, I would hear Marie spit out the phrase "… and that damn son of yours!" which would escalate things to an even higher level of intensity. Her words were like acid, and she knew it. Marie realized full well I could hear her every word. She really did hate me for being me. This went way beyond rejection. I felt the same way toward her but being a kid, I kept silent. My dad though, always stood up for me; he couldn't or wouldn't let her say the stuff she did without voicing a rebuttal. I was the reason they fought and for that I wanted to disappear.

Dad would sometimes escape the now frequent chaos by climbing up on the roof. His back against the chimney looking out at the twinkling stars above the tranquil vastness of the ocean. It was a peaceful oasis full of possibilities. "On the roof, the only place I know. Where you just have to wish to make it so. Let's go up on the roof ..." Ah the Drifters! They had it right. I would join my dad up there. We sat quietly next to each other lost in our own thoughts, him puffing away on a Winston. I wondered what he was thinking about. This was his second marriage, and it was shaping up to be an unfortunate copy of his first.

In addition to smoking cigarettes, I started drinking alcohol too. Other kids were doing it so why not me? When Dad was a little tipsy, I'd pour a little of his CC into my own bottle. It wouldn't take too long before I'd have enough to get a buzz on with my friends. Whiskey was too strong for me but there was no way I could snatch a bottle of beer without my dad knowing. Beer was more my style though, but how to get some was tough.

 We (my friends and I) solicited people to act as a "buyer" to get us some beer, any beer. It would cost us more (buyer's cut), but we had no other way. Once in our possession I would stash it in a lobster trap to keep them, bottom of the ocean, cold. The rims may have been a little salty, even if you wiped it off first, but hey! Being out on the boats was also a safe place as you could see any trouble coming from a long way off. Lots of reaction time.

When I was fourteen, my dad was in a car accident and lost his sense of taste and smell. The last thing he remembered was hitting his head on the car roof. He was lucky it wasn't worse. With his senses compromised, I knew he would never smell booze on me, so I was emboldened. I could smoke cigarettes or drink beer and he'd never know it. He did catch me (visually) smoking a cigarette once and told me flat out it was better to smoke in the open than to lie to him about it. I started smoking at home right after that, then a carelessly dropped match set the field on fire next to our house. The fire department had to come to put it out. Not good. Dad carried the newspaper clipping about the fire in his wallet for years. I quit smoking after that, but it only lasted a week.

My friend Nick and I built a small fort we called "The Hut" on some wooded land near my house. The hut grew from something Nick and I built from some scrap lumber and a couple of barn doors my dad didn't need anymore, into something much bigger. We dug a rectangular hole and used the doors as walls at ground level. There were two old chaise lounge chairs the Magnolia Manor had tossed out in a pile that were perfect for our needs. We made a little fireplace so we could have instant coffee. Then we added a frying pan so we could cook eggs and bacon for breakfast. We added a dry sink in the ground for washing plates and pans. Friends liked what we had done, and we began to expand. We raided new construction sites in town at night and brought whatever we could find back to build an addition. It was a project that took on a life of its own. Kids loved to contribute and hang out there. My dad didn't mind the noise because we were close to the house. He never asked where all the wood came from. One night we had about a dozen kids there with beer, who comes walking into view but my dad. Word spread quickly and we hid the goods. My dad saw some kids smoking cigarettes and asked what we were all doing. Some sodas passed through our hands and kids began talking to my dad. "Mr. Stedfast, hi! We were just having some tonic and talking. Hope we weren't too loud. Would you like to stay for a while," etc. My dad was just checking on us and had no intention of staying. He made sure we kept the campfire low before leaving and warned us to be careful with the cigarette butts. He couldn't smell any beer. We were all sweating bullets while he was there as we thought this would be the end of the hut. Lots of great nights laughing with friends there.

Other kids in town heard of the hut but didn't know where it was. "Membership" was by invitation only. We outgrew the area when there were uninvited people showing up and soon it was out of control. Once the camel gets his head under the tent …. Kids were showing up when I wasn't there. It was odd for the neighbors to see so many kids walking around our small neighborhood. It wasn't a secret anymore and the magic faded quickly. We did have a small fire weeks later and the damage kind of put an end to the hut, but it was great while it lasted. I was cool because it was my idea, and it brought my friends to me. We sadly tore it down and cleaned up the debris so there was no reason for anyone to trek out there anymore.

I did okay in school. I was no fan of homework, but my memory was good enough to make me a B student as long as I paid attention in class. Each summer a friend of our family named Connie (I called her *Aunt* Connie) would send me textbooks for the next school year. She worked for a publisher or a distributor, I can't recall which. They were for different subjects and occasionally I got the teacher's addition which had the answers to every question included. Seldom were they the specific ones I would see in class, but it did give me an idea about what was going to be taught. I was prepared every year to meet the challenges headed my way. Having the answers to math problems helped me understand how to approach the problems in a more organized manner. There was one year where the class was issued the same Algebra book Aunt Connie had given me the teacher's addition of… Jackpot!

ROTC (Army) was mandatory my sophomore year of high school. We wore regulation army uniforms (with a colored patch on the lapels) twice a week with polished black shoes and brass coat buttons. We drilled with M1 rifles (minus the firing pins of course) and watched film in class. At the same time this was going on, many of us became immersed in the counterculture. My hair got longer (my dad was not a fan). A plan was hatched and a huge number of us in full dress uniform protested the mandatory nature of the ROTC program by walking off school grounds just as drill began...This appeared in the Boston newspapers. ROTC became elective in my junior year, but I was then attending school in Manchester. Student body protesting got results.

Age 14-15-16? I started tearing up pictures of me wherever I found them. I knew I was different than other kids. I got to thinking about how my family was spread out and splintered. Though I made new friends when I moved to Magnolia, I never felt like the kids who lived their entire life in that small town. I had a few very close friends but there was always someone around who treated me like an outsider... usually an older kid, a bully. Marie didn't help build my confidence at all. She was critical of me and my father for standing up for me. Bickering and arguing was almost a daily event; I wanted to fade away and become invisible. If I came across a picture with me in it, I tore it up. Pictures were disappearing and no one noticed... so I continued.

I felt like I didn't matter, and as much as I loved my dad for coming to my defense, I didn't want to be the reason for their constant arguments. I just wanted it all to end. Marie was purposely unpleasant to me and made damn sure I felt unwanted. She tried in vain to poison the minds of her own kids against me and this frustrated her immensely. She was willing to allow harm to her children if it was a means to do battle with me. I recall repairing the floorboards to my skiff on the driveway. Dick was just a toddler and he wanted to see what I was doing. I loved having him watch me and I explained what I was up to and why it was necessary. When he reached for a handful of nails, I told him he couldn't play with those because he could get hurt. Marie jumped in and said it was not up to me to tell him what to do. I pointlessly attempted to explain the concern over him putting nails in his mouth, but she didn't care and told me not to do it again. Of course, Dick moved in for another try at the nails, and not seeing Marie intervene, I told him no again. She went livid and called me a bitch, a bastard, and slapped me across the face. I picked up my stuff and quit the project for the day. I didn't know what to do any more. Every chance she got to make me miserable she exploited. The clothes she bought me for school were not like what the other kids wore and if I told her, she'd just buy more like them. I felt like I was out of sync with the world. I just couldn't take it anymore and knew I had to do something to change things before I went insane.

1967 Monterey Pop festival …I read about it a little and saw some clips on TV but didn't appreciate the significance of what was happening yet. I was on the cusp of another major change in my life. If I only knew then what I know now …..

In March of 1968 WBCN radio switched to a rock format… AM radio played the same 50 or 60 songs over and over again with pointless banter and commercials in between. FM was new to all of us …. the music and the people who played it on 'BCN were different, and it was everywhere. New albums were appearing and being shared by the people I grew up with. We would play them for each other in bedrooms or basements. Cream, Santana, Jefferson Airplane, The Mothers of Invention, Jimi Hendrix, Janis Joplin, Grateful Dead, the Byrds, Buffalo Springfield, Mamas and the Papas, The Who, Electric Flag, Rolling Stones, the Animals, Blood Sweat and Tears, Bob Dylan, Joan Baez, James Cotton Blues Band, Jethro Tull, John Mayall, The Yardbirds, Led Zeppelin, the Beatles, Pink Floyd, the Doors, the Kinks, Procol Harum, the Velvet Underground, the Moody Blues, Traffic, Small Faces, Canned Heat, Steppenwolf, and so many more were getting airplay on 'BCN radio… The American Revolution. Songs with grittier more meaningful lyrics and emotion. I loved it all and couldn't get enough. This music had an edge to it and it spoke to me. There were stories here that rang true to life. There were fantasies, romance and longing, sex and drugs and politics. The DJs related the stories behind the songs and the artists who wrote them. They played album tracks other stations wouldn't touch. They played full sides of records and on occasion entire albums. A new world was opening up to me and it resonated way down deep. It was a release and there were suddenly a lot of people "just like me." I didn't feel so alone.

The counterculture was exploding among the student population in Boston … bell bottoms, long hair, flower power, peace signs and marijuana. This new wave was quickly expanding out from the city and into the suburbs. Magnolia was ripe for a change. College campuses were powder kegs. Underground newspapers increased their circulation. The Vietnam War was escalating, President Johnson was a major factor in this expansion and was repeatedly called to task for it. Nixon reentered the political picture for the Republicans with Humphrey and Wallace as his opposition. Humphrey was popular in the Boston area and would take Massachusetts in the presidential election. The only state Nixon lost. Remember the bumper stickers that read, "Don't Blame Me, I'm From Massachusetts"? These powerful events were percolating, and they shaped my oh so mushy little brain and future forever.

June 1968: My Freshman year of high school was coming to end, and I was looking forward to a summer in the sun on my boat. On the last day of school, we received our report cards and for the first time, they were printed on computer paper. Gone was the heavy card stock in just as heavy a paper sleeve. I decided to hitchhike rather than take the bus home. I think it was George O'Brien who was with me as we left the school grounds (could be wrong on that). We walked past the Sweet Shop, over the Cut Bridge and out toward Kent Circle, where I took out my flimsy new report card to look at my marks yet again. They weren't bad! A gust of wind took the delicate paper from my hands and blew it straight up about ten feet above the ground. I waited for it to come back down but instead it stayed aloft and began crossing the street with me following. I was ready to snag it the moment it came low enough but instead it kept moving toward the harbor. The closer it got to the seawall the more anxious I became. Soon it was obvious it was not going to come down in time for me to grab it and I watched it clear the railing then drop straight down into the ocean! I was going home without a report card and a story no one was going to believe.

That summer was great. I spent most of my time in my boat, hauling the few lobster traps I owned to keep the gas tank full. Up early each day and out to the seine boat for bait. I loved watching the fishermen pull the nets into a tight circle then dip a smaller net on a winch into schools of fish before dumping them on the deck to be sorted, stowed, or sold as bait to us kids. 50 cents a bushel was a very good deal for bait. Mostly pollock. We would wade knee deep in flapping mackerel, cod, herring, monkfish and of course, pollock (considered junk fish back then). I never saw pollock for sale in a store, ever! It was not unusual to see a shark or two in the nets and they could quickly do a lot of damage to the gear (nets) and catch. With the fishermen in their dories, we kids would take turns using a gaff at the rail to snag sharks when they swam over the hook. We would be covered from head to sneakers in sticky scales when we left with our bait.

On days when the fishermen needed to repair the nets it might take hours before they hauled the day's fish catch on deck. We would keep our small skiffs close to the dories and talk with the fishermen as they sewed. I remember one guy plucked a squid from the section of net he was working, held it under water then quickly pulled it out when he felt it swell in his hand. He'd aimed it at us when it discharged water --- a living squirt gun! He threw us a few and we started doing the same until one released some ink which got all the fishermen laughing.

There were times we would stay out of sight behind their boat and drop lines in to catch our own bait. It was illegal to drop a line within so many feet (I forget how many) of a commercial net. Once we hit a school and filled our baskets in half an hour, maybe less. We had more fish than we needed and ended up having a fish fight! There were three or four skiffs involved. Each of us running in intersecting circles, picking just the right moment to fire a fish at an opposing "skipper." Fish were flying every which way. When we ran out of ammo, we collected floating "rounds" from the water and had at it again in earnest. Seagulls entered the chaos hoping to get at the fish before we collected them for yet another volley. We laughed until the fish were gone. We were filthy and wet. I remember going to Archies Restaurant and him yelling at us to get out as we were so dirty and smelly. Life was so good when I was out of the house.

That summer we had a huge party on Kettle Island. We gathered piles of gray, sun bleached driftwood for a huge bonfire. It roared to life, and we kept feeding it more and more wood before letting it die down. With a thick bed of red-hot coals established, we dumped mounds of seaweed on top then layered lobsters, crabs, mussels, even periwinkles on it before adding another layer of seaweed to lock the steam in. This was a feast for all the kids in town. Beer was kept cold in lobster traps... Nothing like a cold one from the ocean floor. We ran a kind of ferry service back and forth from the pier to the island and more kids kept coming. The fog rolled in during the afternoon, but we partied on, adding more driftwood to the fire after we all had our fill of fresh seafood. Kids were coming and going with regularity despite the fog. When night fell, the fog was so dense we cast huge shadows against it as we danced around the fire. We made so much noise we could be heard on shore. Someone called the Coast Guard and suddenly a bright blue light pierced the fog, and we heard them over the bullhorn telling us to put out the fire and leave. We thought it odd they never came ashore and soon realized the fog made it impossible for them to navigate safely past the rocks. We did calm down and they left. It was funny that a bunch of kids could safely head out in the fog and return as many times as we did but they couldn't land. Great times on the island.

In May of 1969 Tommy was released and it seemed to be playing everywhere. We all knew every word to each track on the album by heart. It was like nothing else. A rock opera for our generation. Everyone was a pinball wizard!

Note to the reader: I'm finding it harder to keep the events of my life chronologically accurate. To facilitate the advancement of this reconstruction, I'm going to bounce a little forward and back at times. Not by too much but you may pick up on it as you progress. This isn't easy!

LEAVING HOME

T hen came the day in 1969 where I had had it with my stepmother. It was early summer, school was out, and the thought of spending any more time with someone who hated me as much as she did, just for being present, came to a head. It had been building for years and I knew I had to get out of the house. I was rejected in her eyes, there was no love for me in her heart, only loathing. She had her husband, and her children and I was something that interfered with whatever she held dear. She loved her kids whom I loved as well, but there was no room for me in that house. I was far too young to establish my way in the world but was desperate for a way out. *Any* way out.

You don't possess me
Don't impress me
Just upset my mind
Can't instruct me or conduct me
Just use up my time

...... King Crimson

At 16, you can't rent an apartment somewhere, and even if I could, I didn't possess significant income to support it. I thought about running away but didn't have a destination and there was always that annoying lack of money thing lurking around. I had a summer job lined up in Manchester at the Essex County Club working in the kitchen. The pay was minimal; however, they did offer room and board for free, and meals wouldn't be a problem working in the kitchen. I planned to pack a few things and get out of the house. My dad was away on a business trip, so I simply got up early while the house was quiet and left without saying a word.

I had a small room overlooking the main driveway to the club. The one window was small, tiny actually, and set well back from the walls. It wasn't something you would sit in front of and look out from. The furnishings were sparse to say the least, a bed, small dresser, and a chair. No sooner had I spread my wings when I was informed that due to my age, I was going to need my parent's permission in order to stay there for the summer. That was going to be difficult. They gave me a few days after I explained my dad was traveling. The fear of telling my dad what I had done was tearing me up inside, but I knew I couldn't go back to the house with my stepmother. I waited until I thought he was back and called him at his office in Boston. When I told him I had run away there was a pause on his end, which I half expected, before he gave me the news I didn't want to hear. Instead, I heard him softly chuckle. I hadn't expected this for a reaction. He then explained he hadn't been on a business trip at all. He rented an apartment in Boston and had moved out of the house too! We both did the same thing at about the same time. He thought my living at the club might be a good thing, but he'd have to see it first and speak with management in person before he'd agree to it. He took a tour and met the staff and consented to let me stay! Third cook in the kitchen sounded good to me. I was on my own for the first time! I never heard Marie's reaction to my leaving abruptly and I don't believe she told anyone. My dad never gave any indication he knew I had left. Let that sink in for a moment.

The staff at the club was great, and they helped me establish a routine. It was like a family there. I learned a lot of valuable life lessons in short order. I had to do laundry and fold clothes... eating was no issue as I had run of the kitchen, and I ate very well. I worked six days a week and the summer went by in the blink of an eye.

There was a huge golf tournament and many of the kids in Manchester caddied at the club to make a few bucks. They came to the kitchen for meals, and I cooked for them, which was fun. I got to meet new people. They were short a caddy one day and asked me if I could fill in. They said I could make a lot in tips, so I was all ears. I had the time in my schedule, but I explained I didn't know anything about golf. They told me not to worry as whoever I was paired with would help me along the way. I agreed.

That afternoon I showed up and was told I would be "doing double 18". I had no idea what that was. I would be carrying two bags of clubs for 18 holes of golf my first time out and I would be on my own. I was not a big kid. Thin, wiry, and only around 100 pounds soaking wet. The clubs were heavy, but manageable, and we were off for a long day in the hot sun.

I was in trouble on the first hill. The weight of the bags was too much for me to get any traction up the small incline! It was quickly pointed out that loafers were not an appropriate choice for foot attire. Try as I may to dig the edges of my shoes into the slope, I simply couldn't make any headway and would ultimately slide back down toward the bottom. One of my golfers was annoyed, disgusted, and barked at me to throw him a specific club, which I had no way to determine. A quick lesson in how to differentiate one from another was in order. As the day wore on, I struggled through every hole. My shoulders were sore, I was tired and thirsty, but I kept going.

When we finally reached the end of the nightmare on grass, it was time to settle up with the golfers. The 'barker" gave me next to nothing, which I expected because I was totally inept. The other golfer said he admired my determination and gave me a generous tip as he looked at his irritated partner with righteous contempt. I really appreciated his words of encouragement, and the cash! I also knew I was not going to do this again. Golf was not my thing; kitchen work suited me just fine.

I learned to help out in any way I could at the club. I cleaned pots and pans, washed dishes, etc. but my favorite thing was helping the other cooks prepare food for the dining room. Loin strips of beef, whole salmon with garnish making it look more like artwork than food. I did some serving on the buffet line too. Harry Sinden of the Bruins was there, and I served him sweetbreads. The head bartender had me conduct inventory of all the liquor in the "Vault." That was a lot of booze! I wore any hat they wanted me to.

The waitresses, Myra and Liz were college girls. We drank beer after work in some room downstairs in the basement. At night we would head to the kitchen for a late-night snack like a roast beef sandwich with bacon and mayonnaise. That summer in July we put a man on the moon, and I remember watching TV and glancing outside into the night sky and wondering what that must be like. For the first time in a long while I was at peace. I no longer had to visit Saxonville, and Marie was not looming large in my headlights (she was in the rearview mirror now).

Woodstock was in the news everyday as tens of thousands of kids made their way to the event. One of the cooks asked for time off so he could attend and was told no. He left anyway and we never heard from him again. The void he created was filled by me and I think a slight raise in pay came with it. I had a few friends that went to Woodstock, and I was certainly interested in going but I couldn't leave the club and all that I had just established. It wasn't in the cards for me, but I sure wished I could have been there.

I had very little life outside of work. The few days off I had, all rained. On one of those days Charlie Toye told me marijuana was widely being used in Magnolia. I was shocked but also curious. He pointed out friends who were high and all I could see were smiles and people having a good time…. they seemed okay to me, not really so different. Maybe they'd had a couple of beers. Charlie produced a joint and we smoked it. First time I got high…. It wasn't the last.

NEW DIGS WITH DAD

My dad rented an apartment on Desmond Avenue in Manchester, MA as the summer came to an end. It was walking distance from the high school. I started in a new school and got asked the same tired questions I had answered in my old school with my other friends. Everyone needs to know who you are etc. Why are you living alone with your dad? Where's your mother? (Which one?) You start getting used to it and blow it off as not that important. What does any of that matter anyway ... I didn't have the answers to many of the questions being asked; never did and probably never would. But people can't help but be curious ... they are compelled to ask. The lack of a satisfactory answer inevitably leads to even more questions. The cycle continues. I knew some of these kids from the golf club, where they worked as caddies over the summer.

I recall an evening on Desmond Avenue at our Manchester apartment, when there was a loud knock on the door. As I turned the knob, the door burst open and two angry men appeared. I was between them and my dad. One of them gently moved me to one side while the other threatened my father. Telling him to stay away from Joyce and not to ruin any more marriages. Most of what he said I can't remember. I even think one of them apologized to me before they left a few minutes later. I was shaking and my dad explained he was dating a married woman who lived in Magnolia whom he had known when he was a teenager in Maine. They had bumped into each other in church. Like my father, her marriage wasn't going that well and they had a lot of other things in common too. She had three daughters and one of my best friends (Charlie) was dating the oldest. I envied those with simpler lives but would never let that be known because it would make me different, when all I wanted was to fit in.

I needed a new coat but was looking for gloves at the Deerskin Trading Post with my dad when I saw this brown suede jacket. It had fringe running along the arms, between the shoulders and along the bottom and reminded me of Roger Daltry of the Who. It was the coolest jacket I had ever seen. My dad said, "no way" and I was crushed. Joyce, his new girlfriend, went to bat for me, suggesting a 50/50 split on the cost, and that won the day. I bought the fringe jacket and people remembered me in it for many, many, years. I still have the tatters of that thing hanging in a closet to this day; I just can't let it go. I think it shows up in one of the Gloucester High School yearbook pictures.

Manchester had a Youth Center, which doubled as a coffee house offering live entertainment on some evenings and weekends. Kids could hang out, play pinball, talk about music, school, whatever. It also served as a place for the local band, Gandalf, to rehearse. I went to school with the kids in the band. Bernie, their harmonica slash flute player, and I became close friends. I helped them transport gear to and from gigs and listened to most of their rehearsals. I loved the atmosphere. Lots of dancing and meeting girls and a personal connection to live music... perfect! Manchester was growing on me.

10/19/69 Donovan played The Music Hall in Boston. This was my first real concert. Nick Benn and Charlie Toye went with me. My dad drove us in and picked us up when it was over. So much fun. The smell of pot wafted through the air while Boston cops patrolled the aisles looking for, I don't know what. Kids were smoking right in front of them, I couldn't believe it. There was magic in the air... and lots of smoke! Donovan was awesome.

When my junior year of school was done, I took a job in the kitchen at the Surf restaurant in Magnolia. I started as a dishwasher, but my experience at the Essex County Club allowed me to do a lot of prep work, like peeling fifty-pound bags of potatoes, making salads, and stocking the cook stations for the line. Eventually I became a pizza cook. I was also responsible for making the dough and sauce, chopping meat and veggies, shredding thirty-pound blocks of cheese etc. I liked it. It was work I understood. I enjoyed syncing with the other cooks, so orders went out complete and at the same time. I felt like an equal.

The summer passed and I bounced between Magnolia and Manchester continually. The restaurant didn't open until 4 PM so I had my mornings to do whatever I wanted. I didn't have a boat anymore, but my friends did. I'd hang out by the pier or on the street corner in front of Vierra's drugstore, a place we all referred to as the "square." Five roads intersected at the square and lost tourists would always stop to ask for directions. The square was where you went if you were looking for anyone in town...eventually everyone passed through the square, you just had to wait.

Magnolia was a very small part of Gloucester with only a few hundred people living there. Everyone knew everyone, front doors were never locked, and all the phone numbers were the same except for the last three digits. As the summer heat built and my friends were getting out of work, I'd have to leave to begin my workday at the Surf. I enjoyed working in the kitchen. There was a logic to what was happening, and people had to work together to be successful. We all needed to communicate. The owner had started the business selling pizza and it grew to be a great overall restaurant, which families came to for a relaxing night out.

Despite the success of the restaurant, Al (the owner) never forgot about its humble beginnings as a pizza place. He insisted our pizzas were of the highest quality. We would entertain any customer request.... ½ done pizza to be finished at home, any combination of toppings, no sauce, extra sauce, whatever. We were also the only place that served lobster pizza back then, which eventually caught on elsewhere.

Shortly after my senior year started, I had the urge to leave the apartment I shared with my dad. The summer of '69 was still fresh in my mind, and I loved the idea of being on my own. I had an opportunity to leave home again. This time I planned to move into an apartment in Cambridge with friends from Magnolia. Steve Amalia went in to sign papers for the apartment, while I packed a few things. I left my dad a note saying I would be in touch when I settled down. While waiting for Steve, I heard the news that Jimi Hendrix had died of a suspected overdose. I was stunned. BCN was paying tribute to his music, and I sat there quietly listening and thinking about the loss to the world. When Steve returned to pick me up, he said everything fell apart when the owner learned he was going to drive a cab for a living. He had no idea why that was a problem, but we didn't have a place to live. He knew a place where I could crash until he could find somewhere else to rent. He took me to an art gallery on Lexington Avenue in Magnolia.

THE GALLERY

I had never been inside the Gallery before, but I had heard about it. Bernie from the Manchester based band Gandalf lived there and was the closest one to my age. The owner was a man named Earnest Braun (Brown). He was from New York City, had long grey hair, was street wise and "hip," like an older beatnik or maybe "bohemian" would be more appropriate. The gallery was full of sculpture and paintings in one large room, which opened onto Lexington Avenue. Behind the showroom was a large "living" area. A small kitchen and bedroom lead to a wide-open space with various portions devoted to painting or sketching, and storage (lots of storage). There was a dining table with chairs, a workbench with leatherworking tools, mattresses on the floor, a ladder leading to a loft, another small room in the back and a short hall, which led to a back door. The whole space was much bigger than I had ever imagined from the street.

Besides Bernie, there was Peter who was also from Manchester. He was older than me, long hair, a beard, and face loaded with freckles. I knew who he was, and he had a reputation as being anti-authority. Phil was from Beverly. He was short, had shoulder length long brown hair, big bushy sideburns, and was a skilled leatherworker (he reminded me of a Hobbit). Bruce was clean cut and from Essex. I was the youngest one there. Earnest agreed to let me stay for a while. I still had my job at the Surf, and I offered to pay for living there. Earnest took a vote, and it was agreed; I was accepted.

The topic of school came up and I knew I needed to let my dad know where I was; you can't hide in a small town for long. He was not happy I had left but understood why I wanted to be on my own again. The Gallery had closed for season, and we moved some furniture from the back room into the showroom. It made for a cool transition. We left all the artwork in place but added couches and chairs and tables wherever they fit. We looked very presentable in the front, not so much in the back. We invited my dad to come over to meet Earnest and see where I was living. He was not thrilled but also knew I would leave for somewhere else if he didn't go along with this arrangement. Earnest tried his best to put my dad at ease, but Dad did not appreciate Earnest in the least. There was zero chemistry there, or maybe just bad chemistry. Having me close by was better than other possibilities so he eventually agreed so long as I returned to school. Now I was back in the Gloucester public school system.

The Gallery was as lively a place as I'd ever seen. We were six guys living together. Girlfriends and other friends were always coming and going at all times. Peter's girlfriend, Sigrid stopped in one day and I was surprised because I had met her before. I was walking in Manchester when I came across a kerchief on the sidewalk with this wonderful fragrance. I kept taking it out of my pocket and inhaling through it. A couple of days later I was hitchhiking to Magnolia and an attractive woman in a VB bug picked me up. She called her car the "bucket." The moment I got in I noticed her perfume and knew it was the same as the kerchief in my pocket. When I pulled it out, she was amazed I had it and thanked me for its return. She produced a joint and we smoked it as she drove. I hated to let that kerchief go but.... Anyway, here she is again at the Gallery!

Phil's girlfriend was Pat, and she was a schoolmate of mine from my one year in Manchester. There was a significant age difference between them. She was also close friend of a former girlfriend of mine. Pat's mother was a psychiatrist or psychologist or something. She practiced hypnosis and Pat learned enough to give it a try on me once. Such an odd feeling, being hypnotized.

Bernie's girlfriend was Pam, and I went to school with her older brother Henry (Hank). She was a ballet dancer and a very warm soul. They seemed perfect for each other. I remember a very personal dance she choreographed to music Bernie wrote and performed in her home studio. She was an excellent dancer.

There was a buzz around the gallery about a simulcast concert featuring the Chambers Brothers, Boz Scaggs and Linda Ronstadt. ... WGBH FM and WCRB-FM along with Channel 2 TV were collaborating to broadcast the event in full quadraphonic sound. They carefully instructed their listeners how to set up the speakers (we had to have two independent stereo systems) in relation to the TV (which was to be broadcast in color). They performed a couple of sound checks to ensure we had everything in the right place. Satisfied, we all got high and tuned into a great concert.

There was always something going on at the Gallery. Earnest was writing a book in longhand. Every night he would sit at a table with a yellow pad and pen, a tall can of Schiltz, cigarettes, and a large ashtray full of butts. Completed pages were torn from the yellow pad and stacked neatly on top of the previous pages. I never read any of them; I don't think anyone did. Earnest was a complicated guy. His marriage had failed, and his wife moved out. He worked across the street for a book publisher (I think) when the gallery wasn't open. He was wise in a way I had never known before. Ernest loved to speak about his art, or what it was like growing up in New York City. He had story after story and could talk for hours. He caught me looking at one of his paintings with geometrical shapes of different colors against a light blue background. I would try to view it from my periphery then snap my head around to look at it straight on. He laughed and asked me what I was doing and what it was I saw. I explained I kept seeing a red block in the painting but there was no red block anywhere! He then went on in detail about the concept of op-art. He had successfully created an optical illusion. My reaction to his work contributed to our bonding.

The Gallery taught me to be myself. I recall one night where the discussion revolved around people being "up-tight" about change and a variety of other things. Ernest looked at me and stated I was the most "up-tight" person in the Gallery. This took me completely by surprise. He went on to say I was always looking for a reaction to anything I said. To him I seemed unsure of myself and needed constant reinforcement. I was speechless. When I thought about it, it didn't take long to realize he was spot on. I sought validation constantly. I made it a point to speak my mind rather than what I thought I had to say in order to fit in, from that point on. We were all very honest with each other and there was a lot of respect too.

I keep lookin' for a place to fit in
Where I can speak my mind
And I've been tryin' hard to find the people
That I won't leave behind

..... The Beach Boys

A musician friend (Dave Toleme... or something like that) of Phil's came to the gallery once looking for a new guitar strap. Dave claimed he had played with Vanilla Fudge, but I couldn't find any reference to him on any album cover. Phil was eager to create something for him and soon began the process at his workbench. When he was done, he showed me this really nice-looking belt with a buckle. Each end had a slit that attached to pegs on either end of the guitar. Phil wasn't satisfied and was looking to add something to make it stand out more. I looked around his bench at all of the scrap leather strips piled there from the edges he shaved off of numerous belts and had an inspiration. I collected a small bunch, folded them in half and suggested making leather tassels. Phil thought it was a great idea and began making them right in front of me. He carefully stained each one before attaching them to the guitar strap. The finished result looked very cool! When Dave saw it, he was delighted. He invited several of us to see him open for Frank Zappa at the Tea Party in Boston.

When we arrived for the gig, the lines were long and stretched around the block. Dave led us in through a side door and the people in the line looked at us wondering just who the heck we were. Back stage was amazing. There was graffiti all over the walls in every room from the various artists who had performed there over the years. I would have been content just staying there and reading everything. Pete Townsend, Johnny Winter, Quicksilver, Peter Green and so on... We met everyone in Zappa's band except Frank. Ansley Dunbar, Flo and Eddie (from the Turtles), and others. We were ushered off and out to the main floor. There was no seating ... no chairs. We sat cross legged on the floor near a concrete support pillar. Pot soon filled the room, and we watched a great concert. This was Zappa's first Boston Concert in a couple of years. He had been banned from performing due to profanity, of all things! The date was 10/18/1970. The Tea Party closed for good just two months later. It was my only time being there. I hope someone somewhere took pictures of the historical graffiti before they tore things down. WBCN used to broadcast from this same location. How they did live radio shows with rock concerts going on at the same time is beyond me. Oh ya, Dave played well too.

Peter Ryan was our revolutionary rebel. Politics was always on his mind. He was a soldier in waiting ... waiting for the day when a war with the "establishment" started. He did more drugs than anyone there and harder drugs too. He had a very different perspective on everyday life. I remember a time walking in Manchester when a police cruiser pulled up alongside of me and asked me to get in. I hadn't done anything, but I complied without protest. They took me to the station where they tried to impress upon me I was hanging around with the wrong crowd and they specifically mentioned Peter! After a while I said I understood and asked if it was okay to leave. I was free to go. As I left the station, I noticed several pot plants growing right under their noses in front of the station. They were about 18" tall... I laughed to myself as I walked away. These guys were clueless.

Bruce was the most inconspicuous person living there. He had short hair, good manners, a sincere smile, and was very responsible. I think he worked at a building center somewhere. Later I would learn his brother manufactured drugs in bulk (Methamphetamine I believe).

Bernie was my closest friend there, my best friend actually. We loved the same music. We were close to the same age. We hitchhiked together. We hung out a lot at the Youth Center in Manchester and had a great time. Bernie's band, Gandalf, rehearsed and performed there. I knew a lot of the kids at the center from attending high school there the previous year. I noticed a difference between the kids living in Manchester and those from Magnolia. There seemed to be more opportunities for Manchester kids. There was also a lot more money in Manchester than little ol' Magnolia.

Being on my own was exciting in so many ways. I was evolving as a person. Influences came at me from the radio, people I associated with, newspapers and magazines, books, music, and TV news. Newsworthy people and groups such as Dick Gregory, Timothy Leary, The Black Panthers, Abbe Hoffman, and the Chicago 8 were routine topics of debate and discussion. The counterculture was in full swing, and I was embracing all of it. Despite all of this, I still made a point to visit my grandmother in Boston often. I'd hitch a ride into Manchester where I got on the train and eventually the subway, then walk to her Beacon Street apartment. I always had time for my grandma! She was not a fan of my choices ... or my long hair ... or the way I dressed, but her love for me never wavered. When I think of her, my eyes still fill to this day though she has been gone for so many years.

I didn't have a driver's license, but it wasn't that important to me as I got around quite well by simply sticking my thumb out. I enjoyed meeting new people. There was always a story to tell or hear and maybe a joint to smoke. Hitching was a social opportunity for me. You never knew who would pick you up. More than once a state politician offered me a ride just to hear my take on the world.

The Gallery had to be the coolest place in the area. Everyone knew about it, but few had been inside. There was a lot of speculation as to what it was all about and who lived there. I felt special to be a part of it. Sunday mornings were generally low energy affairs for us. We were usually hung over from Saturday night. Ernest would allow and often encouraged puns up until noon when they would suddenly become taboo. A good pun got a major grown and a raised middle finger. We all shared a love of intelligent word play.

Phil's girlfriend Pat was pregnant and desperately wanted an abortion. They planned a trip to New York City to have the procedure done. Earnest and I came along for support. Peter gave me his no picture ID so I would appear a little older than I was. I recall walking on the runway toward the plane at Logan and passing a table with several men sitting behind it. They pulled me out of line and searched me... no one else, just me. I removed my boots and my fringe jacket etc. They found nothing and let me board the plane ... I had a joint hidden in the lining of my coat sleeve they never discovered. Close one!

Pat and Phil were already in New York and had rented a room for all of us to stay in at the Van Rensselaer Hotel (I think) located in the East Village. When they left to have the procedure done, I went outside to see what was happening and wandered around Tompkins Square. Seemed like a tough place. I noticed a lot of bandages on people's heads and was offered nickel bags every few hundred feet I walked. Everything everywhere felt off-putting. I'm sure Earnest felt right at home. I headed back to the room as I was very uncomfortable.

Pat was exhausted when the procedure was over. Phil stayed with her while Earnest and I returned home. Just before we left Magnolia, we got word the cops were planning on searching the gallery for drugs. They wrongly assumed we were supplying the locals with something; we don't know what. We planned for the event by hiding little notes tied to strings hanging from cardboard tubes stored in the loft. The string would be pulled and instead of drugs there would be a note "Nothing here...try again" or "Sorry, all sold out" and so on. We had these stashed all over the place. We were not dealers, but we did indulge. Anything we had was stashed elsewhere. The cops came while some of us were in NY. I would have loved to have seen their frustration when it became obvious, we had been tipped off, and they wouldn't be finding anything incriminating! A cat and mouse game for sure.

Earnest knew a bookie whose name escapes me. He always had a big wad of cash and another guy along for protection. The muscle was not the brightest guy, but he was big... and quiet. We got him stoned once and he turned into this gentle giant. It was an amazing transformation. He always wanted to get high whenever we saw him after that. His boss always said no!

Stories of the gallery could go on and on but the point I want to make is I was part of a family. We were friends from different towns, different ages, different backgrounds but we all got along. We had fun, laughed, debated and so on. One last story.... When joints were passed around and munchies kicked in, a call was made to the Surf if I was working. A large plain pizza for "Bartholomew." When I saw that name on the order slip, it was my cue to load it up heavily with assorted toppings. No one was ever going to open the box to look inside when it was at the front desk waiting to be picked up. The guys ate well when I was working!

Sometime in January Earnest sold the gallery so he could move to Ohio to be with a woman he'd met while she was visiting in Magnolia. No one wanted to go with him but me. I told my dad I planned on moving and he was adamant that I would *not* be going. He said he would call the police and have me or Earnest arrested as I was underage. On a snowy evening, a couple from Gloucester who owned a VW van drove Earnest and I to Youngstown Ohio. I defied my dad and started a whole new adventure. No police were seen.

YOUNGSTOWN

When I left my home and my family
I was no more than a boy
In the company of strangers
In the quiet of a railway station running scared
Laying low, seeking out the poorer quarters
Where the ragged people go
Looking for the places only they would know

..... Simon and Garfunkel

It was my senior year at Gloucester High School, and I left during the winter for Ohio. I had no job and was told by Earnest I had to complete high school. I was not allowed to attend day classes unless I agreed to cut my now shoulder length hair. I tried using my "Native American" or "Indian," as it was called back then, status as rationale for an exception, but that wasn't going to fly with the administration. I had no idea it was untrue either. I wasn't about to chop off my hair, so the only other option I had left was night school.

Most of the students who attended nights had been kicked out of day school. Friends were hard to come by at first. White was definitely the minority color as I was one of only three white kids in the school. Youngstown was a tough town with a deeply depressed economy. I endured a lot of stares and whispered comments along with the occasional "white lady" remark. Even those who had no problem with me did not want to approach out of peer pressure.

I only had to take one class, English, in order to graduate as I had accumulated enough credits through my junior year back in Massachusetts. I needed four years of English to get a diploma so that was all I intended to do. It wasn't until I was in a classroom setting that I actually made a friend. I was very much a pacifist, and my teacher had an alternate perspective. We played what if games in class to show how differently we viewed things. Once he presented a scenario where someone broke into my home and held a knife on my mother, then asked what I would do to protect her. We debated to the class's delight. The toughest kids would jump in and say if that was them, they'd blow 'em away. Those kids thought of me as weak, but others saw the way I spoke to the teacher and thought I had backbone.

One day the teacher decided to have a spontaneous spelling bee and I had just enough advance warning to open the back of a dictionary to find the word "Zygote." The rule was if you correctly spelled a word you were given, you got to offer one of your own. If someone couldn't spell it, they were eliminated, and the next person was given a chance. I was doing okay and maybe half the class was eliminated when I decided to spring my ace in the hole. There were groans and snickers when I placed "zygote" into play. "He's makin' that up, there's no such word," someone said. "What's it mean?" came from someone else. My teacher looked at me and simply said, "Well?" I said it was a fertilized egg cell. He smiled, opened his dictionary, and informed the class I was correct. I won the spelling bee with that word. One of my classmates gave me a nickname and started calling me "professor."

We were given an assignment to write a short story. Mine was about a sick child who was riddled with disease. A team of doctors desperately tried to save him, but he was too far gone, and he succumbed. The child's name was "Earth," and my goal was to draw attention to the pollution of the planet. A few of the students thought it was a cool story and with that began a path to friendship.

One day I was sitting in a car with my new friends outside the school, when someone approached the front passenger side. As the window rolled down, the guy outside pulled a gun from somewhere, and fired a "blank" at my friend's head. We all jumped and screamed while the guy outside laughed as we watched smoke slowly swirling through my friend's big afro. It wasn't funny to us, a really sick prank, but that's what passed for humor on the streets of Youngstown.

One day I saw James Brown's tour bus parked in the street prior to a gig. I had really wanted to go to that concert but was advised it was probably not a good idea to attend because I was white. I didn't go. There was considerable racial tension in Youngstown at that time.

I found my way around this new town by hitchhiking. I'd go in a specific direction only to the point where I knew my way back ... going a little further each time as my confidence grew. Two girls picked me up one day and informed me I was being kidnapped. I went along with it. We went to the driver's house where I met her mother. The girl played guitar and we talked about music for a couple of days. Her mother brought home some "blue" and I watched her shoot up. She offered to let me "clean the cooker" so I could have a hit. I accepted and felt the rush. This was a very different experience for me.

Weeks later I was in a similar situation in an upstairs apartment somewhere in the city very unfamiliar to me. I sat at a table with some strangers in a sparsely appointed kitchen when there was a loud knock on the door. Suddenly this guy in the room leaps to the side of the door and pulls out a gun from somewhere and asks who's there. I instantly knew I had to get out of there as this guy was strung out and stressed. Overwhelmed with fear, I held my breath and looked for the safest place to be if things turned for the worse. Seconds later we were relieved to learn the knock was a "friendly" and I allowed myself to relax a little. Bad situation.... I was doing crazy things I never had done before. I knew it was wrong but did them anyway. Deep down I knew I was heading for a bad end and made a deal with myself to slow down.

I met a couple of guys who played guitars and sang together. Byrdie and Val. They introduced me to their circle of friends and soon I was with them almost every day. Music was our connection. Someone suggested we take a road trip to see The Southern Ohio Folk Festival in Athens... two days (May 7-8, 1971) of music. We had no money for tickets but thought the atmosphere would be fun, so we headed south and hung around outside the event, singing in small circles with strangers.

We "singers" were a community, and people would stop and listen to us for short stints. A young couple left the show very early and offered us their tickets. They hadn't been punched so we were able to walk right in the main gate and they didn't punch or mark the tickets in any way (again)! An idea quickly formed, and we began asking people after they cleared security if they would part with their tickets. A few agreed and these weren't marked either. The exit doors leading outside were "closed" with chains (that would never fly today due to stricter safety laws). These could be opened just far enough to pass the tickets through. As we handed out the tickets, we told people to hand them back to us once they were inside. We managed to get over 50 people in before we decided to pass the role on to others and enjoy the rest of the show ourselves. I remember seeing some great artists... Kate, Livingston and Alex Taylor, Doc Watson, Country Joe, Odetta, Pete Seeger, and others. The show closed with the Youngbloods. This was my first music festival, and I had a blast.

I planned a trip from Youngstown to Marietta to see Liz Wick who worked with me at the Essex County Club. I had one fat joint wrapped in purple (grape flavored) paper tucked into the lining of my fringe jacket sleeve (this was now my go-to hiding spot). I figured on hitching south along the Ohio river then cutting across to Marietta. The weather was good when I stuck my thumb out and collected my first ride.

I saw some dirty depressing towns along the way. Steubenville was one of them. A windowless van pulled over and the driver flew open the side door, excitedly waving me in then instructing me to close the door and stay low. He said his name was "Hump" and informed me there was a huge drug bust underway and anybody with long hair like mine was being pulled off the street for questioning. Hump had short hair and thought it unlikely he would be stopped. He asked if I had a place to stay until things quieted down. I didn't, but he said he did. He asked if I minded crossing the river into Wheeling, West Virginia. It was okay with me. I kept my head down until we were out of Ohio.

Hump took me to a bar called the Choo Choo Inn. Seemed a friendly place. Everyone there knew Hump. The only other name I remember was "Panther." I let him know I was underage, but it didn't seem to matter to anyone. I had a beer at the bar and listened to all the talk about the bust underway in Ohio. Friends of theirs had been arrested.

When it got late, I rode to a farm somewhere where I met more people. We passed around a bottle of something and smoked pot and hash until I nodded off on the floor. In the morning I looked out the window through barely open eyes. Directly above me I came face to face with a cow! That was a first for me. Where the heck was I?

We had something to eat, and Hump said he would drop me back over the river so I could resume my trip. He thought I would be okay. Shortly after being let out of the van, I had another ride. Eventually I made it to Marietta and found the address I had for Liz. I knocked on the door, but it wasn't Liz who answered. The girl who did answer said there was no Liz living there. I apologized for bothering her and explained who I was and why I was looking for Liz. She asked me to wait a minute while she made a call.

Turned out she knew Liz but couldn't get ahold of her right away. She said I could come in for a short time while she tried again to find Liz. She explained Liz was just using the address to get her mail. She was living with her boyfriend and didn't want her father to know. There were actually a couple of girls in their early 20s living there. I stayed overnight and left the next day when they had places to be. Liz was supposed to come by to collect her mail. As I walked down the sidewalk, there she was! She was shocked I had come all that way just to say hi. I told her I had a joint, but she wasn't interested as she had things to do. We talked for a just few minutes and that was that. I never saw Liz again. I decided to head back to Youngstown via a different route to avoid any trouble that might find me. I remember going north and being let off in Canton, outside the Football Hall of Fame. I didn't go in.

I recall other shows while in Ohio: John Mayall, Poco, and ELP (Emerson Lake and Palmer) May 15, 1971, in Cleveland.... Jerry Jeff Walker, Livingston Taylor, ELP (again), and Cactus playing at Kent State I think... or maybe Akron.

On April 24, 1971, 500,000 people demonstrated against the Vietnam War in Washington, D.C. It was the largest-ever demonstration opposing a U.S. war. I was there and on my own. My thumb got me everywhere. This was like nothing I had ever experienced. People from every walk of life were there to have their numbers counted in opposition to the war. The media had warned of riots and hostilities in an attempt to keep people from coming, but the numbers just grew.

We marched in the streets with entire families and freaks from across the country. I passed a jeep parked on the side of the road with Massachusetts plates. It was Steve Amelia's! Steve was the guy who first brought me to the Gallery. Sometime later I saw Steve, actually, I saw him twice! Imagine being in a crowd of half a million people and bumping into someone you knew! I saw no rioting. The president never came out to address the citizens who were outside the doors. He may not have even been in Washington at that time.

5/1/71: Biggy Rat opened for The Velvet Underground at Struthers Fieldhouse. Biggie was a large woman who sounded like Janis Joplin, really strong voice. The Underground seemed to be in slow motion, probably heavily sedated. The drummer was a girl and it looked like it took every ounce of strength she had to lift a drumstick. Lou Reed sounded okay but what a strange vibe they gave off.

Unknown date: A "newcomer" named Alice Cooper performed at Struthers Fieldhouse in Struthers, Ohio. Alice's props were inexpensive but used very well. Lights flashing through stage smoke, a floodlight at the end of a rugged extension cord, which he spun around above his head while singing. He slit open down pillows and filled the front rows with feathers which eventually found their way everywhere. We all had feathers in our hair and clothes when we left. It was a good show. Brownsville station (Smokin' in the Boys Room) was the opening act and somehow, I got talking to them and they asked me if I wanted to join their road crew. I declined.

5/4/71: Kent State one year after the shootings, I joined a group of protesters on campus as they attempted to shut down the ROTC building. I remember sitting on the grass listening to speakers like Jesse Jackson and the students who had been shot the previous year. There were news crews mingling through the crowd. Music played. Someone said we were all being photographed from one of the buildings. The girls in the crowd took out compact mirrors and reflected sunlight into the windows where the cameras supposedly were. The vibe of Neil Young's "Ohio" was genuine and felt personal:

Gotta get down to it

Soldiers are cutting us down
Should have been done long ago
What if you knew her
And found her dead on the ground?
How can you run when you know?

I was compelled to be present, but also concerned if a riot broke out and I happened to be detained or arrested, I might be charged as an "outside agitator," then be subjected to a more severe punishment. Kent State did not welcome radical thinkers or kids with long hair. Cops vs hippies was a real thing everywhere. Locals in Kent would greet you with four fingers raised, meaning "we got four of you so far." I was out of place until I met a guy who sold unique candles. He got me off the street and showed me how he made them. In his basement were long troughs filled with sand and holes dug in where he would pour melted wax over wicks. Each candle was unlike any other and the sand coating was left on the outside. I left the next morning for Youngstown and never returned to Kent except to see a concert.

I have heard the voice of evil
Speak to me alone
Sitting cold and lonely
And so far away from home
In the darkness of the prison cell
I can hear the angry screams
Calling out to no one
In a place where no one dreams

God won't you deliver me
I've never been before
People say you're watching me
But I'm not really sure

..... Sonja Dada

I attended my graduation at Rayen (night) High School. As they called the students up in alphabetical order to receive their diplomas, my name wasn't called. I knew I had graduated and figured because I started the session late, I was probably at the end of the list. I was not. I was informed of the error and that my name should have been there. They apologized and assured me they would take care of it. I was given a diploma where the name was filled in by hand, rather than printed like everyone else's. I think it was my mother who later asked if it was a real diploma. I was done with high school ... probably done with school altogether!

Youngstown was all about Earnest getting together with his married girlfriend and me finishing school. I had friends, but no job. I panhandled for spare change and hung around fast-food places at closing where they would send out bags of food that hadn't sold. Music was the one thing I had that made me happy. The James Gang was big in Ohio. The Glass Harp was another band I heard all the time. There wasn't much else for me out there, so I decided it was time to head east again. I left Earnest behind in Ohio.

I don't know why
The trees grow so tall
And I don't know why
I don't know anything at all
But if there were no music
Then I would not get through
I don't know why
I know these things, but I do

..... Shawn Colvin

RETURNED TO MAGNOLIA
---LYNN PROJECTS ---

When I arrived back in Magnolia, Gloucester schools were still in session. Just for the heck of it I decided to enter the school and follow my old schedule. In a couple of classes, my seat was still empty, so I sat down like I hadn't missed a day. The kids were all buzzing with questions: "Where have you been?," "What are you doing here?." I didn't broadcast my departure for Ohio before I left. One teacher didn't even realize I had been gone for months. I informed my surprised classmates that I had already graduated (though my diploma looked a little sketchy).

My dad was happy to see me back home and for a graduation present gave me a wristwatch engraved with "congratulations" on the back. He was proud I hadn't quit school in Ohio. I felt good about it too. We never talked about Ohio much. I know the way I left was not good and his feelings for Earnest were lower than dirt. We were both ready for a restart.

My summer was underway even though many of my friends were still in school. Those who had graduated in prior years were busy working. I left Ohio to be with people I knew but they weren't available until later in the day or in the evening. It was good to be home though. My roots have always been grounded in Magnolia. I needed a place to live. I needed a job too. I had a friend from Peabody named Jimmy who was married to Barbara. Barbara's brother Kenny was a good friend, and I went to school with their younger sister Anne. Jimmy and Barbara had a small place in Lynn (the city of sin), and they offered to let me stay with them for a while. How could I say no? I had no other viable options.

The projects in Lynn (America Park) was not a good place; there were a lot of good people, but some bad ones too. When I walked through there at night, I always had rocks in my pocket just in case. I also carried a harmonica, which sounds strange but once I was confronted by a loud Great Dane who kept coming closer while barking. I hit a high note on my harp, and he stopped, cocked his head, and just stared. When I stopped, he resumed barking, when I blew again, he stopped. I used this trick a few times on other dogs, and it always worked.

There were people down and out in every building. Jimmy and Barb were on food stamps and ate government surplus food. I remember #10 cans of peanut butter and powdered milk and processed cheese etc. in the cabinets. It wasn't good, but you do what you must to survive. I didn't have much money but gave them what I could and helped out with anything they needed. The long and the short of it was I certainly got more than I gave. Jimmy and Barbara wanted to get away from the projects and a plan slowly took shape. If things were this bad here, why not try life somewhere else far away.... Like California. I was up for anything, and Jimmy started putting the pieces together. We needed a car, and gas money, and a destination. This was going to take some time.

July 2, 1971 was the first day of the annual Newport Jazz Festival. The event was sold out, but I learned you could hear the music from outside the venue if you were up on the hill outside the fence. There were even some areas where you could actually see the stage from that distance. There would be a place to camp in the woods on the hill as well, so I decided this was something I wanted to do. I went there alone. The Allman Brothers were scheduled along with B.B. King, James Cotton, T Bone Walker, Ray Charles, Aretha Franklin, and others. I had never been to Newport before and had no clue where the festival was located. I followed the line of young people knowing it would lead me to the music eventually.

I came across a welcoming hippy "community" camped out in the woods. Makeshift tents were scattered throughout the trees, little campfires, freaks from everywhere in various states of consciousness. Drugs were consumed, sold, given away wherever you looked. The vibe was good. I still had no idea where the stage was, but I could hear music in the air... I had to be close!

Casual conversations began as I made my way deeper into the crowd; there had to be thousands of people in the woods. At one point I did manage a view of the concert below the hill, but it wasn't a spot where I'd be comfortable if I had to get some sleep later on. I continued wandering around looking at this strange collection of humanity and wondering where everyone came from.

It grew dark and I recall climbing a tall stone tower. It was tricky getting past the iron bars around the door, but once they were cleared there were steps leading to the top where you could look out over the scene. There were not too many of us adventurers up there. Someone asked me if I could roll a joint. Of course, I could! It was difficult in the dark until someone else pulled out a flashlight so I could see what I was doing. As I licked the glued edge of the paper to seal it, I realized it was a cop holding the light! I thanked him and put it in my pocket. We all vacated the tower, and I never heard a word from that cop on the way down. No harm, no foul. The tower was now off limits though. That would have been an ideal spot to watch the event from.

It was late at night and dark, so most people stayed put for the night and just enjoyed the sound from the stage below without being able to see anything. The next morning, we woke to commotion going on below the hill while Dionne Warwick sang "What the World Needs Now is Love." Word spread quickly the concert was being shut down and everyone had to leave. There were lines of officers combing the woods, "tapping" sleeping people on the feet in order to get them up and moving. The remainder of the event was canceled. There were a lot of us out on the street all looking for rides at the same time. I did a lot of walking before I eventually got a lift. What was supposed to be a fantastic event ended abruptly, leaving you to imagine how good it could have been. I think the affluent residents of Newport didn't appreciate the endless stream of young people who arrived for the event. I didn't know it yet, but I would see the Allman Brothers just a few months later, thousands of miles away in a gymnasium on the campus of UCSB.

CROSS COUNTRY TRIP
TO CALIFORNIA

Back in the projects, our plan for another life in a different place continued to grow. Jimmy and Barbara purchased an old VW bus which we dubbed "Magnolia West" (the name painted in white letters below the windshield). "Maggie" was our nickname for "Magnolia" and "West" was obviously the direction we would head in. Our plan was to cross the country with San Francisco as our ultimate destination. Still short on funds we added several more travelers to help with expenses. Newt, Scot, and Arnie rounded out our adventurous group of cross-country travelers.

Before we left, the van experienced a brake failure, which forced us to intentionally hit a stonewall in order to stop. Thank God we were driving slowly at the time and there was little damage. We had this fixed immediately! Used cars are always a risk. We modified the air vents based on someone's suggestion so we could force more air into the engine for when we crossed the desert. There was no gas gage in that VW model, but if you felt the car was starved for fuel, you could flip a switch allowing the one-gallon reserve tank to kick in. This was also your cue to find a gas station immediately. We watched our mileage religiously to ensure we didn't run dry.

Since I was the smallest and also the lightest member of our group, I was responsible for tying down all of the gear we stowed on the roof. With six people inside, we needed all the room we could find. I knew where everything was and if needed, I'd be the one to get it. We put as much up there as we could, but the inside was still cramped quarters. Six people in a VW driving for thousands of miles was going to be more than a little interesting! We were going to get to know each other a lot better. What a trip!

The curse of the used car bit us somewhere near the Ohio border. The transmission failed. Fortunately, we were right outside of Youngstown, and I knew people there who put us up for a week until we could make repairs and be on our way again. This was a lucky break for us. I got to visit old friends and did some catching up. We visited junkyards for spare parts and the best prices. With a little help we were back in business and heading west again!

We came into a little town called Gilead (still in Ohio) on our way to route 70 and stopped in at a small tavern to have a quick bite. We took seats at the bar and felt a little uncomfortable as the few people there kept looking at us oddly. Eventually one of these locals approached us saying something about longhairs not being welcome and that "Sherriff Buddy Bradford" isn't going to like us being there. This one guy looks us in the eye, reaches into his shirt and pulls out a clump of hair (or fur) from his chest and placed it between us on the bar saying "this is how long hair gets in Gilead" …. We wanted no part of this twisted wingnut and made our way out asap. What a creepy place! The nice woman tending bar never said anything to keep the tension down.

The miles rolled by every day. We pushed on through heavy rain and hot sun, stopping where we could find cover so as not to spend any money on campgrounds. We would pull over and cover the van with branches at night. Newt was driving during a severe rainstorm when one of the wipers froze in place halfway through a sweep. Newt gave the windshield a gentle tap with the back of his hand, and it cracked! We weren't stopping to fix that!

Well over 100 miles outside of Amarillo, Texas we began seeing large signs for the Big Texan Steak Ranch. They offered a 72 oz steak for free if you could eat it in an hour with a baked potato and side vegetable. None of us had had a good meal in a long spell so we were intrigued, and the signs kept coming every few miles. We decided to give it a look. It was like a set to a western movie inside. There were swinging doors separating the dining rooms and the staff wore western clothing including holsters with fake sidearms. Jimmy couldn't resist a grand entrance and hit both doors with the sides of his fists. They swung open forcefully and slammed against the walls on either side of the opening. Everything stopped for a moment and then Jimmy laughed as did everyone else. Jimmy apologized and said he just couldn't resist. We looked at the meat display as we were shown to our table. They had every cut and every size steak you could think of, and they all looked delicious.

We weren't the only travelers seeking a meal on the road that night. We noticed several other long hairs at tables. One patron was being served the 72 oz steak advertised on the road signs, and the thing was huge! He asked if it would be okay if someone cut it for him while he chowed down, and they agreed. The large cubes of cut beef filled two oval plates to heaping. There was a second guy being served the same huge steak at a different table just a few minutes later. If you failed to eat it all in time, the bill was high, so we wisely decided against trying, but we continued to monitor the progress at the other tables. Our waitress took our drink order, and I was shocked I wasn't carded. I think we all had glasses of Coors. Reasonable size steaks were ordered, and I relied on Jimmy to pay for me, as I had nothing at all in my pockets.

The first guy was still plowing through his first plate of beef and guy #2 was right behind him. We were having a great time and were all a little on the loud side. We asked some of the other patrons where they were from and where they were headed. Our waitress brought our steaks and told us we were lucky to hit the restaurant on a slow night because usually the place would be full of cowboys who would not be so welcoming to a bunch of hippies like us. She wasn't mean, just politely explaining things the way they were, and we appreciated her honesty. Mt Gilead, Ohio hadn't faded from our memories yet.

A quick check on guy #1 showed he was into plate #2 while guy #2 was showing signs of slowing down. Our meal was great, and the beer, cold and refreshing. All eyes were on guy #1 as he was getting close to finishing. I noticed guy #2 slipping some steak into his boots! When the final bite of steak departed the last plate toward the lips of guy #1, the place erupted with applause. The waitress jokingly asked if he was interested in strawberry shortcake for dessert and he replied, "Give me two please." We all roared again and guy #2 dropped more meat in his boots. #1 finished both desserts and none of the staff noticed #2 cheating so he managed to get his dinner for free also. We got back on the road well fed, full, and headed for Albuquerque.

Interstate 40 followed the same path as the iconic route 66 and we saw some great old signs from the past still in place along the roadside. It was a cool feeling traveling that historic route. Steadily we rose in elevation as the miles ticked by. The mountains were beautiful and unlike anything any of us (except maybe Arnie) had ever seen. The entire trip across country we had listened to only the half dozen 8-track tapes we had. The radio played mostly country music and the weather reports we heard could be for hundreds of miles from where we were. We had Hendrix and Rod Stewart and a few others to keep us company. The van was old, but it kept us rolling on to our destiny with California.

The mountain pass kept each of us focused and alert; it was a long way down. We were on a downward slope when Jimmy called out "The brakes are gone!" We all watched in horror as he slammed his foot to the floor, but we didn't slow down. As panic took hold, Jimmy confessed he was only joking, and he wasn't on the brake pedal when he slammed his foot down. We were all pissed he would even think of joking about something like that. We had the brakes fixed after they failed in Manchester before we left. They should be in great shape. Going off the road into a stone wall would not be an option up in the mountains. We all calmed down as we saw signs for Albuquerque up ahead.

Just as we got to relatively flat land, Jimmy informed us the brakes were gone again. Of course, we didn't believe him at first, but shortly we came to realize he wasn't joking this time as we gradually coasted to a stop. It was quite a walk to find a tow truck, but the man who came to our rescue also repaired vehicles. He was blown away by our "accent" as he originated from the Boston area. He felt very comfortable around us and fixed the van for cost. While we waited, there was a cloudburst that flooded the streets with near knee-high water in minutes. A short time later, the streets were bone dry and where all the water went is unclear. Once repairs were sorted out, we were on the road again. Nothing was going to stop Maggie West!

We passed through several towns we had heard of along the way, and it felt like a dream. The elevation rose yet again and this time higher than we were before. We all hoped that brake job was solid. Were we all really doing this? On our own and far from home, we relied on each other to make the trip work. It felt great. Despite the length of time we had already experienced getting across the country, we decided a detour had to be inserted. How could we not stop at the Grand Canyon? We headed north and as the day wore on and evening settled in, we found a place along the roadside to bed down for the night. The canyon was close by.

In the morning it was cool and damp with an overcast sky. Thick fog blanketed everything. Signs told us we were close to the canyon, but we couldn't see it. There was a parking area with signs saying the canyon was so many "feet" away now, but the fog was too thick to see across the parking lot. How could this huge canyon be so close and stay invisible? We got out of the van and started walking. Finally, we reached the edge, but you couldn't see across. We could barely make out a wall jutting out just to the right of where we were standing. We were so disappointed after taking the time to go out of our way for this. We had seen our share of fog when living in Magnolia, and it was no big deal. Fog was fog, no matter where you were.

Suddenly, a shaft of sunlight burned through the mist at a severe angle and briefly lit up the wall to our side. From the gloom came these beautiful colors exploding off the stone face of the cliff before the fog took over again. We were all amazed at what we saw. Like before, another shaft of light appeared but this one slowly moved across the stone showing even more color before being swallowed up by the fog again. Another shaft appeared and then another and still another. The fog would close on one shaft while light burned through elsewhere. The frequency of this dance continued with the sun slowly winning out. The light would stay visible longer and watching the canyon walls light up was spectacular. Off in the distance we could see even more of the canyon as the fog burned away ever so gracefully exposing this magnificent canyon. As the minutes passed, our awe intensified. The view widened in every direction. We saw blue sky above now. The whole show was like a fireworks display, complete with the "OOHs" and "AHHHs" from us, the only small crowd on hand to witness nature's wonderment.

The grey morning turned into a beautifully bright day. We saw a couple more people there, but they missed the spectacle we were so fortunate to have seen. Several of us wandered out onto a jetty of rock attached to the wall near the parking area. This narrow sliver went out quite a way, and the drop was impossible to estimate. Jimmy and Newt grabbed my shoulders so I couldn't move then lifted me up and turned me parallel to the ground near the edge of the cliff. I was terrified but didn't struggle. The last thing I wanted was to get free and fall in the process. Somewhere there is a picture of this, but I don't know who has it. They slowly set me upright and I yelled at them to never do anything like that again. When it was time to leave, we were reluctant. The magic of the canyon had us in its grasp, but we also knew we needed to press on.

We were almost through Arizona and the landscape was desolate and barren. It was hot and dusty, and the van was full of pot smoke when we spied a road sign warning us to prepare to stop and be searched at the California border up ahead! We frantically rolled the windows down to dispel the smoke and began anxiously stashing our stuff. There was no alternate road we could take, and we didn't want to stop before the border as that would draw unwanted attention. Panic set in and as we crawled to a stop at the checkpoint. A man looked us over and asked if we were carrying any fruits or vegetables! We weren't, and he informed us we were free to cross over into California. Just like that, our horrible panic was immediately replaced with nervous laughter. We had all feared the worst and were relieved when nothing actually happened. Fruits and vegetables were what they were after? Who knew. I bet we weren't the only ones to have reacted that way.

We now had to change direction slightly as we proceeded to Costa Mesa. Phil and Peter had moved there after the Gallery was sold. Phil owed me some money (from Pat's abortion) and I desperately wanted to turn it over to Jimmy. We surprised Phil at his apartment and learned Peter was at work. Phil took us down to a food truck where he gave us an idea of what Mexican food was. I had my first burrito, and it was good. Good food, filling and inexpensive, just what we needed. We caught up on what each of us had been doing since we were last together, then reminisced. We got the lay of the land and learned there wasn't much work in the area. We were there for five days before the smog lifted enough to see foothills in the distance but not *too* far away. Smog was very new to us. We had made it to the Pacific Coast.

We decided to take 101 (sections of which were also the coast highway) north to San Francisco. The Haight-Ashbury district was calling us. We had been talking about it since we left Massachusetts. The center of the counterculture was at the heart of this area. Sex and drugs and rock 'n' roll! Summer of love, the influential bands, the freedom to just be you. The summer of love had come and gone but the vibe still had to be there, right? We were so wrong. While at the corner of Haight and Ashbury we were stunned by what we saw. Junkies strung out on the sidewalks or lying in the park down the street. It was dirty and dead and dangerous. Our dream of a better way of life was decisively crushed, instantly. You could see the sunken hollow eyes of the street people. It was not a safe place to be, and we stood out as "not from around here." We had to go, but to where?

Forty thousand headmen couldn't make me change my mind
If I had to take the choice between the deaf man and the blind
I know just where my feet should go and that's enough for me
I turned around and knocked them down and walked across the sea

...... Traffic

We tried San Jose, but there was no work and rent was high. We made our way south again on Coast Highway 1 and eventually to the college town of Isla Vista. Rents were affordable, but work didn't seem to be abundant. We didn't see much of an alternative, as farther south meant more smog, so we settled there to see if we could make a go of it. We couldn't go back home without trying to make it work.

ISLA VISTA

We settled on an apartment in Isla Vista as it was more affordable than Santa Barbara. Next on our list was to let Phil and Peter know where we were, then begin looking for work. There wasn't much of anything in the newspaper. I think it was Arnie who left first as he saw no future at all for him in California. I believe he found someone who wanted his car driven back east so that became his ticket home. Newt left shortly after him for the same reason. Work was depressingly scarce and so was money. Scott wanted to stay but moved out of our apartment to find a place on his own.

One afternoon I was playing foosball at the Campus Cue with everyone I knew in front of me when I felt a pair of hands grab me at the waist from behind. A bit in shock, I turned around and there was Peter! And Phil! Big surprise. They stayed a couple of days before heading back home. Phil gave me *some* of the money he owed me but when I tried to give it to Jimmy, he told me to keep it and find a place for myself. It was time he and Barbara had a home of their own. She was pregnant when we left the east coast, and they hadn't had any quality time alone since. What little money I had was not enough to rent a place, so I really needed to find work fast. It was very disappointing being turned down constantly. I had no address, no job, no transportation... nothing. I slept outside on a bench that first night. After that I crashed wherever I could. This had to change and fast.

I hitched into Santa Barbara with the intent of pawning the

watch my dad gave me after I graduated high school. I was that desperate. The man who picked me up offered me a temporary job finishing some shelves and cabinets in a store he was about to open. It wasn't much but it was good for a few bucks. Shortly thereafter I took another part time job in the mornings at a Motel 6 or Super 8 cleaning the parking lot. The Santa Anna winds were dropping ash every night all over the city from the fires burning in the nearby foothills. I pushed a broom from one end of the parking lot to the other, kicking up dust and ash as I went. I could only keep the broom damp for so long before it dried out again. Watching the fires at night was eerie, an orange line of flame rose to a hilltop before disappearing behind another, but the glow was always there.

I answered an ad for a part time position pulling weeds at a nursery up on the mesa. Santa Barbara was the only place to find any work. It was backbreaking and exhausting, hunched over all day, but I made an impression on the boss (Tony). The job was temporary, and only supposed to last a week or two, but when we had completed our task, I was offered a fulltime position. There were a few "hippies" working there and several Hispanics. Tony was a short round man with a small mustache and a little dog named Penny who followed him everywhere. His personality was similar to Archie Bunker, he was prejudiced toward Mexicans, though in their presence you would never know it.

One morning we had "potting" stations set along the road in the main section of the palm house. The task that day was to take seedling palms from little 2 ½" clay pots and place three or four of them together in a 6" pot. You added soil and firmed them in place with a "potting stick" which was little more than a blunt end wooden shaft that was comfortable enough to grip. After we finished each 6" pot, it was placed on a shallow wooden flat with the others. Once the flat was full it was rolled out of the way via a set of raised metal rollers and replaced with another empty flat. Nothing to it. I tore into this simple assignment and established a rhythm quickly.

After a couple of hours, a small group of co-workers approached me saying I was done for the day. I didn't understand and they informed me I had already reached the day's "quota." Stunned, I looked back in disbelief. I was making them look bad by being so productive. They had been doing this for years and apparently the boss had no clue they could be far more productive. In order for me to continue working there, I needed to be very careful how I paced myself with everything. I quickly learned the "art" of always looking busy even when I wasn't. I had to pick and choose my moments for demonstrating what I could really do to impress the boss. I always produced the most work, but by a very small margin for the sake of my own safety. If given a nonroutine task, I got it done quickly and correctly, which delighted the boss and inspired him to give me more to do. It also earned a modest pay raise.

I was always at work and on time every day, even though I had to hitchhike to get there. The boss would bark at anyone who was late and point to me being on time despite not having a car. My co-workers just shrugged his rambling off and didn't make any effort to change. Eventually I became the crew leader of a very interesting bunch of guys. We had one coworker who was AWOL from the service. When law enforcement arrived to take him away, word spread like wildfire when several black cars showed up that "immigration" was here. Half the crew ran down the face of a 150' cliff to the narrow beach below, scattering in both directions. We never saw them again; our AWOL buddy was arrested and removed in handcuffs. Art was a Mexican Indian who believed himself to be a victim of the white man. Once you got past all of that baggage, he was a nice guy at heart. We had alcoholics, potheads, straight people, and one guy was operating on fumes, literally (I think he inhaled too much insecticide).

We had a long wooden planter of marijuana growing on the roof of the tractor garage that had just been watered when the local police showed up out of nowhere, confiscating our precious plants. We have no idea who tipped them off and we never saw anything in the paper about it either, so what happened to the pot? I'm sure they were disappointed they missed seeing whoever just watered those plants. We grew pot in several places. We had a great growing spot on the face of the cliff about 30 feet down from where we ate lunch as it seemed very safe there. No one from below could see them and the way down from the top was on our property which was locked at night. We had everything we needed to grow an excellent crop at the nursery. Lots of sun, fertilizer, and water. They grew pretty tall and then they were gone too. I never learned what happened but believed it had to be a co-worker. We grew good healthy-looking plants, but never enjoyed any of it.

I don't know how I was introduced to Tom Hawk, but we somehow ended up renting an apartment together in Isla Vista. We were strangers with very little in common. He loved muscle cars and owned an orange-colored Road Runner with a black roof, while I used my thumb to get from place to place.

He had family in town, and I had none. He knew the area and I didn't. We both had jobs though and agreed to keep the apartment clean and we were responsible for paying all our bills on time. We both liked music and pot. He introduced me to his friends, and I made some of my own. He worked 4 days a week for 10 hours a day, so he had more days off than I did. We made it work and over time became very good friends.

Keeline-Wilcox nursery was located on an area known locally as "the mesa" and covered about 70 acres abutting the Pacific Ocean. It offered a spectacular view of the Channel Islands. We had a small wooden bench at the edge of the cliff where we ate lunch and on occasion watched killer whales just offshore beyond the surfers. The main building covered four or five acres under a lath roof to restrict some of the sun's rays from scorching the delicate Kentia Forsteriana palms growing beneath. Much of the property was undeveloped. There was a ring of tall pines surrounding a field at the far side of the acreage away from the main gate. This was rumored to be the spot the owner had set aside to build a house for his daughter as a wedding present. The pine needles were so thick on the ground it felt like you were walking on a mattress. The beach below was a hot spot for local surfers. I used to go up there on my days off just to take in the view. It was fantastic. The waves, the smell of pine, the sun, and the surfers... heaven.

Santa Barbara was an unusual place and certainly not like any I had ever seen or lived in before. I heard the term "land of the newly wed or nearly dead" in reference to the distinct age groups living there. Isla Vista was a small part of Santa Barbara and comprised mostly of students attending UCSB or City College. Car travel was restricted on certain streets in IV.

Law enforcement either walked or rode bicycles. You could smell pot in the air everywhere and deals were often done in the street. People's Park was a gathering space where free live music routinely played with little or no notice. The rent was affordable. It bordered the beach, and you could walk right on to the UCSB campus. The best bands in the country played on campus or nearby, and tickets back then were cheap, $4.00 or $5.00 would get you in to see anyone. The vibe was very much like what I had hoped to find in Haight-Ashbury.

What I wasn't aware of when we settled in IV, was the extent of the tension between the Santa Barbara police and the student population, as there had been riots about a year prior to my living there. The IV foot patrol police got along reasonably well with the local residents as I recall. There was a pool hall called the "Campus Cue" where some hardcore drug users could be found. Needle tracks clearly visible when their shirtsleeves were rolled up. There were restaurants and head shops, a movie theater, and a college radio station. The air was alive with activity at all hours of the day and night. There was no alcohol sold in Isla Vista, but you could have it delivered from a nearby town as long as someone of legal age paid for it. Politics were discussed everywhere. This was a hub of the counterculture I came to identify with and I fit right in. I was completely free to do as I pleased. My job was my #1 priority, as without it, I couldn't do much of anything. I had to have money in my pocket. Drugs and music were everywhere.

We can be together
Ah, you and me
We should be together

We are all outlaws in the eyes of America

In order to survive
We steal, cheat, lie, forge, fuck, hide, and deal
We are obscene, lawless, hideous, dangerous, dirty, violent, and young

We should be together
Come on all you people standin' around
Our life's too fine to let it die
We should be together

All your private property is
Target for your enemy
And your enemy is we

We are forces of chaos and anarchy
Everything they say we are, we are
And we are very
Proud of ourselves

Up against the wall
Up against the wall, motherfuckers!
Tear down the wall
Tear down the wall

Come on now together
Get it on together
Everybody together
We should be together
We should be together my friends
We can be together
We will be

We must begin here and now
A new continent of earth and fire
Tear down the wall

Tear down, getting higher and higher
Tear down the wall
Tear down the wall
Tear down the wall
Won't you try?

..... Jefferson Airplane

Scott was looking for work and I got him a job at the nursery. It started out okay but then he began showing up late. Tony told me my friend wasn't reliable and it was on me that he was hired in the first place. I had no control over what he did but felt guilt or shame every time he punched in late. Then he became a no show a few times and was eventually fired. He let me down and cast a bad light on me with my boss. I learned right then to be more selective with my recommendations in the future.

Jimmy was unable to find any meaningful work. Barbara had her baby and named it Dylan. With no prospects for work, they decided to head back home. They asked me if I wanted to go back with them, but I declined. I had a job and a place to live. I was going to stay. Six of us went on an adventure together, and one by one they turned around and went home. Not me, I needed to prove I could make it on my own, if to no one else but myself.

I need to regress for a moment. During our travels somewhere in Arizona, we wandered into a headshop and saw this game called "Beat the Border." The goal was to smuggle pot into the country without getting busted. It was a cheesy little board game but the concept inspired Tom and I to expand upon the theme and create something bigger and better. We added a European trip to purchase hashish while still needing to "beat the border." The game board we made was much larger and involved the rolling and smoking of joints as part of the game (a refreshing departure from the original). We had fun drawing each block by hand and creating the messages for each of the steps. The popularity of our version quickly developed a life of its own. People really wanted to play, and we had to restrict the number of players. There was a "waiting list" for those who wanted in on game night. Those who couldn't play, still wanted to watch, so we had an exuberant audience laughing loudly in the thick, smoky haze, of our IV apartment. That board stayed in California when I left; I have no idea where it is today, but I will always remember the wild times around that game. Oh my God, was that fun!

Timothy Leary escaped from Lompoc prison in September of 1970. News spread through Isla Vista like wildfire. The Weathermen had executed an elaborate scheme to set him free. TV news covered it but not like the underground newspapers in California! Leary was like a God in IV. The Weathermen could have been anyone, you just never knew. He was on the run, and no one believed he would be found, because no one was saying where he was. He had a loyal following of "true believers" supporting him. His bizarre story was discussed at length with those who had "tuned in, turned on and dropped out." Timothy Leary represented a large percentage of the Isla Vista community. I'd have to say I was on the fringe of that sentiment. I certainly respected the feeling, but I also thought the guy was way, WAY, out there …. *but what if there was an astral plane?*

Though the people I came to California with had left, I was not "alone" as I did have family out there. Since I was very young,

I always had a soft spot in my heart for my "rebellious" Aunt Joyce. It was always a treat when she came to visit my dad, or more likely, my grandmother in Maine. She retold the most outrageous family stories and got everyone laughing with such ease. This would inevitably lead to more stories about her from my dad's perspective, and it would go on for hours. My aunt was full of life and adventure. I decided to surprise her by showing up unannounced at her home in Palos Verdes. It was a fancy neighborhood where I felt out of place in my humble and faded denim attire. I knocked on the enormous double door entrance to her home and waited. The door opened a crack and there she was! "I paid for the paper already," she stated matter-of-factly. When I didn't respond, she hesitated staring into my eyes until the recognition finally took hold. "Danny?" she asked in disbelief. She was stunned! Just the emotion I was looking for!

Once inside, she naturally wanted to know what I was doing there, had I eaten, etc. She insisted on washing my clothes too! I recounted my journey to California and ate a sandwich while my laundry was being done. I wore pants and a shirt that belonged to Peter, my oldest cousin. My aunt's house was full of artwork. Some was her own, she loved to draw birds. Later she devoted much of her time to sculpting. She and my dad were both creative thinkers and artistically inclined. Eventually she took me for a driving tour of everything from Hollywood to Watts. She showed me earthquake damaged streets and where the riots took place and on and on. She was full of information. It was rare that I had one on one time with my aunt, and I ate it up. It was getting late in the afternoon and my cousins would be coming home from school soon. I hadn't seen them in a very long time.

We returned to Palos Verdes before Peter and Byard (no longer called David). The laundry was done, and I got back in my more comfortable clothes. When my cousins came home, they took me outside on their patio armed with firecrackers and a slingshot. Byard lit the fuses while Peter lobbed explosives into neighbors' pools who lived downhill! They were Hellraisers just like my aunt and dad! They roared with laughter while I looked on with astonishment. My uncle Ted came home from work, and we all had a great family dinner. When Uncle Ted asked about where I was living, he proceeded to tell me a story about him rowing a boat into a cave on one of the Channel Islands off the coast of Santa Barbara. He said there was a beach at the end that was full of seals. The noise from their barking echoed so loudly off the cave walls, you wanted to cover your ears. He asked me if I liked sailing. "Absolutely," I said.

The next day they took me out on a sailboat and headed in the direction of Catalina Island. It felt great to be on the water again. It was a warm day with just the right breeze. When I looked back toward shore, I was shocked to see about four rows of clustered housing before losing sight of anything further due to the smog! Land bearings disappeared into the brownish haze quickly, so you had to use a compass for navigation even on a sunny day. Back home I used direct sight and dead reckoning. I had a great visit over the course of a few days.

10/10/71: I finally saw the Allman Brothers after missing them perform in Newport. They had a gig at the UCSB gym. I stood center stage a few rows back. Dickey Betts was right in front of me tuning and warming up when Duane hopped on stage, grabbed his guitar, and said into the mic, "C'mon Dickey these people don't want to hear that!" He went immediately into their first song, and it never slowed down from there! The gym was rockin'! Amazing show, but no Whipping Post encore! The Elvin Bishop Group opened, and they were very entertaining too. "My little ol' sweet patatah." I believe Elvin performed a couple of songs with the brothers at the end of the show. Duane died on 10/29/71, just nineteen days after I saw him. This may have been the last concert Duane performed with the Allman Brothers.

CROSS COUNTRY HITCHHIKING

In late October of '71, Peter said he was going to return to the east coast and asked if I wanted to hitchhike with him. I wanted to visit my old friends, so I agreed. I was always up for a little adventure, and I had some time off coming to me at work. I sent a box of clothes ahead to my dad's office in Boston, so I wouldn't have to carry them with me. Inside I stashed a pound or so of pot. This would ensure I had a little spending money and partying time when I got back home. Peter and I scored a ride to Lake Tahoe on the first night. We were dropped at the beach next to a sign indicating it was closed at night and there was no sleeping allowed on the beach. We slept there that night as we had nowhere else to go.

I woke early in the morning to a stunningly beautiful sunrise. It was dead calm with no wind at all. Half the sky was cloudy and the other half clear. The clouds were bright pink in color and the water of the lake was still and mirror flat, reflecting the clouds on the surface. Lake Tahoe was pink! I woke a groggy Peter and walked off the beach before any cop had time to spot us.

We got back to our journey and the next ride dropped us in Sparks, Nevada. It was warm and sunny as we waited patiently on the sidewalk for someone to pick us up. A local cop pulled up to the curb and asked us what we were doing. We explained we had been dropped off there and were on our way to the east coast. He went on to inform us there was no hitchhiking allowed in the state of Nevada. We were at a loss. How were we supposed to get out of Nevada? He strongly suggested in his most sarcastic tone, we start walking, when another car pulled alongside and asked what the problem was. The officer started to explain hitching was illegal, when the driver interrupted and said he was talking to us and not the cop. The cop was pissed, and we quickly explained our dilemma. The driver turned to the cop and asked if it was against the law to offer the two of us a ride. He was told there was no law against it; the driver motioned us to get in. The cop was boiling mad. The first thing Peter and I noticed after we thanked the guy, was he had a telephone in his car. We had never seen one in a car before. Turns out he was a prosecuting attorney for the city of Indianapolis, Indiana.

He was looking to make good time and wanted us to take turns driving. He was disappointed I didn't drive but was glad to hear Peter did. He stopped in Salt Lake City, booked a luxury room, and allowed us to sleep on the floor. It sure beat sleeping under the stars. Peter and I walked through the central park in the city and saw the monument to the seagulls and read some of the history of the Mormons before returning to the room for the night. We stayed up late watching movies on TV before eventually turning in.

We were back on the road early the next day. Peter and the Good Samaritan lawyer took turns driving. In the afternoon we pulled over for a break and some lunch. The lawyer had sliced ham and cheese for sandwiches and gallon bottles of Cribari wine in his trunk. We were so fortunate to have had him come to our rescue in Sparks! He took us all the way to Illinois before he needed to change direction and head south. It was a great ride, and we covered a lot of miles in short order.

I remember it was raining and we kept getting quick but short rides. We'd hitch from under bridges to keep as dry as we could, but eventually we got tired and had to get some sleep. We crawled up under a bridge as far from the road as we could so we wouldn't be seen. The mosquitos were driving me crazy, and I just couldn't get comfortable. Peter was already blissfully snoring away. The bugs couldn't penetrate his thick beard. After an hour of this, I woke him up and said we had to keep going. He'd had a refreshing nap and was ready. Somewhere in Will County we received a written warning from an Illinois state cop for hitchhiking and were warned not to be caught doing it again. I remember folding the warning up and placing it in my wallet, then forgetting about it. We had to keep hitchin'! We got another ride immediately.

Our adventure continued. We got creeped out by a guy who picked us up and asked if we had any pot. We didn't and told him so. He asked that we open the case behind the seat, and it was full of marijuana. Then he started asking if we knew people who had pot. Something wasn't right with this guy, and we couldn't be sure if he was just strange or perhaps was working with local cops. We got out at our first opportunity.

We never waited more than an hour at any one place when we were actively hitching, and we were making great time. Somewhere in Connecticut we got a ride with a guy and his dog. We hadn't gone too far when he apologized and said he couldn't take us any further. He also said someone traveling behind him was going to pick us up. Peter and I wondered how that could be possible and just dismissed the guy as a quack. We did get picked up by someone who had a friend traveling with a dog in another car ...weird.

Our next ride was a cabbie on his way home to Danvers, MA! We knew this was going to be another great ride. The driver just wanted to be entertained by our stories and said as long as we kept talking, he would drive us all the way to our Magnolia destination! Talk about luck! We had our old familiar WBCN (104.1) on the radio as we neared Boston and just as we left Manchester for Magnolia, "Closer to Home" by Grand Funk came on. Wow, this was amazing. "I'm getting closer to my home .... I'm getting closer to my home ....." True to his word, he drove us right to my house. He was tired and still had to backtrack to Danvers. What a fantastic ride that was.

We went across country in five days using our thumbs; you

couldn't drive it much faster than that. It was early in the morning when we pulled into my driveway. I didn't want to wake anyone, so we went around to the back yard (or the front as my dad would say) then rolled out our bags to get some much-needed sleep. We got up a while later when I heard movement in the house. Joyce saw Peter, a stranger, through the window and was scared until she noticed me. She let us in and made us a big breakfast while we recounted the parts of our trip we were comfortable enough sharing. I was home again. The ocean never looked so good!

Later in the day Peter and I parted ways. I walked into the Table Four, a local bar in Manchester, and saw several of my old friends. It was great to see everyone. I felt like a rock star as everybody wanted to know where I had been and what I was doing back etc. I'm sure I saw Newt at some point. I knew I wouldn't be staying long as I had a job and friends waiting for me back in IV, but I wanted to soak up this attention for a while. I felt like I had been missed and this gave me a feeling of joy. I felt like I mattered. It was the kind of feeling I had craved for years. I was somebody.

My dad brought the box of clothes I had sent ahead home from the office, and I nervously noticed the damage. It was partially open, and I felt sure the pot had been discovered, but it was still there. Thank God he didn't try to repack everything in a better box for me! It wouldn't take long to sell a few lids and have a little spending money. California pot sold quickly.

Tom Rush's version of Joni Mitchell's song "Urge for Goin'" swam around in my head. Time passed in the blink of an eye I knew these good times had to come to an end.

And all that stays is dying all that lives is gettin' out
See the geese in chevron flight
Flapping and racing on before the snow...
They've got the urge for going

And they've got the wings to go

I got the urge for goin' and I had a thumb to help me go. The weather in Magnolia was nice but fall could descend quickly, and I knew I had to be on my way before it got too cold. I didn't want to be hitching in the snow.

When it was time to return to California, my dad gave me his Coast Guard duffle bag. It was in excellent shape and perfect for carrying the clothes I'd sent ahead weeks earlier. This would also save me a freight charge. I rolled my clothes tightly (a trick my dad taught me to keep them wrinkle free) and packed up what I had. My stepsister Laurie baked me a big batch of toll house cookies for the road, and they were wonderful. My dad also gave me $20.00 which I tried to refuse. He made a joke and told me to take it for "bail money." I folded the bill and pinned it to the inseam of my jeans and was on my way again. Dad dropped me off at an on ramp to 128 south. Peter was staying behind. This would be my first trip across country alone.

I had one ride which made me very nervous. A box truck pulled over and the driver told me to throw the duffle in the back. I didn't like being separated from my things but did it. There was no problem in the end, but I was completely on my own and at the mercy of those who stopped to "help." It's something you just had to get used to.

Just outside of Chicago I was holding my "California" sign against my chest when a cop pulled up with a stern expression plastered on his face. He wanted to see some ID. I opened my wallet, and he shined his light on it so I could see better. "What's that?" he asked when he saw a small piece of paper folded inside. I couldn't recall and pulled it out to get a better look. It was the written warning I had received in the neighboring county only weeks before. The cop looked at me and noted I had already been warned not to hitch in Illinois. He stoically informed me I would be riding with him to headquarters in Cook County, and likely spend some time in "the crossbar hotel" (jail!). Just great.

At the station I had to fill out some paperwork. Another cop informed me the officer who brought me in hasn't so much as smiled since he'd been there, and I could be released on bail if I had $20.00! Thank-you Dad! He must have been clairvoyant. I wanted to take a different route to California, but my first trick would involve hitching out of Cook County without being arrested again. A trucker picked me up and I was once more on my way.

I headed south to get on route 70 to avoid the colder weather I was sure to experience on the northern route. I was in Missouri on a fairly nice day with my thumb out, facing the scant oncoming traffic when a semi crossed over into the breakdown lane as it approached doing the speed limit. I figured the driver must have dozed off and was glad he recovered in time to miss me. Minutes later another semi crossed the same line but a little further into the breakdown lane than the first truck. This was no coincidence. Another truck was heading toward me and this one was completely in the breakdown lane! I had to jump out of the way to avoid being hit. I now knew I was a target and they had to be talking on CB radios. When you're alone, you have no one but yourself to count on. This was not good. All I could picture was a convoy of trucks taking bets to see who would nail me first! I could be dead by the side of the road, and no one would know.

A very kind young woman in a station wagon stopped and picked me up. She had two kids in the back seat, and she said she had to drop them off in town but would continue down the highway after that. She asked if I minded the detour. I said it would be fine as I really didn't want to be standing out in the open on that particular stretch of road.

She dropped off the kids and asked if I had eaten anything. I said I was fine, but she said she was hungry and wanted to grab something before traveling. I went with her to a small restaurant, and I felt every eye in the place on me... and her. Why was she with that long hair? She wanted to pay and wouldn't accept anything from me. She took me down the highway a way and then said goodbye, wishing me luck. She was a kind Samaritan just doing her Christian best by me and nothing more. I will never forget her for that reason.

Eventually, I took a ride with a young man driving a brand-new, yellow-orange, full sized school bus. This was a first. You just never know who is going to stop for you or what you might be riding in next. He was on his way to deliver the bus to the Kearney, Nebraska school system. He had pot and we fired a joint up then watched the country roll by, just the two of us in a shiny new school bus. I had to make a choice. Staying on the bus would take me a long way, but it also meant taking route 80 which I was hoping to avoid. So much for staying on interstate 70, 80 would be just as good.

I was let out somewhere outside of town in the middle of nowhere in Kansas. There was no traffic and I decided to get some sleep then resume in the morning. There was tall grass or hay growing just off the shoulder of the road. I swung my duffle by the laces in a circle to mat it down then crawled into my down filled mummy bag for some sleep. There was no traffic, so it was quiet until I heard voices off in the distance talking, but I couldn't make out what they were saying. I wasn't alone.

In the morning I got up and started thumbing again. I think it was a Sunday as many of the people I saw in the passing cars were very well-dressed. Kearney was not the friendliest town. I saw old ladies giving me the finger as they drove by me more than once. Contorted faces mouthing something indistinguishable, which I'm sure I didn't want to hear anyway. No one was stopping. This was going to be a long day; I could just feel it.

From off the side of the road I heard voices again, they were close by too, closer than what I heard the night before. Two guys emerged from the tall dry grass, approaching the ramp with backpacks. Just what I needed, competition. I figured I should break the ice, so I looked at my watch purposefully, then directly at them and said," You're late!" They laughed and it was then I noticed I knew one of them! I had seen him at a party somewhere in Santa Barbara some time back. We figured out we kind of knew each other and it was their voices I had heard the previous night. They were headed to California too. Both had hitched from West to East through Canada that summer and were now on their way home like me. We agreed to travel together the rest of the way.

As I anticipated, it was a long day. We stayed at that onramp for hours absorbing more than our share of verbal abuse from the passersby. At some point we called it quits then walked into town. We found a cheap place that had pizza, then found a liquor store. I was the only one old enough to buy a bottle of whiskey. This had been a waste of a day and our thoughts turned to getting out of sight for the night before trying again in the morning. We found a place off the road to bed down, then passed the bottle around until it was almost spent.

Sleep came easy and when we woke the next morning, I noticed my hair that was outside the sleeping bag was frozen, it had lightly snowed during the night. The next lucid moment was unsettling, as I spotted men with long rifles walking through the woods and tall grass. Apparently, it was hunting season for something, so we really needed to get back on the road. We were all hungover, as we hastily gathered our gear as quietly as we could and got back to the relative safety of asphalt.

Shortly after getting ourselves safely to the on ramp for what we assumed would be another long day, a pickup truck stopped. There was only room for two of us in the cab, so all the gear and yours truly hopped in the bed. We would do anything to get out of that town. We took turns in the back as we began a slow but steady ascent into the Rocky Mountains ... I must say my bag was plenty warm, even with the wind and occasional snow. Looking up at the rock cliffs hugging the roadside, it seemed as though they were ready to fall at any moment. It was beautiful and I probably had a better view of things than anyone in the cab. I really didn't mind being in the back.

We were somewhere near Denver when we stopped at a hotel for the night. It was the first time I had been comfortable in quite a while. We had a good meal, and a couple of cold Coors on draft. It was getting late, but we had nowhere else to go, so we just enjoyed sitting and talking. With just a few regulars left, the girl behind the bar asked if we wanted anything else before she closed for the night. We settled up, and then she said we could stay after closing if we wanted. We said why not. She locked the front door of the bar and pulled out a guitar, then came around to where the tables were and began playing and singing. Great way to end the night, and we felt privileged to be allowed to stay.

The next morning, we got an early start. The mountains were beautiful, and I was in the back of the truck once again. We eventually came upon Las Vegas, the older Las Vegas, with huge neon signs in every direction. The bright lights of the city were a stark contrast to the mountains we just came through. I had never seen lights like these. We stopped for gas and that was all. No gambling, we were just passing through. I do remember seeing a slot machine in the gas station bathroom, I didn't give it a try.

The long ride would terminate in Redlands, California. We all parted company and went in different directions. I was on the road shoulder in Alhambra when I saw a police helicopter buzz by overhead. Minutes later a police car pulled up without even looking in my direction. I think word came to them from on high, that a hitcher was on their freeway. I was given a ticket for "occupying space," then they dropped me off in a neighborhood near the freeway. My destination was close now and I desperately wanted to get back to IV without any further incident. I saw signs for route 101 and my energy was renewed. The long trek back was almost over. My job was waiting at Keeline Wilcox up on the Mesa.

(Note: I returned to the courthouse later on to pay my $100.00 fine.... of course, I hitched to get there.)

RETURN TO SANTA BARBARA

Christmas time in Santa Barbara was so odd seeing the Santas at various parking lots ringing bells for charities wearing Bermuda shorts. It didn't feel right. I wasn't cold, there was no snow... I really felt out of place and with no family close by, I was feeling alone and lonely. I saw some snow on top of Figueroa Mountain and decided to hitch into the hills outside of town to see if there was any snow there or at least maybe feel a little chill. It may have been Christmas Eve, I'm not really sure.

I was out on San Marcos Pass when it started raining and I figured it was time to head back. The rain was cold, and I was soon drenched. There were no lights out that way and traffic was nonexistent probably due to the holiday, so I walked and walked. It sucked being alone, cold, soaking wet, and a long way from home. This turned out to be a terrible idea. I had been walking for a while when I finally saw a set of headlights approach from the distance. The rain appeared steady in the twin headlights and the car was slowing to get a good look at the drowned rat walking the side of the road. Maybe some holiday magic was going to provide a lift down the mountain at last. As the car got closer, I could see it was a police car and the cop inside had a really good long look at me before he decided to keep on going. I couldn't believe a public servant would leave someone out on the road like that in that weather! It took me hours to get off that road and out of the cold. I did get a lift eventually and I was ever so grateful, but it was still going to take some time to get home. Not my favorite Christmas holiday.

You poisoned my sweet water.
You cut down my green trees.

The food you fed my children
Was the cause of their disease.

My world is slowly fallin' down
And the airs not good to breathe.
And those of us who care enough,
We have to do something.......

Oh... oh What you gonna do about me?
Oh... oh What you gonna do about me?

Your newspapers,
They just put you on.
They never tell you
The whole story.

They just put your
Young ideas down.
I was wonderin' could this be the end
Of your pride and glory?

Oh... oh What you gonna do about me?
Oh... oh What you gonna do about me?

I work in your factory.
I study in your schools.
I fill your penitentiaries.
And your military too!

And I feel the future trembling,
As the word is passed around.
"If you stand up for what you do believe,
Be prepared to be shot down."

Oh... oh What you gonna do about me?
Oh... oh What you gonna do about me?

And I feel like a stranger

In the land where I was born
And I live like an outlaw.
An' I'm always on the run...

An I'm always getting busted
And I got to take a stand....
I believe the revolution
Must be mighty close at hand...

Oh... oh What you gonna do about me?
Oh... oh What you gonna do about me?

I smoke marijuana
But I can't get behind your wars.
And most of what I do believe
Is against most of your laws

I'm a fugitive from injustice
But I'm goin' to be free.
Cause your rules and regulations
They don't do the thing for me

Oh... oh What you gonna do about me?
Oh... oh What you gonna do about me?

And I feel like a stranger
In the land where I was born
And I live just like an outlaw.
An' I'm always on the run.

......Quicksilver Messenger Service

For Christmas gifts, I bought tickets to a Quicksilver Messenger concert scheduled for early February and gave them to a family that had sort of taken me in. I think it was through them I met Tom Hawk, my roommate. They were delighted with the gift, and it made me feel good too. They were the closest thing to a family I had. "What About Me" was a theme song for my life at that time. I was dating the youngest of the two daughters at the time.

February 2, 1972, was the day for the draft lottery for men born in 1953. This was my year, and I was glued to the radio at work. One of my coworkers at the nursery and I were the same age. I remember listening to the numbers being drawn and called out. It didn't take long before I saw his expression drop. His number was 6 and he was bummed. I had to wait quite a while for my birthday to be called. My number was 186, chances were good I wasn't going to be drafted. The draft was officially abolished in 1973. I did not serve in the military; ROTC in high school was as close as I ever came. I had burned my draft card some months earlier as part of a demonstration in People's Park. I didn't believe in the war and saw no justification for fighting or dying there.

02/05/72: Dan Hicks and his Hot Licks opened for Quicksilver Messenger Service at Santa Barbara City College. I had been waiting for this concert for weeks and now it was finally here. Our seats were fairly close to the stage. Dan Hicks and those very Hot Licks had us all in a good mood with their unique brand of humor. Primed and ready, we waited for Quicksilver to fire us up. I was a big fan of this band when I was on the East Coast and seeing them was huge to me. Not long into their first set we were all getting into the music when the whole place went dark. The power was out. We could still see by the dim light coming through the windows. Everyone was milling around, and someone said we would resume shortly. Presto, the lights were on, and you could hear a hum from the equipment on the stage. The band was smiling, and they picked up where they left off and as soon as they got up to speed, BANG, the power was out again. They killed time with some drum solos and a little acoustic guitar..... Lights returned and they began again only to have it all go down once more. The band started passing out lit joints to those of us close to the stage and started playing the few instruments which didn't draw power.... They really tried but it wasn't what we all expected. I was disappointed for a couple of reasons. First because these were Christmas gifts I had given and secondly, they were one of my favorite bands. I felt like I let everyone down. What was supposed to be a great gift, was closer to being a major dud.

04/26/72: Leo Kottke opened for Van Morrison at the Granada Theater in Santa Barbara. This is a majestic venue with a rich history. Great place to see a concert. Leo performed three encores and we enthusiastically called him out for a fourth; he was willing and appreciative but told us Van was anxious to come out, so that was it for him. What a performance he gave us. Van was also amazing, but barely moved a muscle the whole time he was on stage. He sounded great but stood like a stone on stage as he belted out the fantastic songs we all knew so well. The energy was full on, but didn't align with what our eyes took in.

5/14/72: My roommate, Tom Hawk, and I decided we would get out of town one weekend and headed for Palm Springs. The traffic was crazy and the heat on the congested freeway was sweltering. We had the sun baking us from above and pavement frying us from below. It seemed like everyone had the same idea. We had the top down on his MG, and we were slowly being cooked alive. We heard on the radio it was even hotter in Palm Springs, so we decided to alter our plans on the fly. Our new destination was Big Bear.

It was dark by the time we got there and with no signs anywhere, we were clueless as to where we could go. We were both tired and figured we should find a quiet spot to sleep for the night. Off the side of a quiet dark road was a grassy area with a slight slope that seemed perfect to roll out the sleeping bags. When we woke the next morning, we realized we were on someone's front lawn! We got out of there quickly without being seen. Who knew!

There was a breakfast place open early, and we pulled into a small, nearly empty, parking lot. We took a booth and ordered some food. The radio news was playing through the speakers in the dining area. We heard Dan Blocker had passed away. He was young, only in his forties, and was my favorite Cartwright on Bonanza. Hoss!

With no real plans we decided to simply drive around looking at the scenery. It was a beautiful day with lots of sunshine and a heck of a lot cooler than the freeway. There were very few houses and lots of thick woods. I had to pee, so Tom pulled over. I walked down the embankment to some bushes and began relieving my full bladder. I had this uneasy feeling of being watched and slowly turned my head to the side and saw a deer a couple of feet away on the other side of the bush. I yelled, "Deer!" and it spooked him into a run. Tom heard me from the road and came barreling down the hill as he thought I said "Beer." We had a laugh and climbed back up to the road then drove off.

We kept seeing signs for equestrian crossings and neither of us knew what an equestrian was. We did notice huge swarms of butterflies cutting across our path as we drove and assumed equestrians were synonymous with or some specific type of butterfly. It all made perfect sense to us at the time. You don't know what you don't know. That evening before it got too dark, we found another place to sleep, which was not on someone's lawn. Tom woke the next morning with an intense pain in his shoulder. When he pulled his collar down to take a look, he found a tick burrowed into the center of this big purple lump the size of a golf ball. He needed medical treatment, so this trip was officially over.

November 11, 1972: I saw Dan Hicks and his Hot Licks again when they opened for Hot Tuna (The Hot Tuna show was the loudest I'd ever heard). I believe the venue was the gym at

UCSB. Dan Hicks was very entertaining, witty, and relaxed as usual. Hot Tuna was overwhelming! Jack Cassidy was wearing red from head to toe, sporting his famous black eyepatch and his black guitar strap cutting diagonally across his torso and a black headband. Rich deep tones pounded out the rhythm. Jorma was otherworldly and mesmerizing. If you closed your eyes and listened, you would swear there were three guitarists on stage playing at the same time. The complexity of the music was so intricate and powerfully loud. It seemed there was a musical bridge connecting me from my slightly elevated perspective (not in reference to the balcony I watched from), to the very stage on which he stood. I wanted to walk across it. Papa John Creach was actively hopping around with his contributions to the magical music. This truly was a supergroup. What a show! Incredible music. I wished everyone I knew could have been there. I recall when Hot Tuna was first played on FM radio no one knew who was in the band. I think demos showed up at radio stations and the DJs went nuts and just started playing it because it was that good. I think the same thing could be said about Derek and the Dominos. Music was just so exciting to me.

12/31/72: Chuck Berry at the Arlington Theater scheduled for 11:30 PM: Anticipation was high for a great New Year's Eve concert with the legendary Chuck Berry. This theater is designed to give you the impression you were in the courtyard of a small Mexican town. The balconies looked like they were attached to villas lining the road, leading to a central fountain. The ceiling was a nightscape with stars. It was gorgeous inside. The show started strong, and the audience was having a great time as he rolled and duck-walked through several hit songs back-to-back-to-back. He invited people from the audience to come up on stage and dance while he played. Security firmly escorted them off as soon as they got up there and Chuck was pissed. He kept waving people up anyway, and security kept removing them. Abruptly he stopped playing and walked off stage. The crowd went nuts, but there was nothing the promoter could do. The band apologized and said they would stay and play, but we wanted Chuck back. They told us he had already left the building. I heard later he was pulling this stunt at other shows too. We saw him for 45 minutes and that was it! Very disappointed.

March 11, Concert (on my calendar): Granada Theater, Santa Barbara, CA: Mahavishnu Orchestra...This was something else. These guys continually traded off leads and you had a hard time following who was actually playing at times. They could make a guitar sound like a violin or vice versa. Same with the keywords. Really a good show. John McLaughlin was phenomenal. This version of the band featured Jan Hammer on keys, Billy Cobham on drums and Jerry Goodman on violin. Strange new music... really good music! The energy was off the charts and the audience was treated to a special sound that wasn't anything they had heard before. We were in rare air. If you've never heard of them before, you need to check them out.

March 17, 1973: The Beach Boys (remains one of the all-time great shows I ever attended) - the Beach Boys played a sock-hop in the gym - pandemonium from start to finish. Their wives and kids were on stage, and it had the feel of a family reunion. They told stories about the music they played and had other family members including kids dancing on the stage. "Kids, this next song was written before I knew your mother" ... A lot of fun, fun, fun for sure. Mike Love had a house on the Mesa in Santa Barbara just a few doors down from the nursery where I worked (more on that later).

February 20, 1973: Mark-Almond on the UCSB Campus. I was familiar with them from when they were part of John Mayal's band. The constant stream of musicians rolling through Santa Barbara and Isla Vista was uncanny. I was in heaven. I could never have seen this many bands back home.

March 28, Concert (on my calendar) ... I have no idea who I saw, but I am sure it was great!

In April I made a call to Ned Werner back in Magnolia. The Nursery I worked for was going to close the Santa Barbara location and relocate to the smog choked city of East Irvine to the south. I was asked if I wanted to work there and had declined. My dad heard that our neighbor and family friend, Ned, was looking for some help with a Hinckley sloop he had recently purchased. I really had nothing much keeping me in California anymore, so I said I would take the job. I had a chance to move back to Magnolia, live on his boat or in his house. It was a job I couldn't pass up, but I wanted to stay in Santa Barbara for one more concert. The Grateful Dead were coming.

Albert King and Freddie King on a date I can't recall. Location (Robertson Gym?). I think there was a third act playing but can't recall who it was (it may have been another "King" but not BB). I think it was billed as the King or Kings of the Blues. I was right up front, and the blues were great!

I attended several other concerts at the Santa Barbara County Bowl but am unsure of the dates.

- Paul Butterfield and Better Days with Sonny Terry and Brownie McGhee opening the show. Sonny Terry is probably the best harp player I have ever seen... and I've seen a lot! I couldn't believe the variety of different tones and sounds he could produce so clearly! We had great seats close to the band. Butterfield was terrific too. His style of harp playing was so different than Sonny's. Super place to take in a show!

- Dave Mason played on one beautiful evening. The crowd outside the chain-linked fence broke through and Mason stopped. He asked people to go back out and put the fence back in place. I thought this was going to end the event but to my astonishment, and most everyone around me, they complied, and the music continued! You could see the lights of Santa Barbara down below the stage and the boats between the shore and the Channel Islands. Moonshine and stars with a few clouds and a warm breeze ...what a night! All along the Watchtower was awesome! He played solo work and stuff from Traffic. Great venue for sure.

Californians are very different than the people where I grew up. They have no concept of staying inside due to bad weather because they don't have much. Card games? Board Games? Not likely. Outdoor activities were always planned or simply evolved out of thin air. Hikes, the beach, long drives, music in the park or on campus. There was always something going on and no one stayed home for very long.

There was a really cool place my friends took me to called the Gaviota Hot Springs. There was a small unpaved parking area off the road as I recall. No lights. No signs. Just a foot trail going up a hill. We arrived late on an overcast afternoon. All I could do was follow as we headed up, I had no real idea where we were. Someone fired up a joint and we passed it between us as we hiked up the path. The air temp was cool and a bit on the raw side. Finally, we reached our destination. I don't know what I expected but there wasn't much to it. We were in a small clearing with a roundish hole in the ground; the grass worn off the edge all the way around. No one else was there. There were no benches. The pungent smell of sulfur was obvious as we undressed and hopped in the very shallow spring. You had to sit on the sandy bottom to keep your shoulders in the warm water.

Soon we were all laughing and bobbing from side to side. It was warm and felt great. Time went by and before long we realized what little sun we still had was fading away quickly.

We shared a couple of towels and dried off as best we could. The lingering warmth of the water allowed us to dress slowly despite the deepening chill in the air. Night was settling in as we gathered the last of our things. We all reeked of Sulfur from the water, especially our hair. Another joint appeared and the glow moved from person to person as we began our descent to the cars parked below. No one thought to bring a flashlight, so we had to be careful walking down the path using the evening sky's meager light.

Someone saw car headlights ahead, and shortly after, a handheld light swept across the parking area. Our guard was up and moments later we had good reason. There were a couple of cops waiting for us as we left the end of the trail. Immediately the intense illumination from a long black Maglite was thrust into our faces, one after the other. Obviously, he was looking to provoke a reaction. One in the group was able to make out the lens was cracked and commented on it. The response was meant to intimidate, "Happened when I struck it over someone's head." The relationship between law enforcement and the younger population in the area, many of which were college students, was strained at best. Most interactions I experienced were confrontational in nature. The riots were still fresh in the minds of all residents of Santa Barbara and the surrounding communities. The cops were unsuccessful in getting any one of us to "flinch" and as quickly as the contact began, it was over. We piled into the cars and slowly left, anticipating the cops were still close by and watching somehow. The cops in the streets were different than those in Isla Vista who typically rode bikes or walked. In IV they were part of the community, and you got the sense they wanted to keep the peace and avoid confrontation at all costs. These guys wanted trouble.

THE NURSERY

I looked up the particular palm tree we grew in the Nursery: Howea Forsteriana, the Kentia palm or thatch palm, is a species of flowering plant in the palm family Arecaceae, endemic to Lord Howe Island in Australia. It is also widely grown on Norfolk Island. It is a relatively slow-growing palm, eventually growing up to 10 m (33 ft) tall by 6 m (20 ft) wide. Its fronds can reach 3 m (10 ft) long.

The Love Foundation (as in Mike Love) considered buying the Nursery where I worked, as did Fess Parker. One sunny hot afternoon I was working outside of the lath house overlooking the Pacific Ocean from the top of the mesa. We were "grinding soil" with a machine that took clumps of dirt, separated the stones and debris, then dumped the sifted soil in a pile where we would cart it off for use in the lath house. There was a slight breeze that sunny day and I was working hard. The finest soil (dust really) was covering my body, sticking to my sweat. Face, arms …everywhere was coated. Through the smallest of slits, I looked out and saw a few well-dressed men headed my way. One waved and smiled at me, I returned the wave …. It was "Daniel Boone!" …Fess Parker! Apparently, he was interested in buying the property…for condos, I think.

I used to hitchhike to work every day and would often be the first one to arrive. I'd have to wait for someone to unlock the main gate before I could punch in and start my day. One morning I saw an MG convertible parked inside the fence by the entrance. I climbed over and was sitting in the car when the crew began showing up. I asked them what they thought of my new wheels, and we all had a laugh. Later that day a woman came to claim the car, her husband's car. They lived a few doors down from the nursery and were driving around the property the previous day when we locked the gate. Her husband was Mike Love of the Beach Boys! His MG convertible (the one that looked like it was used in the ads for Craig car stereo) was very comfortable. The Love foundation was also interested in the property I think as a rehabilitation locale for ex-cons.

As far as I know the property (or most of it) eventually became a public park. The Actor Michael Douglas may have had something to do with that, I'm not really sure. It was a beautiful place. Twenty-foot-tall bird of paradise plants lined the main drive to the office. They were overgrown and neglected, but impressive, nonetheless. I think we had four or five acres of palm trees in the lath house. We also grew azaleas in greenhouses. There was a dirt road which terminated at a field on the far end of the property ringed with huge pine trees. The fallen needles were never cleared and piled up over the years. The house that was never built would have been located here. I never knew the story of what happened. I loved to go there to watch the surfers far below. We could see seals and killer whales occasionally just beyond where they were riding the surf. It really was a place special. I would love to visit here again just to relive the feelings, sights, sounds, and smells. That property is worth a fortune.

Just outside the lath house near the edge of the cliff was a bench where I would sit and watch the ocean during lunch. There was a huge unpruned avocado tree at the far edge of the property where I would climb to pick my lunch sometimes. The avocados were smaller and more rounded but oh so good .... I would add some salt, that is all.

I learned to drive various tractors at the nursery, but never took the time to get a real driver's license. The roads under the lath roof were straight with each intersection at 90-degree angles. The main road which ran through the center of the building was the widest. The rear wheels of the tractors had independent brakes which would allow you to turn on a dime. Jam on the brake for one wheel while still using the throttle with your other foot and you could pull a 180 turn on the main road. I got pretty good with the tractors. It was a fun place to work and the characters who worked with me made every day more interesting.

The lead salesman was a greedy slimeball who would literally rub his hands vigorously together when he made a big sale. He was not against overcharging either. The more profit the better and the more enthusiastically his meaty paws rubbed. He and I never got along but my boss and I did. We all suffered the misfortune of having Julius cover for Tony when he went on vacation. I ended up getting fired because I punched in a couple of minutes late from lunch! He loved firing me and smiled with delight while he did it. When Tony returned, he said he would find a way to get me back. He also found me another job to get me by until then.

A new experience for me was picking Gypsophila (Baby's Breath) in Carpinteria. I had to crouch or stoop, cut stems, gather bundles before wrapping a piece of wire around each one before setting it in the row for someone else to collect. Swarms of bees were all around while you did your job. They also grew Cymbidiums (orchids) in a greenhouse which smelled very strongly of perfume. Surrounding the rows of Baby's Breath was farmland. I recall them harvesting celery one day and the air was pungent with that distinct smell. The air was saturated with varying smells.

After a couple of weeks, I learned Julius was gone, and I was rehired at the nursery. A decision was made to consolidate the Santa Barbara location with the one in East Irvine. I was given the opportunity to relocate with the move but declined as the smog down there was horrible and I didn't want to live in a city. We began the process of packing up the palms and loading them onto semi-trailers. I developed a knack for quickly and efficiently building, then loading shelves inside the long trailers. When we started it would take most of a day to load one truck, eventually we did it in about two hours. I told the crew where to position themselves and where I wanted the flats of seedlings placed and we flew! The boss had no problem letting me take charge. We dismantled sprinkler systems and clay pot inventories were moved. There were black widow spiders everywhere and a few scorpions too. What started as a temporary job pulling weeds ended up being two years of employment, but it was now time to move on...

It's so easy to slip
It's so easy to fall
And let your memory drift
And do nothin' at all
All the love that you missed
All the people that you can't recall
Do they really exist at all
Well my whole world seems so cold today
All the magic's gone away
And our time together melts away
Like the sad melody I play
Well I don't want to drift forever
In the shadow of your leaving me
So I'll light another cigarette
And try to remember to forget
It's so easy to slip
It's so easy to fall
And let your memory drift
And do nothin' at all
All the love that you missed
All the people that you can't recall
Do they really exist at all

..... Little Feat

A FEW MORE CONCERTS AND
ANOTHER TRIP CROSS COUNTRY

May 2, 1973: Beck, Bogert & Appice was scheduled to open for Tower of Power.... Jeff Beck was "late" so Tower of Power opened the show, and they were fantastic. Many of us thought Jeff was intentionally late because he felt TOP should have opened for him anyway. The crowd was very into Tower of Power, and they played with a ton of energy. We wondered if Jeff was going to show up at all and then word spread rapidly he was in the building. When he took the stage the vibe changed dramatically, and he was simply awesome. He filled the gym with sound from his great band. His rendition of Superstition blew us away and that was just the beginning. He rocked the house! There is no one like Jeff Beck and there never will be. He can do anything with a guitar. He was in complete control and having as much fun as we were. I saw one of my favorite guitarists of all time. What a night!

May 8th: Boz Scaggs played in the Gym on the UCSB campus. So many good shows there and they were just a short walk from where I lived. Boz was awesome. Great band, great sound and the guy could sing! This wouldn't be the last time I'd see Boz! I was going to miss going to concerts at the gym. It was so convenient for me to walk over, listen to great music, then walk home.

May 13, 1973: Loggins & Messina: I think the first set was just Kenny sitting on the edge of the stage with his legs hanging over, singing House at Pooh Corner and a few others. There was a soft and very intimate quality that was special. When Jimmy Messina came out with his electric guitar, he directed the sound engineers to raise or lower the sound from each of the instruments on stage. He was all over the place listening and pointing up or down and then they started rockin'! Lots of fun. It was like two totally different shows rolled into one.

5/15/73: Our rent ended, and we had to find a place to live for a few days until the Dead played.

5/20/1973 (Harder Stadium): New Riders of the Purple Sage opened for the Grateful Dead...Jerry Garcia played in both bands. There were many problems associated with getting this concert to happen from the beginning. I stayed on in Santa Barbara just in case they finally pulled it all together. I had my bags packed, the lease on the apartment was up, we had moved out and stayed with friends, as it looked like the concert was really going to happen. It was overcast with periods of rain for days leading up to the event, which was uncharacteristic for the area. We thought there was a chance it would be called off at the last moment due to weather, but no, they were going to play! .... NRPS opened and performed for a couple of hours. Loved their music. Dirty Business and Somebody Robbed the Glendale Train being my favorites and let's not forget Panama Red! ... And then the Dead appeared... and the sun came out! Deadheads were blown away by the change in weather and if they had any doubts about Jerry being God, they were laid to rest at that moment.... The band played for hours in a typical Grateful Dead manner; jamming and extending songs, and when it was over the clouds returned...amazing. "Playin'... Playin' in the Band." Having fulfilled my desire to see this band perform, there was nothing holding me back from leaving California and returning to the east coast. Driving with friends this time rather than hitchhiking, was going to be so much better.

5/21/73: I left California for the East Coast. There were three of us, Tom Hawk my roommate, and Curtis Guthrie. Tom owned a black El Camino at the time. We stored most of our gear in the back under a tarp to keep the weather off. We also had some clothes tucked behind the front seat for easy access. I had a very good feeling about this trip as there would be no hitchhiking involved. We were on our way. My fourth trip across country!

We stopped in a dry dusty town somewhere in Nevada for a bite to eat. The owner took our order and when he returned, he asked if we would consider staying on for a while as he was looking for help. We were surprised and it must have shown on our faces. He continued by acknowledging "There isn't much to look at right now, but when the workday ended, places like his filled with cowboys and the atmosphere was markedly different than what you're looking at." We respectfully declined saying we had people expecting us on the east coast (true for me but not my co-travelers). It was really like a ghost town, and we wondered what the nighttime would be like, but didn't stay to experience it firsthand.

We purchased a couple of cases of Coors Beer as an investment to be resold when we got to Magnolia. Coors wasn't sold east of the Mississippi back then. People paid top dollar for Coors on the east coast. The weather was fantastic. We smoked pot, listened to music, and enjoyed the spectacular scenery that was our enormous country.

Flashing lights from behind gave us pause, as we pulled the car onto the shoulder. The officer asked us where we were headed and where we were from. I don't recall what his justification was for pulling us over. He asked what was under the tarp and when we showed him, he noticed the Coors and asked for ID. Fortunately, Tom and I were old enough to buy alcohol in whatever state we were in. He asked if it would be okay to look around in the car, we didn't want to seem like we had something to hide so we agreed (what else were we going to say?). He picked up a bundle of my clothes from behind the passenger seat and poked around on the floor before placing it back where he found it. The whole time my heart was in my throat; I had an ounce of pot tucked inside that tightly rolled bundle! Attached to the rearview mirror something else caught his eye. We had left our roach clip there for easy access. He nodded at it and asked what "that" was. We explained how Tom knew macramé and the only way we had to display it was by using an alligator clip. He accepted the answer without noticing the "teeth" were charred black with soot (aka residue). He told us to take it down as it could impair our vision while driving. Once we complied, he said we were free to go. We all knew how close we came to being arrested for possession. We also had to be careful driving through states where the legal age to buy beer was 21, none of us were 21.

We made great time heading east. We drove into Youngstown Ohio so I could show them where I lived when I was with Ernest. As we pulled to the curb across the street from my old apartment, we heard yelling; a guy was walking backwards through a doorway of a store on our side of the street. He was holding a handgun out at arms-length. The guy doing the shouting was walking straight toward him saying "I know who you are motherfucker!" He had no fear, we on the other hand, wanted to drive off immediately, but we also didn't want to attract any attention being so close to the action. The guy with the gun ran off, we took a breath, and I explained it wasn't like this when I used to live there. It was a tough town, but I didn't see much of that at all. We decided there wasn't anything else we needed to see and got back on the interstate.

We made it to Massachusetts where we parted company. I stayed with my dad while Tom and Curtis found a temporary place to stay in Gloucester (I think). I had places to go, people to see, and a new job on the horizon. We crossed paths at night in various places for a short time before they eventually returned to California. I never saw Curtis again. Tom returned for my wedding, but we didn't spend any time together. Years later I received a late-night call from Curtis telling me Tom had committed suicide. He blew his brains out in a closet. We talked for a long time. It was so hard to believe. I relived the times we spent together and resigned myself to the fact there would never be another one to add. Such a waste. We shared a lot of good times together.

RETURN TO MAGNOLIA

J ust as I had done the last time when I went back east, I sent a large box of clothes ahead. This time I wasn't sending them to my dad's office though. I addressed it to "Ben E. White" c/o Daniel Stedfast and used my Magnolia address. My dad was once again living in our old house (Marie was *not*). This box was better sealed than my previous parcel. When my package didn't arrive, I made an inquiry with the freight company and learned it was sitting at one of the distribution centers outside of Boston. I made arrangements to pick it up and was extremely nervous considering the moment I claimed it, I might be arrested. A couple of friends agreed to drive me in to collect my stuff. Once I had the box, I had to center myself, stay calm, and walk slowly out the door. We got in the car and headed back. I didn't want to open it, as it was still addressed to the fictitious Mr. White. My thought being I could claim it wasn't my package if I had to. Silly me!

Jimmy was driving the car (like old times) and to my surprise he said the brakes were gone and I looked at him with a "really?" look that clearly showed I wasn't buying it. He said, "no shit, they are gone." Great, we have a box full of pot and we are about to crash somewhere. Good news, I got the box in the car without being arrested; bad news is the cops will find it in the wreckage! There was a rotary coming up and we went around it more than once to make sure we would not need the brakes as we exited. That was just the first of many hurdles. There were plenty of traffic lights ahead, so we were all nervously sweating bullets as we approached each one. We tried to judge the right speed to either fly through or slow to a crawl if space allowed, hoping the red would turn green before we got there. How we made it all the way to Manchester was nothing short of a miracle. We arrived at the Youth Center/ Train Station parking lot and went around in circles until we could gently apply the emergency brake to bring us to a complete stop. Someone was smiling upon us from above.

I went through all kinds of changes
Took a look at myself and said that's not me
I miss my pad and the places I've known
And every night as I lay there alone I will dream

...... The Beach Boys

I planned on staying in my old home until I figured out what I was going to do with myself and the new job at Eastern Point in Gloucester. I don't think the boat was even in the water at that point, so I had some time to visit and hang with friends. I didn't actually have a room anymore. My dad had married the woman he had been dating and she had three daughters. They occupied all the bedrooms, so I slept in a bed at the bottom of the stairs in the basement for a while. Susan and Dick were living with their mother in Danvers at this time.

I settled on staying at my new boss' house in Magnolia, not too far from my dad's place but a little closer to Gloucester. I was given a small bedroom and free reign of the kitchen and no curfew. My Boss, Ned, had been married before and I knew his ex-wife. His new wife had to get used to me. Together they had a toddler daughter. Ned had an indoor charcoal grill that was vented outside via a blower and hood. He loved cooking steaks for dinner, and I loved eating them.

Work for me was performing maintenance on a Hinckley Sou'wester moored at the Eastern Point Yacht Club in Gloucester. The sloop was about 32 or 34 feet in length with teak wood decks and a lot of brightwork. I would polish, sand, varnish, paint whatever needed attention. Take out the trash, stock the galley with block ice from the icehouse deeper in the harbor. On a hot summer day, I loved climbing the ladder to the warehouse where ice blocks, bigger than me, stood in rows like frozen soldiers. All I needed was a little chunk, which was lowered down via rope and ice tongs to the small Boston Whaler I used to get around with.

I was on call and ready to crew the boat whenever Ned had the urge, but I would usually get a heads up in the morning before I left for the club. If it was gloomy, I knew we wouldn't be going anywhere. I was given a book of chits to use for food while at the club. I could order whatever I wanted but I tended to have cheeseburgers and frappes mostly. Typically, I would row a pram from the dock to the sloop, I was in very good physical shape. Often, I would just row around that part of the harbor for exercise and fun. There is a certain peace that comes from rowing. It's good for the soul.

I avoided most of the club members, as many of them were wealthy and carried a certain air about them that rubbed me wrong. I did talk to the people who worked there or on other boats and some of the younger kids who were members. I wasn't hanging around with anyone I knew from Gloucester or Magnolia there, that's for sure.

Sailing days were great. Ned would take his family or friends out to Rockport, Marblehead, or other towns nearby. Sometimes we would simply head "out" then come back. I would often sail past my dad's house in Magnolia and wave to anyone who might be watching. Occasionally I would see a return wave from the porch.

One morning late in the season we dropped anchor off Misery Island outside of Manchester harbor. Ned was talking to a man he knew or just met (I was never sure about that). This man seemed to know very little about the boat he owned. He had a couple of wild kids running around the boat and at some point, he asked if I would take them for a ride in the small whaler we towed behind the sloop. I knew quickly this was not a good idea.

These kids were spoiled brats who listened to no one. They were standing when I asked them to sit, they were shifting weight abruptly and moving to the same side of the boat at the same time. Finally, I had it with them and pulled up alongside some rocks and ordered them out. They were stunned at first, then thought I was kidding. Once they realized I was serious, they became brats again and told me I would be in big trouble if I left them there. I told them to stay away from the water and motored back to the anchored boats to explain my actions. Ed, the kids' father, saw me coming without his kids on board, so I quickly explained what I had done, fully expecting to draw his wrath, but the opposite happened. He laughed and asked me if I wanted a Bloody Mary. I passed but did come on board where we talked for a while. Something clicked with him, and he asked what I was going to do once the summer was over. I said I had no plans as yet. He told me he was looking to hire someone like me, and I should come by the business in Salem for an interview. After we talked, he asked me to bring his kids back. When I found them again, they were wet. Obviously, they hadn't listened when I told them to stay away from the water. I told them to sit still and not say a word. They listened as they didn't know what I might do if they chose to do otherwise.

I am not the person who is singing

I am the silent one inside

I am not the one who laughs at people's jokes

I just pacify their egos

I am not my house or my car or my songs

They are only just stops along my way

.... Paula Cole

GISELE

8:45 AM on 8/22/1973 I was in Salem, Massachusetts to interview with Ed Meam. Ed was one of two partners who owned a semiconductor chip inspection business. They also had a major stake in another venture called Creative Technology, which manufactured a screw-in lamp socket dimmer. They needed someone to supervise the assembly of these devices. When I first walked in, I spoke with a couple of young secretaries and then shown the way to Ed's office. Once that was concluded I was escorted downstairs for my next interview with Ed Rodriguez. I entered a hall with large well-lit windows on both sides and young women sitting in front of microscopes in a cleanroom environment. Several glanced up as I walked by and smiled. This was looking very promising!

Downstairs, I met the inventor of the dimmer who explained how it worked and what was required to build one. I remember he also examined my handwriting for certain characteristics as part of the interview (very odd). I was hired! I walked up the stairs, past the station where my future wife worked and asked the young woman supervisor which way was the exit. I walked past the female filled clean rooms again, took a right as directed, opened the door, and walked into a closet! I had been set up! I paused, then confidently walked in the opposite direction past giggles on both sides of the hall and left for home. I had a job that paid almost three times more than anything I'd had before, and it was mostly girls my age working there. I thought I had died and gone to heaven. My dad was happy for me. I had moved back into my old house and told him I wanted to contribute something until I found a place of my own, but he didn't want anything. Eventually he accepted something small, as I wasn't taking no for an answer.

On 9/4/73: I started working for Semiconductor Services Inc/ Creative Technology Corp. There was a girl in Magnolia who worked for the phone company in Salem who agreed to give me a ride in each day. I was on my own getting home though. I was usually one of the first ones to work in the morning. I liked the girl who unlocked the building bright and early. I would anxiously wait with anticipation for her green dodge with the turtle in the back window as it approached and wondered what she would be wearing. Her name was Gisele. A pretty name for a very pretty girl.

The fall went by quickly. I spent time with old friends at night and on the weekends, but my primary focus was really on the new job; there was a lot to learn, and I wanted to be successful. Gisele was the shipper and receiver for the parent company on the ground floor. I was responsible for shipping the few units we made downstairs and had to learn that process. The logical choice to train me, much to my delight, was Gisele. I was constantly peppering her with questions, many of which I already knew the answer to. I loved walking up the stairs to her work area. She wore these jeans with a heart shaped patch on her bum that I couldn't stop looking at. I think she was puzzled as to why I couldn't retain her instructions. We had lunch together a couple of times, actually it was more like a group of us from work, but I was just happy to see Gisele.

The company Christmas Party was on Friday December 21, 1973. Gisele attended with her longtime boyfriend, while I came alone. Gisele wanted to dance but her date declined, complaining about a bad leg. I notice him dancing a short time later with another girl from work, the same one who directed me to the closet after my initial interview. It seemed his leg was feeling much better. Gisele was upset, and for good reason. She and I sat together during dinner, and we talked with her friends. As the party concluded, she asked me to meet her at a friend's apartment, because there were plans to keep the festivities going. She wanted to drive her boyfriend home first.

I tagged along with one of her girlfriends and waited for Gisele to arrive at the apartment. The party went on until the sun came up and Gisele gave me a ride home. We started dating shortly after.

I enjoyed being with Gisele every moment I could, and I saw her a lot since we worked together. She knew many of the girls whom I supervised at CTC, and both businesses were growing. When I was a crew leader in California, it was very easy and loosely organized. This was markedly different. At one point there were 40 women and maybe two or three guys working at CTC. I was still very young and suddenly the boss over women old enough to be my mother, or grandmother. Many were my age too. The older ladies knew I was green at this, and some helped me while others took advantage of what I didn't know yet. Some would complain about any and everything, others brought their personal problems into the workplace. Some loafed, some excelled, some didn't feel well, and some experienced personal loss. I was dealing with problems every day and learning valuable life lessons that would stay with me in the decades to come.

Creative Technology had a small office staff. I was responsible for shipping and receiving, inventory, assembly and rework, quality control and payroll, I even did some sales at trade shows. I was the first one there and the last to leave every day. The owners had an idea to help boost production and cut some costs by farming out a portion of the operation to Mass Rehab in Boston. We set up meetings and I brought in parts then showed a member of their staff step by step how the assembly went together. They in turn broke the steps down into very simple functions and had trainers show the challenged employees how to perform their specific task. I was amazed to see the quality of work they could turn out. The pride on their faces was obvious when they completed a unit. It was an amazing experience to see what they could accomplish. Whatever doubts I held when I first walked in disappeared quickly.

Each time I dropped off more parts and collected completed assemblies I saw more proficiency; they were getting better every week. They were doing so well, we decided to lay off some of the CTC staff. This proved very difficult for me. I had never had to do anything like this before. It was just a few at first, and I explained to those that remained how we needed to boost output to compete with our new counterparts in Boston. They responded and the increase in productivity was there. They wanted to keep their jobs, so they worked extremely hard. Despite the effort everyone put in, we continued shrinking the CTC workforce. It was not pleasant, but that core of hardworking people continued to give it their all.

Gisele and I were almost inseparable at this point. We went into Boston to watch Al Pacino in the movie Serpico. When the show was over, I was surprised to hear she wasn't that impressed. When I asked her why, she said it could never happen in real life. I suddenly realized she didn't know this was based on a true story about a very corrupt New York Police Department. We talked about this and many other things for hours at the top of the Prudential Building. Somewhere during the discussion, Gisele made an offhand comment about my long hair. She loved it but said I might be hiding behind it. I naturally protested and cut it within days. It had been years since I'd heard scissors clipping around my head. My hair did not define me. I settled on a shag. Quite different than what I was used to seeing in the mirror!

I was at a local bar with a good friend and the conversation kept coming back to Gisele. Bernie finally just looked me in the eye and stated matter-of-factly, I was going to marry Gisele. The word "marry" hit me strangely, so I begged to differ. Bernie said he had never heard me talk about a girl so much in the past. He just knew it was inevitable. I never realized he was so intuitive ... or psychic. Bernie got to know me quickly and he knew I never stayed with any girl for long. What he didn't know was I was always looking for the right girl. Since I was first interested in girls I always looked for someone from a stable home who wanted to commit to a lasting relationship. Anything short of that represented the foundation for a one-night stand. Sometimes girls weren't interested in me, other times, I wasn't interested in them. It wasn't a like or dislike thing either. When you are looking for chemistry, there is a certain expectation. In retrospect, I would say I didn't have a real girlfriend until I moved to California. I met Collette and her family and was welcomed in their home. Things were going very well, or so I thought, until they weren't. For whatever reason, she drifted away to be with someone else and then someone after that. What I believed was meaningful and real, faded into illusion. We remained friends but never were the same again. Gisele was from a traditional French Catholic family. Very respectable, stable, and religious. I on the other hand came from a dysfunctional family, didn't go to church anymore, had long shoulder length hair when we met and probably represented the antithesis of what her parents wanted for their daughter. Gisele and I had something in common, we were both looking for the same thing at the same time and managed to find each other. We grew close in a very short time and Bernie saw the change in me. I don't think I realized just yet that I was ready to leave my wild days behind, settle down with a wife, and raise a family. Bernie, on the other hand, did.

5/8/74: Boz Scaggs and Steve Miller played the Music Hall in Boston. Both bands were great but what made the show exceptional was when they played together for an encore that lasted about 45 minutes. Such great music. They still had chemistry together and history. It was awesome! It was nice to share the experience with Gisele.

Hitching a ride from Magnolia to Salem every day and back again was getting to be a pain. I decided to move to Salem and found an apartment on Leach Street which was easy walking distance to work as well as Gisele's parents' apartment. When Gisele and I went out after work, she didn't have that long drive to Magnolia and back anymore either. My apartment was large for a single guy, with three bedrooms, a large kitchen, living room and dining area. The place was furnished with very inexpensive used furniture bought in town and I made a couple of pieces too. I began putting down some roots in Salem. Gisele and I were from different worlds but there was something strong connecting us.

Groovin' is easy, baby, if you know how
Groovin's so easy, baby, if you know how
You don't have to keep yourself forever slavin'
Go out and chase whatever you're cravin'
You know it doesn't have to be (so hard)
No, no, no, no it doesn't have to be (so hard)
So hard on you

There's nobody stopping you, baby, there's just yourself
And if you can't see that, baby, girl you need help
I could teach you things you never could learn
Show you just exactly how you got burned
It doesn't have to be (so hard)
No, no, no, no it doesn't have to be (so hard)
So hard on you

It's easy to see, baby, you're nobody's fool
But you won't gain nothing, baby, by staying cool
Better leave all your uptight worries behind
Get into something will excite your mind
You know it doesn't have to be
No, no, it doesn't have to be
So hard on you

             .... Electric Flag

7/12/74: Gisele and I saw Eric Clapton with Yvonne Elliman at the old Boston Garden. Fabulous concert. Eric was in control of the crowd. You could hear a pin drop as he performed "In the Presence of the Lord" and then everyone would roar to the first notes of "Layla." Couldn't have been a better show. There was tremendous energy as well as respect in the crowd. I saw another guitar hero of mine.

9/13/74: Little Feat opened for Traffic at the Garden. The double bills back in the day were so good. Lowell George was awesome, and the band was crisp and tight. They had an infectious vibe people there loved. A very energetic audience anxious to greet Steve Winwood was not disappointed. It wasn't lost on me that I saw Eric just a couple of months back and together they were 50% of Blind Faith! Traffic was incredible. An amazing concert. The combinations of artists we were seeing at that time spoke to their personal evolution and growth. Miller and Scaggs were solo artists who were once bandmates, Clapton and Winwood the same, Winwood and Mason, the same. I love music....

9/30/74: Eric Clapton added another Boston show to his tour, and we were fortunate enough to get tickets again. This time he had Yvonne and Marcy Levy with him. It was not a repeat of the earlier show we attended. Some songs were played at both, but he did perform several that were different. The end result was another outstanding performance. Eric Clapton was so poised, so professional.

Oct 13 or 14, 1974, Kansas opened for Jefferson Starship at the Music Hall in Boston. Kansas performed every song from both of their albums. The violin was LOUD. A good show. Jefferson Starship was also loud. Papa John Creach's violin wasn't as loud but sure was sweet. He was literally hopping/jumping around the stage. You could feel the walls of sound booming from the group. I thought back to California and seeing Hot Tuna and how different that sound was compared to Starship. Somehow Gisele managed to fall asleep during the show. Grace Slick was awesome. I wished to God I had seen Jefferson *Airplane*.

Gisele and I were in love and very comfortable together. Late one evening, without any hype or drama I very casually asked Gisele if she wanted to get married and she calmly said yes before dozing off while leaning against me on the couch. My life had already changed and now marriage was on the horizon. Bernie had called it right! A friend's mother from Magnolia worked at a jewelry store and I dropped in to find an engagement ring. It was a single diamond with six smaller ones surrounding it. It looked like a six-pointed star or a snowflake. We planned on announcing our engagement at the next company Christmas party, still a couple of months away.... 12/23/1974.

We made every effort to keep our secret and acted as normally as we could, though we were about ready to burst with excitement. Somewhere along the line I had to let Bernie know, since he informed me it was going to happen before anyone else did. I asked him to be my best man and he agreed. Gisele and I belonged together, and I was keenly aware of the pitfalls my dad went through with his marriages and they were not going to happen to us. This was the real deal!

Gisele and I were in my Leach Street apartment when a call came in that took me by surprise. A social worker was on the other end telling me I was the father of a baby girl. I didn't think it was possible and when I heard who the mother was, I was even less sure. I had been with her one time at a party and never went out with her again. I didn't really know too much about her either. Getting together that night had been her idea, and I simply went along with it. I didn't know if I was one of several guys she may have been with. What made her so sure it was *me*? How could she *know* it was me? *Was* it me? I didn't even know how they determined who the father was in situations like this. In hindsight, we were both young and irresponsible. Neither of us used any form of contraceptive. If the baby was in fact my child, I would have to face that, but to me there was no real evidence; everything was purely circumstantial. If this child was mine, it was not conceived in love, it was more accurate to say the passion of the moment. I was in the process of planning a wedding with Gisele, the woman I had been looking for my entire life. Gisele was right there listening to everything being said, there were no secrets between us. When I hung up the phone, we stared at each other lost in thought about what could or might happen, if anything. Gisele knew I was a rebel who bounced around the country, was hooked on rock music, took drugs, and spent time with other women, but I turned a page in the book of my life when I met her. Gisele and I clicked, and we each helped the other live fuller lives. My life was finally grounded with Gisele, and it had meaning. We needed to be together and eventually we would have a family I could call my own. We didn't know if the story we had just heard was true or not, but if it was, we knew one day we might hear a knock on our door. We put it behind us and continued planning our future together.

We had lots of friends in Salem, and we spent quite a bit of time with them when we weren't working. I would go to Gisele's house often for dinner. Her mother was one of the kindest people I had ever met. Gisele's grandmother lived in the apartment with them; she spoke no English, or so I was told. Gisele's family also took in a young girl after her mother died unexpectedly. We all had lively conversations and lots of laughs. I felt accepted and was very grateful to have all of them in my life. Gisele's older sister was married, and we would visit them in their home in Salem too. I remember a family reunion at a place called Paradise Park. It was my soon to be brother-in-law Marc's side of the family, and almost everyone was speaking French. There were probably hundreds of people there, campfires and grills, food and drink, and music. Guitars and singing. People coming up to me speaking words I could barely translate, but the vibe was obvious and needed no translation. There was a lot of love in this group, and I was finding a niche. My constant need to feel accepted was satisfied and it felt great.

We were over at her parents for dinner on the day when Gisele divulged to her mother we were going to be married. I was in the living room with their two Pekingese dogs listening when voices were suddenly and sharply raised. "But he's not Catholic!" There was some back and forth but, in the end, Gisele had made a stand and it was with me. I had never seen her exert her will like that before, and to see her do it in support of me was felt deep within my core. This was to be my wife. Gisele's mom also realized we were meant to be together, and I never felt the slightest resentment from her, ever. In fact, I think it made our bond that much stronger. She was more like a mother to me than anyone else I had known. We grew very close, very quickly.

The 1974 company Christmas party came and with it our announcement was finally out in the open. Everyone was genuinely thrilled for us. We were the company sweethearts. Gisele wore her engagement ring for the first time in public. A special night for us.

March 2 – 9, 1975 I represented Creative Technology at the Home Show in Boston's John B. Hynes Civic Auditorium. It ran from 1 pm to 11 pm each day except the last, where we closed up early. I set up my booth with a couple of nice lamps I purchased, placing a dimmer in one, and a photoelectric cell in the other. As I dimmed one lamp, the other would instantly come on. People were drawn to it, smiling, and wondering what the "trick" was. I was selling quite a few of both units.... retail. I had to have someone from another booth watch mine, just so I could go to the bathroom, because I was alone. We had no other salespeople in the company. When it was slow, a guy from a neighboring booth would stand in the middle of the aisle and dramatically demonstrate his awe of the products to draw more attention. He'd loudly exclaim he had to buy one of them for everyone in his family. He "bought" a case, and suddenly I had a small crowd again. When things died down, I would return his money, and he, the case of product. He should have been on commission!

Gisele would come to Boston each day as soon as she got out of work and join me. It was great having some company. She was helping me, but not on the clock, even after I mentioned what she was doing to our boss! I met Dave Maynard at the Hill Foods booth and gave him a dimmer. He talked about it on his radio show the next day. I kept seeing him at odd places throughout the week. I recognized a face in the crowd heading my way one day. It was Terry O'Reilly of the Boston Bruins. He saw what I was doing with the lamps and bought a dimmer. I had no way of knowing Terry and I would cross paths again later in life.

The show was finally over, and I was packing up what little inventory I had left, when a woman bought both lamps I had been using, for more money than I paid for them originally. I decided Gisele should be treated to dinner for her efforts in helping me and found a nice place near the Prudential building where we could relax over a good meal. I ordered a large bucket of shrimp on ice, and we dug in. Not too long after, Gisele started feeling "off" and was turning red. She was having an allergic reaction to the shrimp and that was the end of the night. She would be fine, but I never saw her eat another shrimp again.

March 14, 1975: Not long after the Home Show ended, Gisele moved out of her house to live with a coworker… the same one who danced with Gisele's boyfriend at our first company Christmas party. The same one who guided me into a closet after my interview. Her parents were upset, but Gisele was determined it was time to go and make her way on her own.

We packed and moved her things under the sad eyes of her mother. Bernie was there to help with the move.

April 7,1975: Bernie and Pam were married. I had known Pam since she was a kid and her older brother Henry (Hank), and I went to school together. Hank's was the only bar mitzvah I ever attended, Bruce Bradley from WBZ radio was the MC (Juicy Brucie). I knew Bernie from the Manchester based band Gandalf and we both lived together at the Gallery. These two (Bernie and Pam) had so much in common, both being creative artists linked to music. Pam was a strong dancer. Bernie would be my best man later that summer when Gisele and I got married. Good friends.

April 9, 1975: Gary Beaton was married to Janet, a coworker at SSI/CTC. He was 1 of 100 people entered in the 7-11-21 Instant Game Scratch Ticket Grand Prize Drawing. The event was televised locally. Gisele and I had gone out to dinner and thought we should check on Gary to see how much more he had won. We knew he was going to get at least $1,000.00 more (minimum prize). Someone picked up the phone and all we heard was pandemonium! His was the last name drawn... he won the grand prize! Janet and Gary would receive $1000.00/ week for life.... On a free ticket! When a reporter asked him what he was going to do with his winnings, the first thing that came to his mind was buying a bowling ball! Too funny seeing it printed in the newspaper! A bunch of us celebrated their winnings at Kowloon on route 1 in Saugus. We had a huge table to ourselves, and we were loud. I remember we all tied our napkins together forming a ring around the table then inserting objects into the knots as it rotated around everyone. You never knew what was going to appear in your lap next! We did it again on the first anniversary of their winning. Such a good time with good friends.

May 3, 1975: We moved my things into a two-family rental home at 14 Spring Road on the Lynn/Swampscott line. It was a quiet neighborhood and far different than my Leach Street apartment. This would be our first home together. We had a small backyard and an even smaller garden, but it was home. Our modest excuse for a stereo was displayed for all to see on unfinished wooden planks supported by cinder blocks, with a plant and a few albums mixed in. We didn't have much, but that's the way it was back then. No one expected to have a first rate *anything* right away. Good things would come as the years went by. We had other priorities taking center stage. Furniture shopping was going to drain our finances; we couldn't look at the stuff I had from Leach Street much longer. The main thing was we were planning our life together and would celebrate each milestone as it came. I moved in and started getting things ready for our married life to start.

May 27th, 1975:   My adoptive mother, Nancy, was an experienced dog breeder when she was younger. We raised Boxers and German Shepherds. She introduced us to a man who had amazing dogs and was still actively breeding them. We checked on a litter of German Shepherd puppies he had, as we both wanted a dog in the family. We made arrangements to stay in touch. Another litter would be coming soon. When we checked these puppies, one in particular stood out. We both fell in love with this cute little thing and had to have him. Holden grew to be 100+ pounds of pure energy. A great dog, but unfortunately, just my dog. He listened to me, but not so much Gisele.

June 7, 1975: Dulcie and Eddie were good friends of ours and on this day, they were married. Weddings were fun and it seemed we were going to several leading up to our own. Gisele and her mother were doing a lot of planning in anticipation of our big day. I did a lot of nodding. This thing was getting real.

July 18, 1975: Joan Baez played a free concert on the Boston Common. When we heard the news, we knew there was no doubt we would go. Gary Beaton and Janet said they were going too and offered us a ride. The crowd was large and eager to hear Joan. The sound quality was phenomenal, and we were close enough to have a good view. What I will always remember from that event was her version of Amazing Grace. I've heard her sing this many, many, times before and since, but this one was different (and the best). She had to have played the Common before or maybe she just figured it out on the fly, but she used her own voice as an accompaniment or a chorus. She'd sing, then wait for the echo to bounce back from MIT across the Charles River, in perfect time before resuming. Gives me chills to this day.

Just before we were to be married, Gisele and I decided to take a vacation in Canada together. We drove our VW convertible on board the ferry in Maine, then headed for Nova Scotia. We toured around NS and took another smaller ferry to Prince Edward Island. We had a great trip, thank God Gisele knew French. English was common enough but there were a few times when it sure helped to know French. I had never been outside the USA before. On PEI we couldn't make a reservation to stay anywhere. We found a night club jammed with people and figured we should give it a go as there was no place else to kill time. Strange dress code... corduroys were not allowed but jeans were. We had to share a small table with another couple and quickly struck up a conversation in the noisy bar. When they learned we had no place to sleep, they invited us to their campsite on a wildlife sanctuary. We accepted. Gisele kept in touch over time and years later we met again in Montreal where they took us on an amazing tour of the old section of town. Old Montreal on foot and at night was beautiful. We also went to a saloon outside of town where the beer was cheaper and came in much larger bottles!

MARRIAGE

Our wedding took place on August 17, 1975, in Salem Massachusetts at St. Joseph's Church on Lafayette Street. What we didn't realize on that same day and on the same street, was the annual Heritage Day Parade. Streets were blocked off with sawhorses in all directions, so no one could make it to the church. Bernie was my Best Man. He met me at the house I rented in Swampscott. We were dressed in white tuxedos, taking out the trash together before climbing into his white convertible and heading to the church in Salem. When we saw the road blocked, we caught the attention of a police officer and explained our situation. He reluctantly agreed to lift the roadblock to allow us on the road, but only after a very stern warning to keep our speed at a crawl. He didn't want any of the people there for the parade to be hurt and reminded us there were little kids everywhere darting into the road. We gratefully thanked him and oh so slowly made our way toward the empty church. Picture this, two young guys dressed to the nines in a white convertible rolling slowly down the parade route. People had no idea who we were but figured we must be important, so they all started waving to us. We smiled and waved back as we were caught in the moment, laughing all the way to the church. We made it! But no one else was there other than the priest and a couple of altar boys. We were all going to have to wait patiently for the parade to pass. With all the planning that took place leading up to this moment, how did this nugget get missed?

I hadn't been nervous at all leading up to the wedding, but now that it was here, my knees were knocking. Gisele, on the other hand, had been nervous for weeks leading up to our special day, but I would soon find out she was perfectly calm and ready to get married. It was a kind of role reversal. I couldn't stay in the church waiting anymore, so Bernie and I wandered out on the sidewalk. A few bystanders asked why we were so dressed up on a hot sunny day and we let them know the wedding party was delayed due to the parade. We bought ice cream for a few kids eagerly waiting for the procession. An older woman in a beach chair told me she would marry me if my girlfriend didn't show up. The wait was maddening but finally the parade passed, and traffic slowly started to move again. The church began to fill, and I disappeared into the wings to wait for my bride to be to make her stunning entrance. With knees still shaking I waited for word the limo had arrived. Finally, I heard Gisele was there. I thought I might need a sponge between my knees to keep them from knocking together. The music played and the ceremony began. It was a beautiful wedding, and the reception at Caruso's Diplomat on route 1 in Saugus was top notch. We were whisked away to a hotel and had very little sleep before boarding a plane for Elbow Beach, Bermuda the next morning.

God only knows what I'd be without you
If you should ever leave me
Though life would still go on believe me
The world could show nothing to me
So what good would living do me

..... The Beach Boys

Bermuda was just ideal for us. We stayed at the Elbow Beach Hotel. Visited night clubs, which didn't open until 10 PM. Had fantastic service and food. Rode mopeds everywhere. Enjoyed the beach and the pool and wore deep dark tans. We left there with almost no money in our pockets and had a blast! Marc's brother Tommy was a travel agent and set the whole thing up for us. He did an outstanding job!

After our memorable honeymoon, we returned to our jobs for the first time as husband and wife. We worked in separate buildings now and would try to see each other for lunch. Gisele's mom worked on the upper floors in an adjacent building to mine in the Mills and would hang out of the window calling my name to say hi whenever she saw me. I can still hear the echo!

CTC eventually laid off everyone but me and was actively trying to sell the company. I kept moving the parts inventory to Mass Rehab where all the manufacturing was performed now and doing odd jobs around the SSI factory. SSI was still growing and there was justification for starting a second shift. They wanted me to be their night supervisor. I wasn't happy. Apparently, they thought nothing of Gisele working days and me, nights. I had no intention working those hours after just being married. The work they had me doing now was not much more than running errands into Boston. CTC had been sold and my future shifted to SSI. I can't recall what mindless task I was asked to do when I just snapped and quit on the spot. I just couldn't do it anymore. The other partner (Jim) thought I was kidding and tried to get me to come back, but I was done. Gisele was in an awkward position due to my action, but fortunately they didn't take it out on her.

October 6, 1975: I took a job with a tannery in Salem, figuring the physical activity was just what I needed. I wanted nothing to do with business anymore. The work was hard, but I was gradually getting back in shape. I worked six days a week sorting large cow hides after they were tanned, but prior to being dyed. We worked on a cement floor which had no give at all, and did a lot of walking, lifting, and stacking of pallets. I eventually messed up my back thinking I was Hercules, and it has never been the same since. We were living in Danvers now and Gisele's mom had contracted ovarian cancer. It was very tough to watch a vibrant woman who embraced life so fully, slowly withering away. It was a horrible waiting game, as the doctors gave us no hope she'd beat this.

10/12/75 We picked up Holden, our German Shepherd puppy, and introduced him to his new home. Loved that dog! I slept on the floor alongside him, so he didn't feel alone for the first few days. It felt good to have him with us.

January 1976, I had a pay raise to $4.50/hour at the tannery. Not a lot of money, but Saturdays were all overtime, which really helped. My annual bonus was based on my average weekly paycheck times two. I worked about 15 hours of OT each week. That bonus was important to us. I was just glad I had a job which didn't involve business situations anymore. I had more time to think. Gisele continued working at SSI. We had one car. Our combined income was enough to seriously think about having a family at some point. We both wanted children and now it was just about picking the right time. Kids .... Blood relatives... unbelievable this could finally happen for me.

August of 1976 (our one-year anniversary): Gisele and I headed west with the idea of seeing the Grand Canyon. I had wanted to return there ever since seeing it with my friends from Magnolia. The VW Super Beetle was small to begin with but add in a large German Shepherd with our camping gear, and it was almost impossible to move at all. Holden kept leaning over my shoulder, dropping his bone in my lap like this was something I was going to throw to him and say "fetch!." We broke down outside Des Moines, Iowa. The transmission blew and we could only drive under 40 mph on the highway. It was ironic to me that we were in a VW enroute to the Grand Canyon and experienced a breakdown! Just like the old "Maggie West" days!

There were no hotel rooms available anywhere near the city due to the State Fair. Jimmy Carter was scheduled to make an appearance and Johnny Cash was playing a gig there. We found a garage and were told it would take days to get the part they needed, so rather than wait, we rented a car. The two of us transferred all our gear into the rental and were off again. We planned on completing our trip in the rental, return to Iowa for the VW, then head home. The rental had a little more room and was much more comfortable.

Once we saw the mountains of Colorado we couldn't get enough. We found a campground somewhere between Estes Park and Colorado Springs. We decided to stay there for a week rather than push on to the Canyon, it could wait for another trip. We drove to the summit of Pikes Peak and witnessed the view from the top of the world. It was a white-knuckled drive up and down the mountain. "Hot Brakes Fail" read the signs (is that why we lost them on Maggie West years ago?). At night we heard wolves howling off in the distance and the occasional echo back. We roamed around the Garden of the Gods, shopped in Manitou Springs, dined in Colorado Springs, and enjoyed the stillness of our campsite. We had to carry our water there as there was nothing flowing for the campers that high up. The mountain elevation actually slowed Holden down. Never seen him tire so quickly. We had a tremendous vacation celebrating our first year of marriage. Good memories.

December 1st, 1976: We moved to Water Street in Danvers, Massachusetts. The owner worked as a registry cop. Nice people but I was always nervous when my monthly copy of High Times magazine arrived in its plain brown wrapper. The house was old and even had a working Indian shutter in the bathroom (no, we were never attacked by Indians). The kitchen had an enormous brick fireplace with a very deep baking oven to the side. Good bones in that old house.

July 16, 1977: Southside Johnny and the Asbury Dukes opened for Boz Scaggs at the Music Hall in Boston. Southside put on a great show. I had never seen him before and left being a huge fan to this day. Boz was into a different phase than I had seen before. All the young teenage girls attending the concert should have tipped me off. He played a lot of disco/pop stuff and I had come hoping for rock and roll and some blues. It was still good, just not what I expected.

OUR FIRST HOME AND A
FAMILY BEGINS

March of 1978: We found an affordable two-family home in Bradford, Massachusetts and on the 14th, we passed papers on our first house. The rental unit on the first floor would serve as income to offset our mortgage. I had never been a landlord before, but we figured this was our best path to owning a one family home of our own someday. Gisele's sister had done the same thing, so we had someone we could talk to about it as the questions came up. Gisele was pregnant when we applied for the loan and we were stressed thinking the bank would realize one of the two incomes documented would soon come to an end, rendering us unsuitable for any significant loan. She kept her coat on in the warm office as we filled out the required forms. The loan was approved, and we passed papers on our first home. We really wanted this!

With Gisele pregnant, I began to reflect more on my life and was reminded of just how little I really knew about myself. Many of the simple things I dealt with routinely as a kid and young adult began bothering me again. Were there genetic illnesses in the family I could pass onto my children? Mental illness? Coronary concerns? Cancer? Gisele and I wanted to know more about my family medical history, but there was nothing for us anywhere. My dad and I weren't comfortable speaking to each other when it came to my adoption, and my mother was dealing with physical and emotional problems of her own. I did ask her about the medical history, but she didn't have much to offer. What little she did offer ultimately proved to be a pack of lies. Seemed odd to me that medical history wasn't provided to my adoptive parents, or if it was, where was it? Who had "custody" of *my* history? I believed there wasn't much I could do about any of it and regardless, nothing was going to stop us from having a family. It was just too important to me/us. How can a society allow someone to go through life without any medical history? Didn't I have a *right* to know? My first blood relative was growing and kicking away inside Gisele, and I was ecstatic. We would deal with whatever happened, as a family.

Daily things fall off like water,
Falling down like summer rain;
We see each other in confusion;
Wonder why we came today.
Sittin' lonely in our prison,
Lookin' out for ways to sail;
What we'd be without confusion,
In our less uncommon way.
Through your hair across my eyes,
The twilight shafts in soft surprise;
Reminds me once again how nice,
It is to be with you.

..... Hot Tuna

Our good news was cruelly countered with the heartbreaking news of Gisele's mom being so very sick with an aggressive cancer. We spent as much time with her as possible. A blizzard shut the roads down throughout the neighboring towns in the area and we decided to hitchhike from Danvers to Salem to be with her. It was a wild ride through unplowed streets marked with deep ruts made from the few vehicles daring enough to venture out in the snowpack, but we made it. Time with her was precious; we all hoped and prayed she would pull through.

She was a very strong and determined woman who somehow managed to attend Gisele's baby shower. She had lost a lot of weight by then, but she found energy on this special day. My nephew Justin took his first steps in the aisle between a couple of tables. One foot in front of the other, as he made his way right to me! I was so proud. Gisele's family, as well as Marc's, had accepted me and to know Gisele's mom was so sick, tore at me deeply. It just wasn't fair. As a kid I always gravitated to my friends' mothers to fill the large void that was always there and ever-present. Gisele's mother filled it like no one else had. I didn't want to lose her. Not now, not ever.

One day a letter arrived from my adoptive mother. In it she had placed a news article about an adoption agency and wrote a note indicating this was the agency that had placed me when I was a baby. My mother was a strange character. She had been a nurse in her younger years, loved the outdoors and performed in local theater. She was an excellent cook. She trained show dogs. She also drank heavily and was mentally and physically abusive to my twin sisters. Throughout my life she had told me my biological mother was of American Indian descent, and too young to keep me. She told me I was sickly and small and that she had to nurse me back to health. Naturally, I believed all of it. Receipt of this letter/note was my pathway to the truth; she knew I would pursue this as far as I could. She also knew it would unravel whatever lies she had fed me. I think it was her way of setting the record straight. I needed to contact Children's Village in Hartford, Connecticut to see what I could learn. I called information and asked for the phone number, but they had no listing for the organization. A mystery right out of the gate? Time to start asking a few questions.

June 3,1978 Gisele stopped by the tannery where I worked after her scheduled doctor appointment to calmly tell me we were going to have a baby later that day! I wondered why she was walking around, driving a car etc. "Shouldn't we be at the hospital right now?" I asked. She assured me we had plenty of time and she was going back to Carmen and Marc's to wait for the contractions to begin. I couldn't think about anything else for the rest of my shift. A baby was coming! Today! It was so exciting. A child was coming in a matter of hours now! True family. Blood family. My family.

Why must every generation think they're folks are square?
And no matter where they're heads are, they know mom's ain't there.
Cause' I swore when I was small, that I'd remember when,
I knew what's wrong with them, that I was smaller than.

Determined to remember all the cardinal rules.
Like, sunshowers are legal grounds, for cutting school.
I know I have forgotten maybe one or two.
And I hope that I recall them all before the baby's due.
And I'll know he'll have a question or two.

.... John Sebastian

Gisele was at center stage; we all were excited and full of anticipation. Finally, the contractions were close enough that we knew it was time. The hospital was busy and understaffed for the number of pregnancies facing them that night. We were prepared as best we could, the birthing classes fresh in our minds. I was suited up and by Gisele's side while the doctor and nurses attended other soon to be mothers in other rooms. I saw the top of our child's head and called for the doctor. By the time he arrived, the head was completely out, and a tiny body followed. Rhiannon was born at 2:18 AM and my first known blood relative was in my arms. I had a family of my own. I could not have been any happier at that moment. Flesh and blood. Most people take this for granted, but as an adoptee it was more than special and to my amazement, Rhiannon looked like me! People have asked how we chose Rhiannon for a name. Many thought it had to be from the Fleetwood Mac song penned by Stevie Nicks. We arrived at the name prior to the song hitting the airwaves and it came from the same source Stevie used... Welsh mythology. I loved the character and never thought of her as a "Welsh Witch." What I recall was a love so strong, she gave up immortality to marry a mortal man. Pretty special, just like our daughter.

I had never seen my resemblance to anyone or anyone to me before. I would always scan faces in a crowd looking for one like mine. There was a time once when I saw what looked like a younger version of me at a bar in Bar Harbor, Maine. When I saw his face, I turned to Gisele to get her attention. When I turned back to show her, he was pointing toward me while talking to his friend. It was freaky, we both had the same reaction within seconds of each other. I hopped off the stool and into the throng of people standing around. I had to ask this guy a couple of obvious questions. He got down from the bar too but was headed in the opposite direction! He walked out the door to the street and by the time I got outside, he was gone. I couldn't believe it. It was like I spooked him. I still think about that encounter after all these years.

6/16/1978: To add to the list of changes taking place in our young lives, we also had a litter of kittens. So many little voices in the house now. We have a great picture of Rhiannon sleeping on the couch with a little kitten curled up next to her. They both looked so peaceful. I felt so blessed.

August 7th, close to 4 PM of 1978 was especially sad, as Gisele's mother finally succumbed to cancer. I was at Carmen and Marc's house getting ready to visit her after work, when Carmen told me the news. Florence lived long enough to hold Rhiannon only once. A huge hurt weighed on me and the entire family. Personally, I felt cheated. I finally had someone in my life who felt like a real mother. I ate the meals she lovingly cooked, I was always welcome, we laughed a lot and talked about our dreams for the future. I had been given up at birth for some reason, Nancy didn't really want me, Marie and I never got along and now Gisele's mom was gone. I felt awful. We were all grieving. Gisele was so strong throughout the funeral and wake. I, on the other hand, couldn't hold myself together at all. I don't know how Gisele did it.

My adopted mother was also quite ill when our first daughter was born. We went to see her at the hospital where she had the only opportunity to hold her first grandchild. She passed away shortly thereafter. Gisele's mom and mine died just a couple of months apart. Gisele's mom's passing hurt me more. Had it not been for Gisele, my life would have turned out quite differently. I straightened out, had a child and recently we bought a home. I had a family of my own and wanted to grow it even more. I also harbored a lot of unanswered questions about myself, but having a family gave me such a good feeling. Medical history was more important than ever, and I wanted to know my roots. With Rhiannon, I was experiencing the same nagging questions I had all my life. Her pediatrician would ask about any history of family illness and of course on my side remained the deepest of black holes. Doctors ask these questions for a reason ... a good reason. I was unable to answer them because someone had decided I didn't need to know anything about myself all those years ago! How many others like me were out there, wondering? I kept thinking about the note my mother sent me and wanted to find Children's Village more than ever.

April 23, 1979: we brought Greta, a German Shepherd/Collie mix, into our home. Rhi had a new friend! What a family! A baby, a dog, a cat, and kittens. There was something going on every waking minute of every day. Our home was bustling with chaos, and we loved it!

THE SEARCH

Sometime in May of 1979 while at work, I happened to hear a talk show on Boston AM radio (WITS) where it was "open lines day". People were calling in on a wide variety of issues and I just caught the end of a conversation about a place where people would help adoptees locate their birth parents. I grabbed something to write with and waited for a name, address, or phone number. Nothing. ... Several minutes went by before a woman called in and gave her name and phone number. She was the Massachusetts President of the national organization. It took two days of calling before I was able to get through on her very busy phone. Her name was Susan Darke, she owned and operated The Adoption Connection, a search and support group for adoptees and birth parents. There was a meeting coming up on 9/9/79 in Boston for adoptees or parents of adoptees or those who had given up a child. It was open to the public and we would certainly attend. I couldn't believe a group like this existed.

To say I was shocked to be in the presence of so many people like me, searching for simple answers would be a gross understatement. I listened with rapt interest to their amazing stories without saying a word. Many knew of "the Chosen Baby" book I had been read from as a toddler. At these meetings we heard stories of joyful reunions with positive results, while others shared accounts of their frustration and roadblocks experienced while seeking the truth about who they were. Susan spoke about her personal story of giving up a child and being an adoptee herself. She represented both sides of the situation. Books were recommended as references or to document personal stories. Dates and places for future workshops were available. Search techniques were discussed (what worked and what didn't and what to try next after a failure). How to make contact with your birth mother without letting someone else know who you are, etc. and why this is important. It was an eye-opening experience, showing me the

things I had only dreamed of, were in fact possible. I knew this would be something I would pursue with vigor wherever it led me.

I'm no longer clear how I learned the Children's Village became Child and Family Services. It may have been through one of Susan's associates. I wrote them requesting my non-identifying information, something I learned I had a right to! In October or November of 1979, I received a letter from the adoption agency along with my personal information. I received several pages, mostly blank, but there was some very good information to start with, and quickly I realized the stories my adoptive mother had told me about my birth were completely false.... I was not premature, small, sickly, not an American Indian, and my mother was not too young to keep me. I think she wanted to clear away her lies before she passed or maybe she just wanted to upset my dad before she died. I chose the former rather than latter, but who really knows? I was stunned to see the blank space for the child's name was filled in! According to this, my name was David! A name! Having these limited facts was uplifting and made me think I would be able to learn even more if I sought the truth. My mother was 22 years old when I was born. 22! Why did she give me up? What happened to her? A thousand "whys"!

I remember feeling an overwhelming guilt associated with searching for my heritage gnawing away at me. I needed to tell my father what I was doing but I was terribly conflicted and concerned it would have a devastating effect on our relationship. That was the last thing I wanted to see happen. My dad was the guy who raised me, taught me things I would use throughout my life, and I loved him. When I broke the news, he was noticeably sad, and I think a piece of his heart broke. He understood I needed to do this but was disappointed I felt the urge to do so, so strongly. I think it was akin to a failure on his part, which was so very far from the truth. My dad wanted me and fought hard to maintain custody of me when he divorced Nancy. He stood up for me against Marie too. Now I'm seeking out who my "real" parents were. To him, I'm sure it felt like a massive kick in the gut. It breaks my heart to think about how this must have felt to him.

He agreed to help me in any way he could and said he would sign anything that was necessary to help in the effort, but he also made it clear he didn't want to know any of the results should I find anything out. I thought it was odd, and sad, but if that was his wish, I would certainly respect it. I don't think we ever spoke about it again.

I told the twins about my searching and was surprised to see they were not the least bit interested. Actually, one of them was slightly curious, but the other was emphatically against it. In the end they united on being totally opposed to the idea in every way imaginable. They even hinted at "knowing" something about their story. It dealt with a family scandal involving our grandfather (my dad's father)! None of it made any sense, there was no documentation to support it, they couldn't tell me how they "knew" either. It was all absurd. I wonder if our mother had fabricated yet another lie, for their benefit. I did bring up the obvious falsities Nancy had fed me in hopes they might reconsider their united and tenuous position, but it fell on indifferent ears. We would not discuss this again. These girls were each other's world. As long as they had each other, they would be fine. I began feeling more distant from them as time went on. We weren't on the same page. We weren't even in the same book! I couldn't fathom the total lack of curiosity on their part.

February 8th of 1980, my job at the tannery came to end when the owner sold the business. I had a wife, a new home, a toddler, was out of work, and had no significant savings. Gisele was a stay-at-home mom, so I needed to find a new job fast. It seemed no one was hiring. I was at it every day, all day long. I made cold calls at various businesses in town and interviewed at the unemployment office. I wasn't eligible for food stamps because I had a little money in the bank. That would soon be gone, as it wasn't enough to cover a month of bills.

March 10, 1980, around noon time, I made a brief statement before the Massachusetts legislature on the subject of adoptees' rights. I dressed in a suit and read my piece nervously as TV cameras rolled, so scared my dad might see my face on the evening news later that day. He didn't (or if he did, he never said a word about it).

5/20/1980: Susan Darke put me in touch with Nancy Sitterly from Connecticut, when she learned where my adoption took place. Nancy called one night to let me know of something a few people had recently tried, which proved successful in delivering their birth name. She urged me to try it quickly, as she was not sure how long it would be before this loophole would be negated. I would need to provide a request for my original adoption decree, but as my father. It had to be notarized and be accompanied by a check and a self-addressed stamped envelope. I didn't need to make an appearance before a judge.

I wrote a letter as my dad, signed it, and went into Haverhill to have it notarized. The Notary told me flat out he couldn't do it because he didn't witness my father's signature. I improvised quickly. Disappointment with just a touch of exasperation, desperation, and a trace of fear shrouded my face. "My dad just left on an extended business trip and asked that I make sure I got this notarized and, in the mail immediately, as it was extremely important. He is going to kill me if I don't get this done!" I gave him the most pleading of faces I could muster, and he reluctantly agreed to do it, but he emphasized what the rules were, and I needed to follow them in the future. Document in hand, I left with a huge sense of relief. I quickly mailed it then anxiously waited.

On May 27, 1980, I received a copy of my original adoption decree which clearly stated my name at birth was "Martin Clarke Decker"! This was huge. I assumed this was the key that would open the doors to the mystery of me --- how wrong I was! Gisele and I drove to the Bureau of Vital Statistics in CT and asked for a copy of my (Martin Clarke Decker's) birth certificate. A young woman headed off into the files and as she returned with a card in her hand, paused while reading it. The subtle hesitation was all it took to tell me this was not going to go as planned. When she returned to us, she said she could not give us a copy but could provide the amended certificate. I explained I was Martin and had a copy of my adoption decree in hand as proof if she needed it. The rules were clear to her; she could not comply with my request. The woman genuinely looked disappointed as she sincerely wanted to help. I told her I was adopted and the card she had in her hand might hold long anticipated answers for me. Her hands were tied, and I was frustrated. Less than two feet away from the names of my biological parents. I wanted to reach in and grab it from her hand! I hoped she would at least set it down in such a way so I could casually read it, but that didn't happen either. My mind just fogged over in defeat. Gisele thought she heard her say something along the idea of "suppose your mother's name was Mary" .... I never recalled hearing her say that, but for years after, we assumed it to be true. We would fruitlessly research Mary Decker over and over again for years.

While in Hartford, we decided to visit Child and Family Services. We met with the same woman who sent me the letter and non-identifying information and learned absolutely nothing new. There was no letter in my file from my mother. For a fee they would initiate a search and if successful, they would ask if my mother wanted to make contact. It seemed absurd to pay for a search which if successful, could end in my mother's identity being withheld from me anyway. I was asked why I felt the need to know who she was and whether my adoptive family experience was good. How could anyone not understand the need to have simple answers? It didn't matter whether my adoptive parents treated me well or not. I just wanted to know where I came from! It was such a waste of time. We went home disappointed and feeling defeated after having such high hopes. I had my birth name but couldn't do anything with it. It didn't open any doors at all. Connecticut was a barrier I just couldn't penetrate.

A NEW JOB

About 80 people answered an ad for two Quality Control positions with Borden Chemical in North Andover, MA. I interviewed for the job in person and thought it went well. A week went by, and I heard nothing, so I called to see what my status was. They wanted me to come in for another interview. I did and thought that one went well too. Time went by again and I was about to call when they called me for yet another interview, this time with the General Manager. I met with him, and he asked some very pointed questions about working as a salesman rather than the Quality Lab job which I had applied for. I told him if I really wanted to be a salesman I could have gone to work at my father's business in Boston. I really didn't want to be in sales. The interview ended shortly thereafter. Again, I waited. A call came asking me to come in yet again and I was compelled to ask if this process was ever going to end. I thought I sounded too forceful, but I think something clicked at the other end. They hired me. I learned later it was my voice over the phone when I was looking for answers, that convinced my boss I was right for the job. I had no problem pressing an issue and that seemed perfect for what they wanted. My first day with Borden was June 6/23/1980. I had been out of work for almost five months! It was the longest stretch of unemployment I ever experienced. Thank God we had tenants as this was our only income during that time.

Borden was launching a new business at a new location and there were only a few of us in the lab charged with assessing the quality of the product when they managed to get a sample to us for testing. The production line was down far more than it was up, which gave me ample opportunity to ask questions of the engineers. I learned more about the process and the product being made. Often, I would go home without testing a thing for 8 to 10 hours. I made myself available on call for any hour of the day or night on any day of the week. There were times I had just gotten home or into bed when the phone would ring saying they had a sample for me. I would drive back in and perform the testing required. There were always gaps in their quality coverage, as only three of us were covering a 24/7 operation. I seemed to get the nod repeatedly when they needed someone during "off hours." I lived close by and could be there quickly. I took on as much responsibility as I could. I wanted this to work for me and my family.

11/28/1980 I learned from the documentation I had that I was born at Hartford Hospital. I wrote them as Martin Clarke Decker looking for a copy of my medical file. A form letter was returned to me asking for signatures from my parents before any information could be released. I was an adult but still needed my parents' permission to get my information! Unbelievable!

12/8/1980: John Lennon died. I had been watching Miami vs New England on Monday Night Football but dozed off without hearing Howard Cosell inform the country John had been shot twice in the back. On my way into work the following morning I fiddled with the radio to learn the final score of the game when I heard the news, I started crying. John was my favorite of the Beatles. I struggled to regain my composure as I walked in the front door to begin my day. Such a loss.

THE FAMILY GREW

G isele was pregnant again. Work was crazy busy. My schedule was two weeks of nights followed by four weeks of days. Night shift was six days at ten hours for each. Day shift was five days a week at eight hours per day. Additionally, there were still overtime opportunities almost every week. In the warmer weather, I came home for lunch to be with Rhi and Gisele. We would often cook burgers on the deck before I raced back to work. Having an hour off and being so close to home was great!

I never knew when I would be coming home so Gisele never knew when to plan dinner. The company gave me a beeper. Gisele now had the means to get in touch with me immediately when she felt it was time to go to the hospital. I had come home for lunch, and it was snowing heavily. I explained what she needed to do to reach me when the time came. I stressed the importance of not testing the device when I gave her the beeper number (I had already tested it). I drove back to work in lousy conditions and shortly thereafter, the beeper went off! I wondered if it was really happening as I had just left her, and everything seemed fine. I called the house a couple of times, but there was no answer. I couldn't take a chance that something might have happened, so I drove home again in the snow. Gisele was surprised to see me at the door. She said she never called me. I drove back to work wondering if I should trust the beeper in the future.

Aaron was born on February 19th at 5:12 AM in 1981. Gisele and I waited at Gloria (the young girl raised with Gisele) and John's home until we had to leave for the hospital. Rhiannon stayed with them while her brother arrived. My family was growing! I had a son! Two blood relatives. Aaron was much bigger than Rhiannon when he was born, 50% bigger! At the time, he was the biggest baby in the nursery at 9 pounds and 1 oz. I loved being in there with all the newborns and rocking my son. He looked a lot more like his mother than me. I still had no idea about my family medical history, but it didn't matter right now. We had two healthy children, and I was on top of the world. Since I chose Rhiannon's name, Gisele had the honor this time and Aaron it was.

FRUSTRATION

I continued to search for a Mary Decker whenever I traveled on company business anywhere. We looked for any Decker who appeared in Hartford just prior to my birth but disappeared shortly thereafter. We did find one or two, but the ages were wrong to be my mother. I was getting nowhere with the search, and it didn't seem worth the effort anymore. I had my family, and we would deal with anything adverse if we had to. I would check in at odd times with Susan Darke or Nancy Sitterly to see if there was anything new I could try. I hired an attorney who specialized in these matters at some point. His report to me was nothing more than regurgitated information I had supplied him or already uncovered on my own. I expressed my disappointment firmly and the bill went unpaid. I was running out of options to explore. I did contact the wife of the doctor who delivered me. She explained he was retired. I asked about any record he might have about me, and she told me if there was anything, it was buried in his old files, and it would be impossible for her to locate them. Another dead end.

I read stories and articles on adoption and reunions which always left me feeling a little more crushed when I realized I couldn't get any traction because I was adopted in Connecticut. Everything seemed stacked and fortified against me. What was so wrong with wanting to know where you came from? Many good books have been written about adoption. They have covered issues ranging from the adoptee's right to search out family history (or not), to birth parents (father and/or mother, even grandparents) trying to learn the fate of those given up shortly after taking their first unassisted breath. The argument of whether or not a birth parent's right to privacy outweighs the right of the adoptee to know the circumstances surrounding his or her birth, has sparked much debate.

We usually hear of adolescents or young adults who are actively battling the legal system of one state or another in an effort aimed at discovering their roots. There is another side to this issue that has not received as much attention. We seldom hear about the families of the adult adoptee and their feelings on the subject. The information denied the adult adoptee is also concealed from his or her family. The children of the adult adoptee are only privy to what the "traditional" parent and their family can provide. These children will "adopt" this half of the total package as representative of the whole. Nature abhors a vacuum. The family heritage and history have been effectively compromised as a result. This new generation becomes one more step removed from the facts and will only pass what they believe on to the next generation and so on. The unknown and once questioned becomes invisible to the youngest in the family.

The adoptee's influence on the family tree remains invisible too. The more progressive states were rewriting the laws surrounding adoption, but not Connecticut! Other states were finally beginning to recognize the drive pushing people to search out their backgrounds and made it possible for these people to learn more about who they are and where they came from. Unfortunately, some of these new laws are not fully retroactive. There are still many adults who are repeatedly denied the knowledge which is common information in most households. Those wanting to seek out the facts were often labeled as weak or insecure by those who have no first-hand idea of what it is like to answer "unknown" on questionnaires for an entire lifetime. By being denied the truth as to one's heritage, is to place this individual in the category of a second-class citizen.

STOPPED SEARCHING AND
JUST LIVED FOR A WHILE

July 24, 1981: The Maddens, Bernie and Pam, arrived from Israel @ 8:21 PM TWA#881. We had a great reunion. It had been a long time since we had been together. Bernie had converted to Judaism, and with Pam, left the USA to live in a Kibbutz. There were many new stories told about a hard life in Israel and many old memories shared with hearty laughter. It was always good to be among such wonderful friends.

9/5/81: Dave Mason and Jim Krueger played at the Paradise in Boston. It was an intimate performance. As great as Dave Mason was, Jim was outstanding. All Along the Watchtower was unbelievable acoustically! Memories of the Santa Barbara concert came flooding back. This was a totally different vibe, but a good show, nonetheless. We had perfect seats at a tiny table with a clear view of the small stage.

12/5/81: Our tenants and now good friends, the Inghams, moved out of our first-floor apartment. They bought a home from within their family and moved across the Merrimack River into Haverhill. Barbara's sister lived across the street from us, so we still saw them often.

12/10/81: The Gosslin family moved into our vacant first-floor apartment. Good hardworking family. Long after we moved away, we learned their son committed suicide by driving his car into the same spot on the brick wall where his friend had accidentally died. Tragic. One of my coworkers at Borden knew the family.

1/23/82 Gisele, Gloria, and John went to see Kenny Loggins in Boston.... I had to work that night. Would have liked to attend but .... you know, work was important too. Things were different when I had a family. My life had changed in so many ways.

6/20/83: My paternal Grandfather died. We used to call him "Grumpa" (not to his face of course), as he was a very demanding and opinionated person. He expected results and would let you know if he was disappointed. He took me tobacco shopping once when I visited them as a child in Florida. It was some old shop where the rich tobacco smells permeated everything inside the store. I loved watching him blend various tobaccos in a large plastic tub and then pour a bottle of rum onto the mix. He'd pack the blended combination back into the individual tins they came in then set them in a cabinet. The smoke from his pipe was sweet and strong. There was a softer side to him too. His face lit up like a little kid when he met Aaron as a baby (I had never seen this side of him!). It was a sad day when he passed, but he had been ill for a long time and my grandmother had no time to herself while caring for him. She deserved to take a breath and live a little too.

In the summer of 1983, we learned Gisele was pregnant for the third time. February would bring us another daughter. I loved my family but also believed I had more out there, somewhere. Why can't I have the information everyone else has a right to? What nationality am I? Why aren't the medical records updated periodically and passed on to adoptees? Why isn't it a requirement if you choose to give up a child? What little history I have represents but a moment in time, which goes all the way back to 1953. What happened *after* I was born? My personal history was now 30 years old. Decades old. I kept circulating the same questions over and over for years. I just couldn't let them go unanswered.

In January 1984, we started attending a few workshops in North Andover at the home of a woman named Ruth Roland. This went on through the summer and into November and December of 1985. It was good to associate with people like me, but it also was a drag because nothing really changed. I wasn't any closer to learning where I came from. Eventually I stopped going, I just didn't see the point.

February 25, 1984, at 8:04 PM Kirsten arrived ... We drove to Beverly Hospital then passed Rhiannon and Aaron over to Gloria and John. I barely had enough gas in the car, but we made it. Gisele was experienced at giving birth now and took charge of the delivery room. She told the staff when she was going to push, and it was the smoothest of all the births. Another miracle entered the world, bigger than Rhiannon but smaller than Aaron, Kirsten weighed 8 pounds 9 oz. The doctors told us Kirsten was healthy. Gisele and I were proud parents of three active and thriving kids. Their personalities were all different. My family grew again! I now had three known blood relatives and I was very happy. I could still count all my relatives on one hand with fingers left over. Gisele and I had alternated in selecting names with our prior children. This time we decided jointly. We loved the Joan Baez song Children and All That Jazz. The lyrics contain two long lists of names. If you listen carefully, there is a subtle inflection Joan uses when she says "Kirsten." We both felt she was telling us something. Kirsten sounded just right.

Gisele and I had our hands full; we were parents after all. On top of everything else, we were also landlords. I took a college computer course in Basic Programming, we went apple picking, took the kids to swim class, ballet, gymnastics, hockey, had parties, went shopping, camping, parades, school for the kids, doctor and dentist visits, traveled for work, the Fiesta in Gloucester, performed repairs on the house, took the kids for haircuts, picked up spring water every week in Haverhill, celebrated holidays ... like all the other parents we knew. I only thought about my roots at odd times now.

I don't remember the year, but early in Aaron's hockey adventures we skated at the rink in Haverhill, MA. Former

Bruin Terry O'Reilly's son, Conner, was in the same learn-to-skate class. When I introduced myself to Terry on the ice, he remembered the lamp socket dimmer I sold him many years earlier at the Home Show. He told me it still worked! Terry played keep away with several of us parents on the ice. It was impossible for any of us to put a stick on the puck as he skated in circles around us. He still had that drive that made him tenacious when he played professionally.

1/28/1986: Challenger blew up after lifting off and we watched it live. Horrible watching Christa McAuliffe's parents' reaction as they realized what had happened. I can't imagine the pain of losing a child. My kids were the most precious things on earth to me.

In 1986 we had a decision to make regarding the house we owned. It needed some serious repair if we planned on staying there. We could instead sell the place as is and move was another option. We had intended to live in our two-family for five to ten years until we had enough equity to afford a single-family home. Having lived there for eight years, we felt it was time for us to make the leap to a single family for the sake of our kids. We didn't want the kids growing up in Haverhill if there was a better option for them, so we started looking around.

Massachusetts didn't have much to offer in our price range. We wanted something a step up from where we were living. We began looking over the border into southern New Hampshire and realized quickly, we could get a lot more land there for about the same money. Every weekend and occasionally during the week we visited properties looking for a place to raise our children. We found a realtor who actually listened to us and what our goal was, and she had an idea. It was a little further away than we had hoped, but she assured us it would be worth checking out.

She took us down a long tree lined road, then turned off onto a smaller side road. The pavement became gravel and then we saw a foundation on a small plot of cleared woodland. We were surrounded by trees and a small starter home was to be built on a 2.5-acre lot. There were a few horses on the abutting lot and another cleared area on the opposite side of the foundation. The builder was erecting two homes. The area seemed perfect. We toured a similar house the builder had made and spoke with the people who lived in it. Everything was falling into place. We would have a say on how the interior would be designed and what cabinets would be installed etc. We had a deal and set things in motion to sell our home and move to New Hampshire. We accepted an offer on our two family on July 22, 1986.

Our builder's wife was also a realtor, and she became our go to person for anything we needed or had to pick out for the house. She'd call us to say it was time to pick out kitchen cabinets, or interior lights etc. as they were needed. She made things so easy for us. The house was finished on 9/14/86 and the electricity was turned on the next day. We moved in on October 4th of 1986. Rhiannon had to adjust to a new school and make new friends. We were all starting a new life. The commute for me went from 10 minutes to almost an hour. I was a little concerned about it, but the advantage to us living in the woods was well worth it. In time I grew to love the commute as it was the only time of the day I claimed as mine. I relaxed between the chaos of work and bedlam waiting to greet me when I got home. It was the best move we could have made.

Epping was a small quiet town, unless the racetracks were open. Much of our gravel road was practically impassable for several months of the year due to mud, ruts, or flooding. The town would regrade it every spring. When people came to visit, we directed them to take the long way to the house. At the opposite end of the road from us was an oval track which we could hear when the super modified cars raced. This was going to take some getting used to. We could also hear New

England Dragway through the woods. The first time we heard the alcohol and jet cars, I thought a gas station in town had exploded! Funny how the realtors always brought us the long way to view the property, which avoided the racetracks and bumpy gravel road. We learned as residents of Mast Road we were entitled to free passes to the oval track (Star Speedway) located at the opposite end of our road. We took advantage of this and enjoyed many free nights at the races. While exploring trails through several hundred acres of woods, I discovered a path leading us to the far end of the New England Dragway strip. I took the family on hikes to watch the drags for free until I learned Epping residents were also *entitled* to free passes for most of their events too! We received passes to both tracks right away. It was far easier to drive to the drag track rather than walking through the woods.

Being so isolated, Gisele wanted an alarm system installed for the house. I agreed. The best feature of the system was a chime which went off every time a door was opened. This was great when you had three children. If the chime sounded, it was time to take inventory of the kids. We lost power often and after any disruption, the alarm would lose its memory and have to be reprogramed, which was a real pain in the ass. We were surrounded by eight hundred acres of woods, on a dirt road with no lighting. If Gisele needed an alarm to feel safe, I intended to keep the thing programmed.

By now I wasn't thinking too much about searching any more. It all seemed impossible to get any answers anyway. Those who knew anything or had access to my records weren't going to tell me a thing. I wondered if my mother was still alive or if she ever thought about me. Was she in good health? Did I have any brothers or sisters? Somewhere deep down I still believed there was a family out there that I belonged to. This was a feeling I had off and on over the years but never spoke about it to anyone. Why would I, it sounded like I was being childish. No one I knew was looking for their long lost or unknown family.

I did fantasize about my mother and why I was given up. If it was an affair, who was it with? Was she famous? Maybe it was my father who was famous. Did they ever see each other again? Did he ever learn she had been pregnant? Maybe he divorced his wife and married my mother years later. Maybe I have full siblings somewhere. Maybe I have half siblings from both my mother and my father. I could go on and on imagining this or that, but the truth had become clear, I was never going to learn anything more. They had succeeded in walling off my access to anything relevant.

6/12/1987 Kirsten split her right palm open running on the flagstone walkway outside our backdoor. The rule was *"NO RUNNING ON THE FLAGSTONES!"* .... and what did Kirsten do? We took her to the hospital to get stitched up. I held her tiny hand still when the doctor put a needle into her gash to numb it. I can still see the surprise and shock in little Kirsten's eyes when the needle went in.... ugh!

6/17/87 Rhiannon broke her left index finger when it was shut in the car door. The tip was severely swollen when we went to the hospital, and she was in pain. She was delighted to learn the doctor could make it feel better until she realized it meant drilling a small hole through her fingernail to relieve the pressure! She flat out refused to have it done and went back home with the same pain she'd left with. It felt odd to be back in the hospital with another child less than a week after Kirsten's misstep.

7/24/87 Willie Nelson performed at Star Speedway. We didn't have tickets but walked from our house to the track and listened to some of it from our side of the fence. It was dark when we headed home using our Coleman lantern to light the way. A long walk with the kids.

March of 88 Gisele worked part time at the Newfields Preschool which allowed Aaron to attend for free (preschool wasn't free in New Hampshire back then). The school was just around the corner from our house. Gisele entertained me each night with stories of the kids at the school. She would go into character and pretend to be each kid. I think she could have taken that show on the road as a comedy routine and made some money!

November of 1989 Rhi and Aaron took on a job for a neighbor feeding their horse, Tinker, after school. This was an excellent opportunity to develop a sense of responsibility for them. They knew exactly how much to feed it and where to place the hay and grain. Very good experience in so many ways. Tinker always knew when they were coming, I think he looked forward to it.

December 23, 1989 was a Saturday. A very cold Saturday at -11 degrees when Aaron and I set out for a hockey game in Wolfboro, NH. The temperature at game time reached 0 degrees and simply stayed there. We had friends (the Inghams) over that night and cranked the heat up high to an uncomfortable level. When they left, we dropped the thermostat way down (big mistake) to cool the house a little. The next morning was even colder (-19) when Aaron and I headed out to Biddeford, ME for another game. I thought the house seemed too cool, so I bumped the thermostat up a little for the girls before we left. When we got home the house was ice cold! The Peros came over for dinner and to celebrate Christmas Eve. I spent much of the day looking for an arc welder to come to the house to attempt thawing our frozen pipes. He was there from 6 PM to 11 PM. I punched holes in the first-floor ceiling so he could reach the copper pipes. We finally found the frozen area and attached the cables to either side. Success! We were able to thaw the pipes without them bursting. It cost us $200.00. We fed him too. I was left with a lot of self-inflicted damage to deal with ... ceiling damage that is. It was a very tough winter! I don't think we had a day above freezing the entire month of December.

March 26, 1991 my grandmother died two days before my dad's

birthday. I didn't find out for weeks and was disappointed I wasn't told right away. My grandmother and I were always close. I brought the kids to see her at the nursing home in Exeter as often as I could. She always recognized the kids though sometimes I think she confused me with my dad. She would shoot Aaron with her finger gun, and he would smile. Rhiannon was very comfortable talking with her, and any of the other residents of the home. The elderly would gravitate to her and engage in conversation. She could light the place up in seconds.

May of 1991, I began brewing beer on Mother's Day. A neighbor across the street had given me a lesson in his kitchen and I was hooked. This hobby would last for years ... and many beers!

In July 1991 Aaron "won" the raffle at school and was now the proud owner of the chicks the class watched hatch. I had to build them a pen, nesting area, feeding station etc. These free chickens cost me about $300.00 in materials and supplies. Our first eggs arrived in late September. Fresh eggs are fantastic.

August 13th, 1991, our beloved Greta passed away. She collapsed outside on the lawn and since it was so hot, I picked her up and placed her on the cool cement of the basement floor, hoping this would revive her. Gloria and John were over that day, and we checked on Greta often until I noticed she had died. We buried her in the backyard. So sad. She was a kind dog, played with the cats, our chickens would ride on her back... never aggressive. The kids would drape a colored kerchief around her neck, and she never seemed to mind. Such a good dog.

September 26, 1991, we brought Moxie home. Lots of energy. So different than our older, slower Greta. This dog loved to run so we took her on Birch Road where we could unclip her leash and let her go! She always came back when we called her, and seldom did we see other people when we were out there.

December 20, 1991, Kirsten comes down with Chicken Pox ....

December 31, 1991, Rhiannon has Chicken pox

January 1, 1992, Aaron has Chicken pox. All plans to gather with family over the holidays were canceled. We celebrated at home with itchy kids who needed constant reminding not to scratch!

1/16/92: Aaron was feeling a lot better and was back playing hockey. After finishing hockey practice, we headed over to another building on the Phillips Exeter Academy campus to see Ralph Nader give a campaign speech as part of his run for the presidency. He was introduced by Jerry Williams; a well-known Boston talk radio host and a personal favorite of Gisele's dad.

2/6/92: Aaron and I attended a speech by Bill Clinton at PEA after his practice.... Aaron worked his way close to the stage while I viewed from a short distance away. He told me later he thought he was lying about something. Interesting impression of the soon to be president.

8/15/92: Livingston Taylor played at the Strawberry Bank in Portsmouth. It was a beautiful day for a concert. Gloria and John attended. Gisele, Gloria, and John headed off to get something at the concession stand while I hung around to keep our spot on the lawn. Walking through the crowd seemingly unnoticed was Liv Taylor. He was headed my way and looked right at me. I smiled and waved. We ended up talking for a few minutes. I told him I had seen him years ago in Ohio and he recalled the specific tour. I also mentioned seeing his sister Kate and brother Alex, but never James. When I mentioned his version of Over the Rainbow, he said it would be part of his set that night. He headed off into the crowd before the rest of my group returned. Of course, they all thought I made the story up of chatting with LT. Yes, he did play Somewhere Over the Rainbow that night. Love his version of the song.

2/26/93: Pipes froze again! (-15 degrees outside). I was able to get the temperature in the garage up just enough to thaw them without a burst. More holes in the ceiling to deal with! The area directly above the garage door seemed to be the most vulnerable. I stuffed as much insulation around the pipes as I could without compacting it too much. This sucked!

4/28-29/93 Gisele and I wanted to do some more searching in Hartford while the kids were on vacation from school. Gloria and John offered to watch them. It was uneventful and frustrating for us, but we heard the Peros had a blast! Nothing had changed as far as searching went. The walls were still in place and just as strong as ever.

6/27/93: Aaron auditioned for music camp at UNH and made the cut. Everyone who attended camp was much older than he was and had more experience. The class was from 8 am to 4 pm each day for several days, followed by a concert at night on 7/1 before one last day of camp. He did well performing with the adults in the concert. The composition the class wrote and arranged sounded great. We were very proud parents! Music was very much alive with everyone in the family.

9/23/93: I had to retire the VW Rabbit diesel with a mere 275,000 miles on it. The engine was still running great, but the body was falling apart. The next day I bought a Saab 900 Turbo from my brother-in-law. This had a lot of miles on it too, but the power was amazing. There was a lot of room inside for hauling Aaron's hockey gear too. The Saab also spent a lot of time in the repair shop. It was an expensive car to maintain. Fortunately for me, my mechanic would provide a loaner car when the Saab was in the shop. I designed a flowchart entitled "A Saab Story" which humorously detailed the steps of diagnosing a problem, bringing the car to the garage, checking the weather before taking the offered loaner etc. He posted this up on his office wall for years. It was a big hit with his customers and staff. The new owner (who used to be an employee there) stopped by the house 25 years later with the chart to show me he still had it!

2/11/94: Gisele had surgery to remove one of her ovaries. Outside it was snowing heavily and by the time she was ready to check out of the hospital, there was a foot of snow in Beverly. The Nurses were concerned with the weather and said we could stay overnight, as there was no demand for the room. With no one on the roads, I decided to drive home with the understanding if it proved too difficult, we could return. I had no issue driving in snow, so off we went. There was no traffic, and the conditions improved the closer we came to home.   6/24/94: Rhiannon went to Rhode Island to see Whitney Houston. All three of the kids have a deep love for music. They all played in the school bands and listened to vinyl records, CDs, cassette tapes and the radio. They were well versed in the music I listened to, as it played constantly in our house. I remember their faces the first time each one used headphones. Their faces lit up with wide eyes and smiles.

7/12/94 Kirsten's favorite cat Ivory, was hit by a UPS truck in front of our house. This lovable white cat was docile and loving. Kirsten used to hold it like a stuffed animal and Ivory didn't seem to mind. Sad loss for the family, but especially Kirsten.

9/15/94: With the kids older and in school every day, Gisele was free to get out on her own. She applied for and was accepted as a driver for Meals on Wheels. She was very close to her clients and was often the only contact they had with the outside world. She took her job and role seriously and made new friends while becoming a vital part of their sheltered lives. She would visit them on her own time and even helped them move. When she lost someone, it hurt deeply. Gisele is a very thoughtful and giving person and was a valued member of the team. She has a heart much like her mother's. Must be in the DNA.

April 5, 1995: Gisele had developed a clear taste for country music. I listened to it when I was younger and liked it to a point, but Rock 'n' Roll was still my preference. Since she always attended any artist I wanted to see, it seemed only fair, I should reciprocate. Vince Gill and Patty Loveless played in Maine (I think). Vince made reference to anyone who wasn't a country music fan and my ears perked up. He went into a set from his days with the Pure Prairie League. I had no idea he sang for them. His band was surprisingly good, and his guitar skills surprised me! The concert was far better than I had imagined it would be. Maybe country ain't so bad!

April 6, 1995 (Worcester, MA I think): Having seen Vince Gill the night before, we were thoroughly entertained by Reba McEntire. Great stage presence and performance. Very different than Vince's show. Once again, I was surprised. Maybe Gisele was on to something!

I believe it was 1995 when I dropped Kirsten off at school for a dance or something like that. She was quite young, but I think it was the school's way of slowly introducing social activities to the younger kids. When it was time to pick her up, my car died after I had just gotten out of the driveway and onto the main road. I pushed it back to the house which should have been no problem, as we live in an area that's flat. I couldn't catch my breath after getting the car parked in its usual spot. I was sweating too. I got in the house and gave myself a minute before I called a neighbor for a ride over to the school. I was still struggling for air when I made the call. My neighbor was eating but said he would finish shortly, then pick me up. I still didn't have my breath back when he got to the house. I had never felt this before. We picked up Kirsten and returned home. I was concerned. Something wasn't right with me.

Later that night I felt fine. Someone mentioned high blood pressure as a possibility, so I checked it out at the local

Walmart. They had a cuff device for anyone wanting to check their BP and it was free. Sure enough, it was high. They had little pamphlets you could take with you detailing what high blood pressure was and what some of the symptoms were. They recommended checking it more than once over a period of time. I did and it was always considered high.

I made an appointment with a doctor, and he confirmed my Walmart results. He also told me I would not be starting treatment with dietary changes as my numbers were simply too high. He went on to say I would be taking medication for the rest of my life. This was unexpected and something I wasn't looking forward to.

It took about a week to get used to the meds. I felt fuzzy around the edges and had difficulty concentrating, but eventually these feelings all went away. I learned hypertension was hereditary. Medical history was now haunting me again. Did my mother have high BP? My father? Am I going to pass this on to my children? Is a heart attack in my future? Is there a history of coronary problems in my family? And on it goes with my overactive imagination. If I had the answers, I wouldn't need to speculate. Is that such a difficult concept for those who keep from me what I have a right to know? Have I said that before? I know, I'm repeating myself.

It turned out cholesterol was my new concern and enemy. High cholesterol was part of the hypertension equation. I was active, but not active enough. I could eat better, but it wouldn't be easy for me. As a kid and young adult, I could eat like a horse and never gain a pound. I also could eat whatever I wanted and often did. I could never adhere to a diet of any sort. This was going to be tough.

9/15/95: I really wanted tickets for Eric Clapton in Worcester, but my sister Susan was getting married. There was a rehearsal dinner catered by Woodman's of Essex at my brother Dick's house in Rowley, MA. It was a great family day. Dave (husband to be) seemed just right for Susan. Seeing my little sister so happy made me happy too. I have a favorite picture taken on that day when I got my dad to crack-up laughing about something I said. I avoided Marie as much as possible but was polite when we did talk....Susan and Dave Married the next day at a beautiful spot on the ocean. A lovely wedding.

10/11/95: Gisele was very interested in learning how to line dance, and on this day, we had our first lesson. I had no real desire, but I wanted to be with her, so I gave it a shot. Yikes! This was not going to be easy. Gisele seemed to catch on right away while I struggled to get the simplest steps under control. "Control" is the wrong word. I was out of control! This wasn't making any sense to me. I could dance, I had rhythm, I could move to the music, but this was crazy. God it was maddening! There wasn't enough time to get my feet to the right place before the next step!

I learned I didn't have the right shoes. I needed to slide a little rather than grip the floor. We tried multiple instructors, at a number of places, but the end result was always the same. I was a step or more behind everyone, could never catch up and the steps themselves were all foreign to me. I was a mess and Gisele got better with every class. I was about to call the whole thing off and let Gisele do her thing alone when she convinced me to try one more class at a different place with a different teacher. This is when we met Ed Blain and Lil.

It was the largest class we had attended, and I didn't want to make a fool of myself in front of so many people. I spoke with the teacher before the class began, explaining my prior failures. He said I would learn a dance from start to end that night. I smirked and said many have tried and all have failed, but I will give it my best shot.

We all formed a big circle filling the gym floor, while our instructor had us walk or shuffle as we moved around the room with his amplified voice explaining what to do next as we went. "You have just learned a dance," he proclaimed. He had us do the same steps again, but this time he called them out with a count and then put on music. It all clicked and as he had promised, I learned a dance that night. I was more than surprised, and I thanked him then shared I was on the verge of quitting because I was so frustrated with my previous efforts. He went on to tell me I would learn a new dance every week for the next several weeks. He was true to his word. Suddenly everything was making sense. He had "helpers" in black shirts scattered around the hall that were eager to assist anyone who was struggling. This opened the door to dancing for me and Gisele; I started looking forward to every class.

We became close to Ed and Lil, and they continued to teach us. Lil took the time...with tremendous patience ... to teach me how to couples dance. It took a while but eventually I got it. We attended demonstrations, put on shows for the elderly and eventually received "black shirts" of our own so we could help beginners who attended their classes. We had come full circle. It was through them we met Bob Grundy. Dance became a big part of our lives. Ed and Lil eventually split up which was sad. Ed passed away a short time later. Lil got married and moved to Maine, but we stayed in touch until she too passed due to cancer. Heartbreaking losses.

March 24, 1996: Gisele and I bought our first pair of cowboy boots! We were doing line dancing and 2-stepping every week and it was fun! It was exercise, social, entertaining, and challenging. We established long lasting friendships through dancing. Dancing was also a way for me to block work out of my head for a few hours. Much needed relief!

4/3/96: Gisele saw a moose in the driveway! I kid her about it to this day. No one else saw the "alleged" moose. I know she saw one, but I couldn't resist giving her a hard time about it. She was on her way to the car when it came up the driveway. She thought it was a neighbor's horse at first, but then quickly realized what she was looking at. It wandered through the yard then out into the woods. In all the years we have lived here, we never seen another one here! We've seen hundreds in Maine and norther NH and have the pictures and video to prove it.

4/21/96: Reba McEntire and Linda Davis performed in Worcester, Massachusetts. I had never heard Linda before and it's no surprise that soon after this concert she went solo. She has an excellent voice and when singing with Reba they sound even better. Great show.

10/18/96: Gisele required a hysterectomy, and our dancing was placed on hold while she recuperated from the surgery. She pulled through soundly, and one of the first things we did together when she was strong enough, was return to line dancing. We made many new friends along the way and began going out as a social activity rather than strictly for lessons. We needed and received a lot of encouragement. This grew to be a major event we planned our other activities around.

11/28/96: Thanksgiving and the oven died! Our next-door neighbor, Ginny, said we were welcome to use hers. Back and forth I went between houses with an inch of snow on the ground. Out our back door across a path between the yards and up the stairs to her backdoor and kitchen. When the turkey was done, I slipped in the snow and almost dropped it on the ground. Disaster avoided; we enjoyed a memorable holiday meal.

8/7/1997: We saw Reba with Brooks & Dunn in Portland, ME. This was a high-octane show. They all sang a set together too. So cool. Each Reba concert was different. We often bumped into familiar faces at these country concerts. People we danced with but didn't know their names. With recognition acknowledged, one or the other would say," Rockingham Ballroom" and instantly we knew where we had been together. It was a small world.

10/4/97: On a beautiful fall day, Gisele, and I, along with Carmen, Marc, Gloria, and John took a train ride from South Station to New York and back to view the fall foliage. I think we got out once in Albany to stretch our legs. It was a relaxing day and fun to be with family not worrying about driving anywhere.

10/25/97: I took a creative writing class at UNH hosted by the SiFi writer, Daniel Patrick Kelly. I had been working on a story for a short time, and thought it was conceptually good. There were only 11 people in the class, and each of us had to submit a story to be critiqued by the group and Mr. Kelly. I was really excited and filled with anticipation when we all finally met to discuss our collected efforts. I was the first one at class and wanted my story to be the first one reviewed. Oh, God! It didn't go well. I was torn apart and then each piece was ripped up too! It was a merciless assault on what I worked so hard on. After class Kelly gave me some advice. He suggested I do a word search for "that" to see how often it showed up in my story. The word is typically unnecessary and if I could make my point without its use, I'd be better off.

I let these words of wisdom marinate while wallowing in a state of solid depression for a couple of days. I didn't want to talk to anyone for some time. This whole thing was a very humbling experience. His advice was sound and when I performed my word search, I was shocked at how often "that" showed up! I began the process of eliminating as many of them as I could. I still use far too many of them to this day and will systematically review my work looking for those dreaded "thats," wherever they are used.

CANCER

Sometime in later 1997 I came to the realization I was not satisfied with my job. I was disappointed with the company I worked so hard for and decided it was time to look around for other options. The holidays were almost upon us, and it was not the ideal time to start looking, but I couldn't think of any valid reason *not* to start. I made some calls, carefully put my resume out there and got a couple of callbacks relatively fast. It was an odd feeling akin to deceit in my mind. I didn't have any experience looking for a job while still employed. The company I worked for (Borden) recently changed medical plans. For the first time, doctor visits were now very affordable, and I decided to have a nagging problem checked out while planning for my potential departure.

I was having problems moving my bowels and would occasionally see blood after the fact. I wasn't overly concerned but it was painful at times. I have a lactose intolerance problem too, which actually helped me pass a stool. A glass of milk when I was having difficulty was my way around the problem. I set up an appointment with my doctor and he expressed his concern after I also shared with him, I had this constant metallic taste in my mouth. He wanted me to submit a random sampling of different parts of my stool which had not been exposed to water. In other words, he wanted me to crap on a plastic bag laid out on the floor at home. When I did it, I was shocked at the amount of blood visible, and I was scared. When the results of the test came in, I was scheduled for a sigmoidoscopy at Anna Jaques Hospital in Newburyport, MA.

11/not sure of the day/97: I had my sigmoidoscopy. The "issue" I had rationalized away for such a long time turned out to be a tumor. I was awake during the procedure and saw the bloody thing in color on the monitor at the same time as my doctor. Regardless as to the results of the biopsy, I was told it had to come out. I went through Thanksgiving without telling anyone other than Gisele, I'd have to go under the knife. I would also need a colonoscopy to ensure there were no additional tumors growing anywhere.

I set up a job interview immediately after Thanksgiving on 12/1/97 (the same day as my scheduled colonoscopy). I had taken "the prep" the night before the procedure and figured it would be okay to keep my interview prior to my screening. What a mistake! During the tour of the production floor, I felt my stomach roaring and growling. No one else could hear it over the din of the equipment, but I knew it was happening. If you've ever taken the prep I'm referring to, you know exactly what I mean. The interview ended in a quiet conference room where I couldn't keep my stomach still. I knew my potential new boss heard it too, he had to. So embarrassing. I was interviewed for a couple of hours, but somehow managed to make it to Anna Jaques on time for my procedure. The drive to the hospital was a lot of laughs, as my stomach never stopped making noises....FYI, I didn't get the job.

12/1/97: I took the oral prep (for the second time) the night before my first colonoscopy. Ugh! I was on the table as the drugs slowly took me off to la la land, when I was told by my doctor the biopsy had tested positive for cancer. After I came around, my doctor asked if this ran in the family and of course I responded with my classic, well worn, answer of "I don't know." Damn it! No medical history and another hereditary illness. Where did this come from, my mother or my father? It didn't matter. I had cancer and could pass this on to my kids. Again, I blamed the system which failed to provide updated medical information to those of us who were adopted. Had I known I was at risk, I never would have let the symptoms go unchecked for as long as I did. Now I wondered if it was too late. The thought crossed my mind I might die due to ignorance on my part. Ignorance born from a system which decided to protect my mother's identity at the expense of my health. What kind of system does that? Who designed it? Who signed off on it as being "good" or "complete"? Was there anyone there to advocate for the unborn? I was sick! The big "C" sick. Cancer is never fair, but this just compounded everything. Why would anyone knowingly keep medical information secret or fail to periodically update it? Why would anyone think a momentary snapshot at the time of my birth would ever be enough to sustain me through my entire life? The only reason I had any information at all was because I asked for it. This was not something offered freely. The adoption procedure was more than just flawed, it was discriminatory; there was an obvious bias in favor of the woman who carried me in her womb. I bear no ill will toward my mother and whatever circumstances led to me being given up. I know things happen in life. But for God's sake let's be fair to the child who was given up. What might he or she want to know as he or she grows into adulthood? Where is the common sense?

After the outrage of what happened long before I was born calmed, I focused on the real issue staring me in the face. I had cancer! My generation was always of the collective mind, cancer equated to death. You don't walk away from cancer; the only question is "how much time do you have?" That's a thought that will haunt you very quickly. Your life scrolls past in slow motion as you feel every high and low in exquisite detail. You do a lot of crying. You feel cheated. Pity creeps in though you try to hide it. You cry again. You wonder about your next few months and what you must do. Once you stop thinking about you, the focus shifts on those you love. What are they going to do without you? How can you prepare to make things as easy for them as possible? What do you have to put in order before you aren't around anymore? Your mind goes to so many dark places in rapid succession .... What am

I going to miss? Weddings of my children. Grandchildren, I'll never know. What is my dad going to think when he hears this? Who do I have to tell right away? What will it be like at work? What repairs on the house do I need to take care of? It just rolls on and on. I'll need surgery. How long will I be out of work? Will I make it off the table or will I end my life in a hospital. God, I hated the space where my head was.

First on my shortlist, were the kids. They needed to know right away. Keeping the secret of surgery to ourselves over Thanksgiving was one thing, but now it was even more serious. Kirsten and Aaron were at home when I was ready. Rhi was with her boyfriend Mike, and I called to ask her to come home. She knew something big was up and refused to hang up until I told her. It was not what I wanted but I didn't see much of a way out. Aaron and Kirsten heard me tell their sister I was sick and needed surgery. I had the option to wait until after Christmas, but I had made it known I wanted this out of me as soon as possible.

Rhiannon was very upset and had a presentation planned for 12/3/97 in the restaurant at UNH. She wanted to cancel it because of what was going on with me. We explained we were looking forward to seeing what she prepared, we already were taking the days off and nothing was going to happen in the next two days. She understood and committed her efforts to putting together something to be proud of.

Alone with my thoughts, I was scared and mad, frustrated, and disappointed. I was not in a good place. The next day wasn't much better. I assembled my staff at work in my office, then broke the news I would be out for a while. It was difficult holding back tears and keep my voice from cracking. Word spread from there and soon I heard from coworkers of their experience with cancer and learned several had firsthand experience I was unaware of. They seemed to have pulled through well, maybe I would too. There was hope!

The next day at UNH went extremely well. Rhiannon was responsible for everything from the food choices being served, how it was prepared and the presentation of the meals on the plates. There was a buffet table set as well, it had a Mexican theme and was very creative. The menu selection was a very good one and to see so many people enjoying what she placed in front of them would make any parent proud. Something powerful came over me. I let go and cast my fate to the wind. I was living in a moment, and it was all good. By the end of our meal, I felt great, and my head was in a much better space. I accepted my fate, whatever it was.

Once I stopped all the speculation, started looking at the facts, and the reality associated with them, I felt differently. How I approached all of this was strictly up to me. I could keep my head up high, using the optimism that was typically my ever-present partner to help guide me through this maze of the unknown and yet to be determined. This was a place I was far more comfortable with. One step at a time. I had to be strong for my kids and Gisele. This would be tough, but they had to see a composed father and husband who was not afraid. I had to notify my boss I would be out for some period of time and there was nothing I could do about it. How they reacted was out of my control.

Gisele was my rock through all of this. She let our friends know what was going on and the well-wishing poured in. My surgeon and I developed a warm and comfortable relationship. I had told him I needed honesty, and any sugarcoating was not necessary. The quality of life was far more important than quantity. He fully understood and respected my wishes. I was relaxed with him, and it helped that he and I were the same age. He was genuinely pissed off something like this happened to me at such a young age. I really enjoyed spending time with him, and he made me feel like I was his only patient on the planet. I felt I was in good hands.

A woman at the hospital spent time with me explaining how everything was going to work so I wouldn't be surprised by anything. She answered every question and made me feel as comfortable as possible. When she finished, she confided in me, "I don't usually say anything like this to patients, but I have a good feeling about you... I think you're going to be okay." It almost seemed a little fire was glowing in me deep down. I really can't explain it but there just seemed to be a wave of positive energy surrounding me. The surgery was on 12/9/97 and it went well. Gisele saw the section of my colon the Doctor removed from my body. She said it looked like a slab of meat.

The staff at the hospital were all fantastic and provided me with great care. My family came and went in shifts. Friends and neighbors filtered in and out too. People we danced with showed, the woman who cut my hair was there. It was good to see everyone, and I felt fine, probably due to the drugs they had me on. My brother Dick showed up with a book for me to read when no one was there visiting. The book was based on the Gloucester fishing fleet which was thoughtful (shades of home). When the room was empty, I opened the book... The Perfect Storm by Sebastian Junger. It was about the Andrea Gail. Right away I saw a list of the crew members and noticed Billy Tyne was the captain. I knew Billy; we went to school together. Gisele met him once when he saw my name on an invoice while he was working in Danvers. Since we lived close by, he decided to deliver the part I needed in person and say hi. That was the last time I saw him. Something about the name of the boat was bugging me. I knew that name from somewhere and suddenly wondered if I heard on the news at one time the boat had sunk. I soon realized I was reading a story about the death of a school mate. The irony of it was palpable. I pulled through my ordeal, but he didn't.

After the surgery there was some concern the cancer had spread, but my surgeon wouldn't accept the report and ordered another test. Follow-up testing revealed he was right; it had not spread to the lymph nodes. He suspected a scalpel was contaminated with cells from the tumor when the nodes were checked. Of equally good news, was I would not be needing any chemotherapy! Since I was young and otherwise in good health, I was informed at the outset, the treatment would include chemo as a safeguard to ensure they got all the cancer. I was encouraged to walk as much as I could and would get up in the middle of the night to walk the quiet halls. One afternoon I walked past the elevator when out popped my dad holding a white poinsettia. He smiled to see me up and about. I asked what was with the plant and he told me it was my guardian angel. I still have that plant today. Gisele knows, how the plant goes, is how I go, so we do our best to keep it alive. It is all twisted and contorted but still clinging to life after more than 25 years in the house.

While I stayed home, Aaron took my car to school each day with Kirsten. We had a snowstorm after they left for school one day, and I fired up the snowblower just to open a small place for Aaron to pull the car in when he got home. Gisele asked me to stop, but I was being very careful due to my stitches. Next thing I know she is handing me a phone, and on the other end was my dad giving me a raft of crap about clearing snow so soon after surgery. I was a grown man getting chewed out by his father! I felt like a little kid being scolded. I stopped immediately and went inside. I know it was all out of love. There were people in the world who cared about me. Not bad!

Each day I would do a little walking on the road. I got tired quickly but also got stronger every day. Christmas was special that year. We wanted to ease back into our routine, but our routine had other ideas. There was always so much going on with our family. Hockey games; band practice, competitions, concerts; writers' meetings, jobs, birthdays, bills, shopping, repairs, and all the things we routinely take for granted needed attention.

I recovered in the hospital in far less time than anticipated and did the same at home. I returned to work in half the time they anticipated. I was alive, working again, and oh so grateful. Looking back, cancer may have been the best thing that ever happened to me. It changed my perspective on many things. I reevaluated what was important and what wasn't. Before cancer, I felt like the world was an adversary and I had a target on my back. I had to step up and prove myself over and over on everything I did. I never slowed down long enough to fully realize all the gifts I already had received. I was a lucky man, with a loving wife and beautiful family. All the things I wanted were right in front of me the whole time. I began working to live, rather than living to work. The job was just a means to an end, nothing more. Life drew us back to normalcy. We had school concerts to attend and a traditional Christmas sleigh ride with the family. We exchanged our secret Santa gifts in the warming room after the hayride and I even managed to dance once around the room slowly with Gisele. I was going to be okay.

Gisele and I resumed line dancing, and the class was so welcoming. We started taking additional classes with other instructors and dancing at clubs. As the years went by, our one night a week session, grew to 3 or 4 nights. We attended workshops that went on all day long, or for multiple days, with free social dancing at night. Country concerts were on our "dance card" too. I still felt funny telling old friends or people at work we were dancing to country music because I was a longtime rock and roller. Things weren't getting done around the house the way they used to, but damn were we having fun!

When I had the time, or better yet, when I could find any time, I wrote. It was something I enjoyed doing. There was something about being in control of all the characters I found satisfying and very appealing. Ironically, I was writing a science fiction story about a planetary moon where there was no cancer present for those who lived there. A mass exodus from Earth to this moon took place as science tried to understand what reversed the deadly effects of this horrid disease. The working title was "Cure" and I had just started it when I was diagnosed. I picked up where I left off once I was "cured." I wrote a lot but was never good enough to have anything published. I really didn't care that much because it was simply an outlet for me; I enjoyed it. Publishing was not my primary goal and once again I felt good hammering away at the keys. I joined a circle of likeminded writers where we would critique each other's work, offering ideas, perspectives, and suggestions.

5/17/98: Rhiannon Graduated from UNH. I remember Fritz Wetherbee (a local historian and storyteller) was the keynote speaker. Rhi had done an outstanding job at the university, despite her high school struggles. We could not have been prouder of her.

6/29/98: My dad passed. It was my first day of vacation. The call came in the early morning, and it shook me to my core. His heart failed during the night. He smoked cigarettes and had tried to quit many times without success. I couldn't believe he was gone. I saw a lifetime of memories flash by, rich with detail. Laughter, tears, frustration, reconciliation, celebration, joy, sharing, love, and on and on. Every emotion under the sun was represented in that flash. It seemed to revolve around me, providing slightly different angles and views with each rotation. He was interwoven into all aspects of my life and all I could do was cry until there were no tears left. There was a huge hole in my heart and the emptiness was like nothing I ever felt before. Being so much older than Susan and Dick, I recalled much more than they and knew things they were not aware of. We all cried together at our house and reminded each other what we had lost. There was a part of me that wondered if my dad had made a deal with God to spare me and take him in my place. My surgery and eventual recovery had gone so well. Maybe I'll get the answer to that someday. I think about him every day, and he frequents my dreams with some regularity.

But Daddy I want to let you know somehow
The things you said are so much clearer now
And I would turn the pages back
But time will not allow
The way these days just rip along
Too fast to last, too vast, too strong
.....Jackson Browne

In early spring of 1999, the company I was working for began downsizing. We had been sold recently and were at odds with the new ownership as they struggled seeing where or how we fit into their overall business plan. Our benefits were steadily eroding. Severance pay was dropped from two weeks to one for every year of service. I got word of a layoff and more specifically who would be let go. It was very difficult keeping this from the people I worked with. Friday was to be the day, but it came and went without a layoff. On Monday I was told this next Friday would be the day, but it wasn't. This went on for a month or more until finally a meeting was called for all salaried employees. This was the announcement, finally. We were told the entire company was sold and *all* of us were affected. The new owners would interview a handful of people they would consider relocating to Delaware. We were to cooperate with the teams that would debrief us, and we were all free to use company resources to find new work elsewhere. We had three months before we would have to leave. We were all free to leave for interviews as they came up. Instead of a small group being laid off, it was all of us. I was asked to write letters of recommendation, which I gladly did for anyone. I also asked for a few for myself from the Staff. I managed to find a position in Winchester as an ISO

Management Representative and began prepping for the job that would open after my time with AEP came to an end. I was there on the last day handing out the final paychecks to the small number of people still there. After 19 years, it was time to start over....4/25/99 was my first day not employed by AEP (formerly Borden).

5/10/99: I began a new job with Metalized Products Inc. This job required a longer commute in much heavier traffic. I took my entire severance (18 weeks instead of 36) and bought a new car as I needed more reliable transportation for this job. I hated the new commute and was often late for work, but so were many others. It was accepted as normal. I made changes and improvements, opened the communication up between the shifts and got a system going which would help grow the quality function. My boss was an ass; he crossed a line that rubbed me wrong during a staff meeting, and I wanted out after just a few months. A friend from my Borden days called me out of the blue and asked if I was interested in a Quality Position in North Andover, MA. I said I was and planned for an interview on my way home from Winchester. It went well. The GM walked me through the plant to see the operation firsthand and many of the employees called to me or waved as I went through. They knew me from my Borden days. I was offered the job along with a nice increase in pay and made plans to give my notice to MPI.

The new job was similar to what I did at Borden/AEP, but the product itself was very different. It felt good to return to the commute I was familiar with for so long. It was late in 1999 now and I was in good health. Dancing was a major part of our life and I wondered about my strong connection to music. The non-identifying information said my father's brother was a music professor. I loved to read as did my mother. These traits came from somewhere and I wished I knew their origin. All our kids played instruments but maybe those skills came from Gisele as she, like her mother, loved the piano.

5/15-16/99: Life went on for us just like everyone else. Our leach field failed and was replaced by Mike's father and brother which saved us a lot of money. There was always something in need of our attention around the house.

8/15/99: We saw the Mavericks at Hampton Beach Casino. They were such an unusual band. You didn't hear them on rock stations, and they weren't quite country either. There was a strong Latino influence in their music as well. We danced to several of their songs. It was a fun show.

8/20/99: Kirsten started working at Burger King here in Epping. We didn't know it until almost twenty years later, but my biological cousin Cathy used to take her kids to the same BK when she lived in Candia, NH. They likely crossed paths several times.

8/31/99: Aaron started college at UNH. He had earned a sizable scholarship to Boston University but even with the financial assistance, it was too expensive for us. We also felt he wouldn't fit in with the affluent student body. He wasn't happy about it, and neither were Gisele and I, but we thought it would be better for him at UNH. He was smart and would do well. I couldn't imagine any door being closed to him based on the school he attended. He turned out just fine and has a good solid job that pays his bills.

9/25/99: With our dancing friends came many parties and cookouts. Gisele and I felt it was time we threw one of our own. We asked Bob Grundy to DJ and he agreed. Everyone brought food. We had the grill going for hours and the deck cleared for dancing. Bob played the music he used during our classes. The day was a huge success, and we had a lot of people show up. As the sun went down, we didn't want to stop. A couple of the women lived close by left and returned with a large number of different types of candles. Gisele and I brought out our own and soon we had the back lawn lit for dancing. It was the best party we had ever had. As the candles burned out, we settled by the huge campfire and learned more about each other. We all had dancing in common but came from such different backgrounds. These were conversations that never came up while we were dancing. We had a great group of friends, and we knew this was not the last party we would have in Epping.

DID SOMEONE SAY ROAD TRIP?

8/19/ to 9/2/2000: Right after our twenty-fifth wedding anniversary, we took a family vacation to Arizona, except for Aaron, who remained in Epping. He didn't want to leave his job and we allowed him to stay at the house on his own. Rhiannon's boyfriend, Mike, came with us, as he was very much a part of our family now. We drove in two separate cars. We ate at some greasy spoon franchise and Mike developed a stomach bug (probably food poisoning). Gisele picked up a pair of walkie talkies before we left Epping and each car had one tuned to the same frequency. We talked back and forth constantly.

As we approached the Rocky Mountains, we saw the looming brown smog of Denver. We stopped for the night and visited with a friend we used to dance with. We met at a bar near the hotel and talked for a couple of hours before getting back to the kids. We drove past Mile High Stadium. There was a lot of traffic. We took a detour down to the Garden of the Gods as it was something I wanted the kids to see. Gisele and I had been there with Holden (our dog) many years prior, and I thought it would be a great experience. We parked and entered the Camera Obscura which was cool. It was a hot day and only Kirsten was up for a little exploring. Rhi, Mike, and Gisele stayed behind while the two of us headed out to see the different rock formations. I was amazed at how many people were there compared to my previous visit. Kirsten was looking pooped, and we didn't have much water, so we made for the parking lot. We came upon a news crew and the reporter, with microphone in hand, approached me. He asked if it was okay to film as he had a few questions for me. I said it was okay and he proceeded to ask the standard questions, where I was from, why did I come here and what did I think of the park etc. When I started comparing my prior experience to what I saw today he became more interested. Kirsten stood to the side and watched as this went on for a few minutes. I have no idea if it ever aired on TV.

We drove through Utah to see Bryce Canyon, then into Arizona and past Lake Powell. I recall Rhiannon being nervous as we crossed the Glen Canyon Dam Bridge enroute to Flagstaff. The scenery in Colorado, Utah and Arizona was breathtaking. We passed several "unnamed" canyons enroute to our rental apartment. The Grand Canyon was nearby but we didn't have time to go there until after we settled in for the week.

We set out early in the morning for the southern rim of The Grand Canyon. On the way, we rose in elevation and saw an inch of snow on the ground. There was a miles-long straightaway with no buildings of any kind, just tall pine trees set well back from the road. Only a few feet from the shoulder, we saw a freshly carved eagle standing on the stump of the tree it was sculpted from. Wood chips surrounded the stump supporting the life size wooden bird. What a treat to see.

We arrived at the canyon. The sheer size is mesmerizing and beautiful. We stopped at every viewing site and climbed the old Indian Tower at the extreme edge. Each angle you looked at the canyon from provided a completely different view. It is hard to put into words what goes through you when you see it. You feel small and wonder what the first people who came across it must have felt. It was hot at the canyon though we had seen snow on the way there. We were told there were several temperate zones to go through as you approached the bottom of the canyon. We didn't have the time or the desire to check them out.

After a full day of sightseeing, we returned to the apartment and had a good dinner. The following day was dedicated to Sedona. The shops were filled with Native American crafts, art, and clothing. There were small restaurants and cafes. Cicadas buzzed in the trees. The red rocks gave the place a unique appeal. We had a great time walking everywhere even though it was so hot!

The next day we headed east to the Painted Desert to see the Petrified Forest with one stop in Winslow first.... I had to be "Standing on a corner in Winslow, Arizona..." at least once! There was a huge truck stop there with a diner and a mall. We had lunch and Gisele did some browsing before we headed back out toward the forest. I think it was Rhiannon who was blown away by the stone logs displayed along the walking path. She couldn't believe these were once trees. Loved seeing her so excited!

On the way back to Flagstaff, we shopped to take in the view alongside the highway. Off in the distance we saw a low cloud steadily heading toward us as the wind picked up. Little grains of sand rode on the wind as the dark cloud grew closer. Soon these little grains were stinging our skin. We were in a sandstorm! Gisele was calling us back in the cars, but we wanted to feel the storm. Eventually we had to turn our backs to the wind, then yielded and got inside until it passed. We had sand everywhere! Our hair, clothes, eyebrows, ears ... it stuck to the perspiration on our skin. *That* was an exhilarating experience!

We had an open day and couldn't agree on where to go. In the end, Mike and I decided to return to the Canyon, while the girls went back to Sedona. Mike and I packed a lunch and were on our way north. We parked and Mike noticed a thick snake slither into a pipe pointing down into the ground. Where it went or exited is anyone's guess, the pipe had to be there for a reason. We ate lunch on the edge and just looked out across the vast opening filled with amazing colors and shapes. Small planes and helicopters came and went, a fire raged way off in the distance, ravens flew below us, and clouds drifted high above. It was beautiful.

At one point, Mike and I were sitting on a rock above a foot path where several people walked along the rim. One couple caught our attention when the guy giggled and said he could feel the hair on his neck standing up. I checked my arm and saw my hair standing up too. Mike said he felt something as well. We were getting primed for a lightning strike! I was just about to shout out to everyone when the hair on my arm dropped back down. Whatever it was, had passed without incident. Bizarre!

We didn't do much talking, but I felt a connection with Mike that day. We both had an appreciation for the beauty of nature and didn't need many words to communicate. We stayed a long time and didn't get back until late. I remember we had a view of a baseball field from the small deck at the condo. I watched some kids play ball under the lights and had a cold beer. It felt really good to have a family. The girls filled us in on their day. I think Rhi did the driving, and a portion of the narrow road was very steep along an enormous cliff. I'm sure she can expand on this.

On the drive home we hit a section of the interstate where there was no speed limit. I put the pedal down on the Saturn to see what it could do. We had a lot of weight in the car but managed to get to about 97 mph, I was hoping to hit an even 100. Rhi was driving Mike's Durango at the time and couldn't believe what I was doing. She stayed with me for the short burst of speed. When we pulled over to eat lunch, she called Aaron and I listened to her tell him how fast she had driven! "I was doing over 90 MPH!".

We drove across Texas and noted the signs for the Long Texas Steak Ranch in Amarillo and stopped to check it out. I retold the story of my prior experience at the restaurant. It was early and they hadn't opened yet, so we kept driving. It would have been fun for everyone to stop there for a meal, but it wasn't in the cards. We spent the night in Arkansas and as we were about to start another day on the road, I hesitated to drive out into the busy traffic because I didn't think Mike would have enough time to follow me. The nose of the Saturn was just over the line into the road, and I couldn't back up, nor did I see the need because the oncoming traffic could clearly see me from far away. Mistake! A car hit me! I couldn't believe it as there was plenty of room to avoid me. I thought he may have deliberately grazed my front end. He pulled over and looked at the minor damage. The police appeared and asked what happened while I took pictures of both cars. Suddenly an ambulance pulls up to take the "injured" driver away. The cop ran our records, and he told me the other driver has a history of accidents and lawsuits. My insurance company was grateful for the photos, and they settled out of court. I don't believe it cost me anything other than time and repairs for my car.

A damaged vehicle while on vacation is never fun. I picked up a few parts that were on the road as well as my bumper and found a place where I could locate a Saturn Dealership. It would be a long drive to Little Rock, but I had to get this fixed if possible. Did I mention this was a holiday weekend? I think it was Saturday morning (may have been Friday, not sure). We made it to the dealership, and they took me right in to look the car over before they closed early for the long weekend. I wanted to make sure it was safe to drive as a minimum. They told me it was safe, and the damage wasn't too bad, but they didn't have one of the parts necessary to repair it. I paused and headed back to the car, returning with a piece I had picked up from the road and they said it was exactly the part they needed! They fixed me up and didn't charge me anything. I couldn't believe it. I wrote a letter to Saturn when I got home praising the crew that took such good care of me before the holiday.

We stopped in Nashville for the night. The kids never left the room and were content with the TV while Gisele and I found the lounge; it had been a long day. The place was empty. I filled a bowl with fresh popcorn from the prominently displayed popping machine just inside the entrance and sat down. We ordered drinks and just took a breath while talking about where our next stop would be. It felt good to unwind. It seemed a shame to be in Nashville and not take in a show, but we had a schedule to keep. Suddenly I bit into something that wasn't popcorn! It was a band aid! A used band aid! Grossest thing I have ever had in my mouth. I showed the bartender, and he said it was his; it had fallen off his finger, but he didn't know where he'd lost it. The drinks were on the house, and I needed it to cleanse my palate. I wasn't thrilled with the compensation, and we left right away. This was a day of ups and downs.... I wanted to just get home!

I think we planned to complete the last leg of the trip in one day so we wouldn't hit the holiday traffic on Monday. It would mean a full day of driving so we got an early start. We made good time and had checked in with Aaron, so he knew we'd be coming. We were in Connecticut when Mike's voice came in over the walkie talkie, "Rhi isn't feeling too good. We need to pull over. NOW!" We stopped in the breakdown lane, right up against the guardrail where Rhi heaved whatever she had inside, up, and out! A state trooper pulled in behind us and I approached him on foot. He told me to stop and get back in the vehicle and get back on the highway. I explained my daughter was sick and we would be on our way in a few minutes. He wasn't sympathetic in the least and insisted we leave immediately. I was pissed at his lack of compassion but saw no way of winning any argument with him. We left as instructed. Connecticut was pissing me off again.

We arrived home a little later than we had told Aaron to expect us, and to our surprise, he had bought pizza for the family and kept it warm in the oven. Rhi did not partake. She was still feeling green. It felt great to be home and we all shared stories of the last two weeks until it was late. That was enough drama and adventure for a while.

9/16/2000: A short time after returning home from Arizona, the kids gave us an anniversary gift. An overnight getaway to Ogunquit, Maine. We were quite surprised. We had a good time and experienced a nice restaurant and some light entertainment. Rhi made a point of telling us not to take our time coming home. We suspected she was up to something and figured she was probably cooking a surprise dinner for us. Normally Gisele would visit the shops along route 1, but on this day, we stuck to the basic plan. We got home and the kids met us in the driveway. They told us to forget about the overnight bags, as they would bring them in for us. They kind of directed us toward the backyard and that's when we heard "Surprise!" The kids gathered our dancing friends and

threw us a party to celebrate our 25th wedding anniversary. Bob was there with his music, they had a campfire ready to light, there was food and drink for all. They even had a cake with our pictures on top of the frosting. All our friends' cars were parked at neighbors' houses, so we never suspected a thing. We were floored. A week or so later, we were presented with a framed picture of everyone dancing in our backyard. Gisele and I were in the forefront. It was signed by those that were there; what a treasured gift. Such great memories of our anniversary party.

5/12/2001: Joe Diffe played at UNH. I loved dancing to the song "Welcome to Earth (Third Rock from the Sun)." He is a clever songwriter with a great sense of humor. We thoroughly enjoyed the night.

6/29/01: Martina McBride played at the Hampton Beach Casino Ballroom. I think she had taken a break from performing and was just getting back to touring. Her voice was strong, clear, and powerful. Not sure but I think Brad Paisley opened for her (I know I saw him there but not sure when... and I didn't know who he was at the time). Always had a good time at the ballroom!

7/13/01: We attended my 30th high school class reunion at the Radisson Ferncroft in Danvers, Massachusetts. I hadn't kept in close touch with many of my old friends and school mates since I had a family and lived in NH. Some came all the way from Hawaii to attend. At one point I went to the men's room and when I looked at the familiar faces lined up in front of the urinals, I thought I should be sneaking a cigarette! There were a lot of laughs for sure. Some people hadn't changed at all since high school …. I certainly had though.

9/8-9/2001 Rhi moved out to live with Mike in Newmarket, New Hampshire. We checked the place out and it would be very different than what either of them had lived in prior. They were determined and ready … and not too far from home. We made a day of it, moving everything in and getting it set up. Lots of up and down the stairs that day. It's tough seeing one of your kids leaving home, even if she was much older than I was when I first left.

9/11/2001: It was just a couple of days after Rhiannon moved out. I was working at Vernon Plastics, getting ready for our morning production meeting when the first plane hit the first tower. A guy from customer service poked his head in the room to give us the news. In my mind I pictured a small two-seater out of control smashing into a building. Then word came in, another plane hit another tower, and they were both on fire. We knew then something was terribly wrong.

The meeting was shortened, which allowed us to check out what was happening. I pulled up a news feed on the computer in my office and saw the first tower collapse. There was no doubt we were under attack. Terrorism was now a reality for all of us. The crash in the field in Pennsylvania, the Pentagon … We heard of planes stopped on the ground with terrorists inside…. Unconfirmed stories were everywhere. I called home to make sure Gisele was aware. There was a lot of talk about box cutters, and I thought of all the times I traveled with flexible blade knives (similar to a box cutter) as part of my job. I carried them for years all over the country. Air traffic was halted … cell phone calls were dropped. I was worried nuclear power plants might be a target. Seabrook Station wasn't far away from us. My kids etc … like everyone else in the United States, were all worried. Most of the people on the production floor were not aware anything had happened, but those of us in the offices were all watching screens in stunned silence and shock. It was a whole new world from that day on ….

11/18/2001: The Lovin' Spoonful played at UNH…. But without John Sebastian! The songs were good to hear but without the distinct voice John had, it wasn't the same. Bummer, I really wanted to see him. The tickets were free, so I guess you get what you pay for.

4/11/2002: Kirsten and I flew out of Boston to North Carolina to tour the East Carolina University campus in Greenville. This was her first time on a plane. The new security precautions at the airport added a another factor to flying, but if it kept us all safe, I was in favor of it. I had only flown a couple of times since 911 myself. I suggested Kirsten might want to remove all the piercings from her ears before going through the metal detector, as I emptied my pockets, took off my belt, and removed my steel-toed shoes. Kirsten elected to keep her piercings in place and walked through the detector without issue. I on the other hand, set off the alarm and was pulled to the side. Kirsten was concerned for me and wanted to be by my side, but security stopped her. They pulled out a wand and ran it up one side and down another. It revealed a tiny piece of a chewing gum wrapper in my pocket! Satisfied I posed no threat, I was allowed to board the plane …. And Kirsten walked on still wearing all her jewelry!

The campus was nice and felt welcoming and comfortable. New buildings and renovations showed they were keeping up with the times and investing significant money in the process.

The town was well laid out with the students in mind. We sampled food from the dining hall, as well as local restaurants, and took in a movie together. I loved spending quality time with Kirsten on that trip. This would be her school.

8/15/02: With high school completed and a scholarship from Burger King, we packed Kirsten up and drove to Greenville, NC. Unbeknownst to us, Kirsten received a tattoo from our next-door neighbor as a graduation gift. An incomplete butterfly on her lower back (it still needed to be filled in). Just what you want for your daughter. Needless to say, it was a distraction for her as she drove a hot car in the summer with fresh artwork on her back. She couldn't get it wet, which meant she couldn't use the multimillion-dollar pool the school had just put in.

We stopped in to see my sister Susan and Dave on the way down and they told Kirsten she could stop in anytime she was driving to or from the university. They were the closest family she had near the school.

Rhi and Mike flew down and met us in Greenville. Kirsten's dorm room was on the tenth floor, and it was sweltering hot the day we moved her in. The elevator stopped working almost immediately, which meant we had to carry everything up ten flights of stairs! We bought a desk and a small refrigerator in town, then lugged them up as well. We had to assemble the desk once it was in the room … did I mention no air conditioning either? We were all soaked when we met Kirsten's roommate … what an impression we must have made. We found a nice Mexican restaurant and had pitchers of margaritas brought to the table. All of us were exhausted.

9/10/2002: I traveled to Butler, NJ on business. I had to approve the first few printed yards of pool liner before they could run the rest of the material we had shipped them ahead of my trip. Next morning the company held a 911 vigil outside in their parking lot on the 1-year anniversary of the twin tower collapse. The employees could see the smoke from their location after the attack by climbing a hill above their business. A coworker and I climbed the hill to take in the view they had on that horrific day. We heard stories of people they knew who died. It was a sobering moment I will never forget, and I thought about it each time I was there on business.

9/14/02: Every winter I dealt with ice dams on the roof and water leaks in the house. We bit the bullet and had a new roof installed. It was the perfect time, as we also needed a chimney for a used woodstove given to us by some friends. I hoped this would be the end of sitting up there in the freezing cold with a hammer and a screwdriver busting up ice ... spoiler alert: it wasn't! The woodstove was such a blessing when we lost power in the winter.

9/28/02: We picked a perfect day to have another dance party in the yard. We were more organized this time and set out tables and chairs around different places in the yard. We had lanterns and candles ready for the evening and plenty of cut logs for the campfire. People played horseshoes, danced, ate, and drank. Bob was in charge of the music. When darkness fell, we gathered around the fire and talked. We bought a huge sack of peanuts (in their shells) and distributed them to those who wanted a handful. I began tossing peanuts at shoulders and knees when no one was looking. Once people caught on, a peanut war erupted. The squirrels had a banquet the next morning! Vic pulled out a guitar and we sang for a while before we called it a night. Another successful party.

1/10/2003: Jay was a line dance instructor and DJ at the Rockingham Ballroom in Newmarket, NH. He was an excellent dancer and when he DJed, he had a knack for getting everyone out of their seats and onto the dance floor. He wanted the customers to have a good time. He also had a drinking problem. By the end of the night, he was usually pretty well lit, but it never was a problem to us. One night, we celebrated somebody's birthday or anniversary (not an unusual thing on any Friday night), but this time someone there was handing out Jell-O shots from a large tray. The owners of the Ballroom were not there that night and when word reached them, Jay was fired. We tried to get him back, but the owners stood firm, Jay's tenure over. We had a lot of fun with Jay and missed him after that. He teaches and DJs in Florida now.

1/13/03: Our pipes froze again! It took a couple of days, but I managed to get them thawed. Less than a week later, they froze again, and it took another day to thaw them. I was so tired of this! All I could think of was the woodstove kept the boiler from firing, as the thermostat was satisfied. The water sat cooling in the pipes without circulating until it eventually froze. I had left the holes in the garage ceiling open, thinking it would be easier to get at these areas if the pipes ever froze again. I needed a solution.

1/28/03: I shoveled the entire roof as we had several feet of snow up there and more on the way. Two days later, we had water leaking from the ceiling in two rooms. The next day, I chipped ice above the leaky rooms for hours.

2/1/03: Space shuttle Columbia broke up just before landing. We were riveted to the television and flashed back to the Challenger and Christa McAuliffe. Heartbreaking loss for the families directly affected and the country as a whole.

2/2/03: It snowed again. I shoveled the roof again. Aaron crashed his car; fortunately, he wasn't hurt. This was turning into the winter from Hell.

2/14/03: Valentine's Day, and the pipes froze yet again! ...I rigged a second thermostat to an outside wall, a foot above the baseboard heater in the girls' room, which would force the heat to cycle on and off frequently, and hopefully prevent the damn pipes from freezing again until I could devise a better solution. It was successful, but the boiler was going on and off every half hour or so. It was better than the alternative. We had to be careful not to rip the wire out from the thermostat in the hall. I had created an obstacle course.

5/27/03 Fleetwood Mac played at the Worcester Centrum and the family (minus Kirsten who was still at school) went to the show. It was fantastic seeing this band. I had been a fan since the Kiln House album and only after, did I explore their earlier work. I also had the Buckingham Nicks album before they joined FM. I loved every iteration of the band (with perhaps the exception of Dave Mason's stint). The ticket prices were high, but we didn't care! Note: days prior, on the 23rd and 24th at the Fleet Center they filmed the DVD "Live in Boston". They were on top of their game.... perfection!

6/12/2003 Gisele and I left for a vacation in Rangeley Maine. We had planned for this months in advance. Vernon Plastics was doing well but the parent organization wasn't. They bled our company dry and we eventually went under that summer while we were away. I had a feeling it was going to happen and had cleaned out most of my desk prior to vacation. I left my phone number with a coworker (Geno Fontane ... the nephew of Frankie Fontane for those of my generation). He called to let me know it was official, we were closing our doors for good. We kept the news to ourselves as we gathered around a campfire with friends and their family. After a few introductions, the question "where do you work" came up. When I said, "Vernon Plastics" someone asked, "Didn't they just go out of business?" Here we are sitting around a fire in the woods of Maine and these people had already heard the news! Amazing. When I returned to work there was just a skeleton crew keeping the office going. I received my last checks and started looking for a new job. They closed their doors officially on 15th.

9/8/2003: It took about six weeks to find a new job. I built a woodshed without any blueprints during the down time. I began work at Advance Reproductions Corp. in North Andover, MA for significantly less pay than I had been making, but it was

DANIEL STEDFAST

a job. My same old familiar commute continued! This job was in the High-Tech industry and was unlike anything I had done before. I learned how to apply skills I learned from previous positions to this new challenge, and right away I saw a logical pathway for me to follow.

One of my resumes found its way to a company even closer to home and I received a call to come in for an interview. This business was more akin to what I had been involved with and seemed it might be a better fit. There was a substantial pay increase for me as well. I really liked the people I was working with, but I needed to think about my family and the bills that needed attention. I gave my notice and was met with a counteroffer. They would match the salary I had been offered, but no more. I opted to remain where I was as there seemed to be more of a future with them.

I had a lot of support from longtime employees which made a huge difference. Everyone wanted me to succeed. I learned what they did and how they did it, then took this understanding and applied it to their unique process. We established benchmarks and tracked improvements. I was offered more responsibility. They wanted me to take on the production manager's role. It would be my choice to keep the quality department or focus solely on manufacturing. I decided to keep both departments, figuring I could apply quality principles directly to the manufacturing process without going through another manager. My pay increased again, and I was now making more than ever before. Quality improved, we had a workable schedule, and everything revolved around it; people understood their roles better and we grew. In all honesty, this was the best job I ever had. I seemed to be involved in everything and I enjoyed it. I offered many suggestions, and they were incorporated quickly.

10/16/2004: The first ever Stedfast Octoberfest Party was held. We had our dancing people, neighbors, our kids, our kids' friends... there were a lot of people. Many brought pumpkins and for those who didn't, we had extras. Carving went on all day while we danced and ate and drank. We lined up the pumpkins and lit them up as night fell then the judging began. The laughter was immense. Of course, we had another peanut war at the campfire and then we settled in for the "Bobtionary."

I must digress briefly. A year or so prior to the party, we were in Maine with Bob and his wife Judy at our rental on Rangely Lake. We were talking about wildlife, when I mentioned something about a wolverine and Bob asked me if I knew what a wolverine was. We had all been drinking, but I was pretty sure I knew what one was. Before I could speak Bob stated, "It's part wolf and part ...." He paused and I jumped in to finish his thought. "...RENE?" I asked sarcastically. "What the hell is a RENE?" I asked. Well, we laughed, and for days and we teased him about "renes," eventually getting his whole family involved in the ridiculous story. Subma-renes, nectar-renes, ur-renes, etc. If we saw an ugly dog, it was a "rene." I thought our sides would split. Since Bob simply made-up definitions without thinking, I thought it would be good for the people in the dance class to submit words to the Bobtionary for him to define in his own unique way.

Returning to the party: We handed Bob a copy of the Bobtionary (there were several copies floating around) and began the process of asking Bob to enlighten us on the meaning of such words as: Pussyfoot, humpback, pricker-bush, you get the idea. Bob obliged for a while and then had had enough. I can't remember laughing so hard.

10/22/2005: Rhiannon and Mike were married (finally!... what took so long, Mike!). The wedding was wonderful. I walked my daughter down the aisle, and we had our father daughter dance at the reception. We survived the chaos of planning and setting up for the event. The theme was all about the fall. Pumpkins and gourds on the tables, apple cider donuts instead of a cake, haybales around the dancefloor and great music. Someone lit the candles on the mantle which were there strictly for decoration. The shellac on the wall paneling caught fire. Mike's father saw it and reacted fast enough to put it out before anyone else noticed. He saved the day from a disastrous ending!

If you ever awake
In the mirror of a bad dream

And for a fraction of a second,
You can't remember where you are
Just open your window
And follow your memories
Upstream
To the meadow in the mountain
Where we counted every falling star

I believe the light that shines on you
Will shine on you forever
(Forever)
And though I can't guarantee there's nothing scary
Hidin' under your bed
I'm gonna
Stand guard
Like the postcard
Of the golden retriever
And never leave
'Til I leave you
With a sweet dream in your head

I'm gonna watch you shine
Gonna watch you grow
Gonna paint a sign
So you always know

As long as one and one is two
Ooh ooh
There could never be a father
Love his daughter more than I love you

Trust your intuition
It's just like going fishin'
You cast your line and
Hope you get a bite

But you don't need to waste your time
Worryin' about the marketplace
Trying to help the human race
Struggling to survive
It's as harsh as night

I'm gonna watch you shine
Gonna watch you grow
Gonna paint a sign
So you always know
As long as one and one is two
Ooh ooh
There could never be a father
Love his daughter more than I love you

I'm gonna watch you shine
Gonna watch you grow
Gonna paint a sign
So you always know
As long as one and one is two
Ooh ooh
There could never be a father
Love his daughter more than I love you

.... Paul Simon

My first born and first blood relative was taking her first step toward having a family of her own, and I couldn't have been happier. I wasn't searching out my roots any longer, as it seemed there was no more I could do. I was resigned to never knowing any more than I already did, and just concentrated on what I had right in front of me. My own family. It made no sense to pursue the impossible, but secretly I still wondered who I was, and what were the circumstances surrounding my mother when she gave me up. My thoughts were mine alone and I kept them tucked away; compartmentalized, like I always did. I would hear or see something that would trigger my imagination into high gear, but as soon as I caught myself, I shoved those thoughts aside. They were not going anywhere and following them would only lead to more frustration. I couldn't control my dreams though, and I had many fascinating visions of faceless people I was supposed to know, or who knew me, but I didn't recognize. You can't hide from yourself for long.

September of 2006, we started work on an addition to the house and completed the job in October. The old porch was gone and replaced by a large room with windows on three sides. Perfect for viewing our back yard. Our little house felt "roomy" for the first time ever. How we survived with three kids in our small "starter" home says a lot about our ability to find creative ways to live together. Five people sharing one small bathroom is not ideal.

SEARCHING WHILE LIFE GOES ON

I heard a company called Ancestry was offering an affordable DNA kit to the public which could be used to locate blood relatives. I was intrigued as this was something new, unexplored, and could circumvent state laws and adoption agencies. Though hesitant, I couldn't help but consider it. I also knew full well it was a long shot, but felt I had nothing to lose. In August of 2009 I joined the early wave of Ancestry subscribers and hoped for a miracle. The autosomal test they provide today was not yet available. They offered a Y-chromosome DNA test and a Mitochondrial DNA test. I don't recall the cost. I elected the Y-DNA test, swabbed the inside of my mouth, sent in my kit, and waited for the results.

After weeks of waiting, my results were in. My paternal haplogroup was identified as R1b. The report I received showed no DNA relatives. Another disappointment. Though I told everyone I had no expectations, I was nonetheless devastated yet again. I shelled out money for a test which fell far short of what I had hoped for. I was given a report as to my heritage which was interesting, but without pointing to a single relative I was disappointed yet again. Another brick wall in my face, and I paid for this one!

Who the heck was I? Why was it so hard to get an answer? Perhaps given time, a relative would take the same test and show as a match. Time went by but it didn't happen. I would check the website from time to time, but never saw any matches. Sometime later I was contacted by Ancestry to see if I was interested in taking another test. I would have to pay again, but this time they were optimistic the results would be more revealing. To me this "science" was just a sad way of separating desperate, vulnerable, people from their money.

I had been burned once and was not about to shell out more money for a second round of disappointment. I declined with the firm notion this whole thing was a scam. I got an email from time to time saying the old account would not be maintained if I didn't take another test. I checked again several more times and downloaded every report I had before letting my membership lapse.

In 2013 Peter came to the house to ask me for Kirsten's hand in marriage. I was quite impressed with the gesture and obvious respect. Daughter #2 was married in May of 2013. What a fun wedding it was! Lots of dancing and laughing and good food. Our youngest …getting married. Where does the time go?

Goodnight my angel, time to close your eyes
And save these questions for another day
I think I know what you've been asking me
I think you know what I've been trying to say
I promised I would never leave you
Then you should always know
Wherever you may go, no matter where you are
I never will be far away

Goodnight my angel, now it's time to sleep
And still so many things I want to say
Remember all the songs you sang for me
When we went sailing on an emerald bay
And like a boat out on the ocean
I'm rocking you to sleep
The water's dark and deep, inside this ancient heart
You'll always be a part of me

Goodnight my angel, now it's time to dream
And dream how wonderful your life will be
Someday your child may cry, and if you sing this lullaby

Then in your heart there will always be a part of me

Someday we'll all be gone

But lullabies go on and on

They never die

That's how you and I will be

...... Billy Joel

April 22, 2013: Just prior to Kirsten and Pete's wedding, our son came by the house. He wanted to let us know he was bringing someone with him to his sister's wedding. Obviously curious, I asked if we knew her. He calmly corrected me saying it was a "dude" then informed us he was gay. The news caught me off guard and sadly, my reaction was not too good. I was blindsided; it was too much for me to take in all at once. My personal struggle with the news was only magnified by the lack of struggle from others who effortlessly took the revelation in stride. I stood out alone, but slowly over time, I came to realize Aaron's happiness was paramount to any feelings I had, and the road to acceptance was there for me to walk. I took baby steps, but continued walking. It became easier. His then partner (and now husband), Jared, is a fine young man, and I'm glad he is part of our family. He has a great wit, so he fits right in! I felt very "old school" and maybe a victim of my upbringing. I seldom use the word "victim" in relation to myself, as I don't like the ring of it. Whether true or not, I felt terrible for many reasons after I got over the "surprise." I thought about the fear Aaron must have experienced leading up to his announcement and the courage it took to tell me/us he was gay. His honesty made me look inside myself ...how much I must have disappointed him.... I didn't make him feel comfortable enough to be open with me about something so important in his life. I couldn't help but feel I had failed as his father in that regard. I have regrets for the hurtful things I probably said when he was younger that steeled his resolve to remain in the dark for so long. Unlike most "victims," I won't be wallowing in my situation. My heart is open now, and I see Aaron is happy with Jared, and there is true love shared between them. Isn't that what we want for all our children? Aaron and Jared have taught me something and opened my eyes to things I've never considered before, and I'm on a better and broader path now.

It seemed things in general were speeding up. Kirsten's marriage on May 18th, was followed by Rhiannon giving birth to Nolan later that year on November 4th. I now had a grandson! Still, I could count all my relatives with one hand and not use every finger. Kirsten soon made this impossible when her first child was born. Belle entered this world on April 24th of 2014. It took a whole hand now to count my relatives.

Working at Advance Reproductions Corp. became more stressful. We survived a hostile takeover from within, but the business remained fragile and pay raises were hard to come by, though we were all working harder than ever. Everything was a struggle and the job I once loved so much was taking too much effort for too little reward. The prevailing wisdom from ownership was we were all lucky to have a job and if we weren't satisfied, we could go elsewhere. When the economy was at its worst, there was some truth to all of that. We shrank the workforce and positioned ourselves to survive while other businesses failed. Sadly, as the economy improved, we did not change. The same, love it or leave it, mentality remained entrenched. The demand to do even more with less intensified, and I seriously looked at retirement as my only way out. I had no plan to start over anywhere else, but the 24/7 grind was finally taking a toll. Management looked to the employees to provide more rather than them providing the resources necessary for us to thrive. There was little acknowledgment for a job well done but a lot of attention on what could have been done better. The right balance wasn't there. There were tools we needed and weren't getting. We lost good people because we wouldn't pay them enough. We couldn't hire people because the pay was too low. Part of my downfall was I was vocal about getting more pay for the hourly workers. I made a point to my staff that we should always submit requests for any equipment we needed (even if we thought it wouldn't get approved), because it was better to go on record with the request, than to have not made it and be questioned later why we hadn't. I spent a lot of time reading resumes as we desperately needed people. I wasn't sleeping well; my blood pressure was rising by the week, and I just felt like the grand ride was over. Had it not been for a few of my coworkers, I would have left some time earlier.

September 15th, 2015: Gisele and I were in a cabin outside of Baxter State Park high above a river when I saw an email from my aunt. I was always excited to hear from her. Quickly I realized it was my Uncle Ted informing us my aunt Joyce had passed away. The news struck hard. I have the best memories and I will treasure them, always.

November 14, 2015: I received word my stepmother, Marie had passed away at the age of 90. I felt for Susan and Dick. Their relationship with their mother was much different than mine. Gisele strongly believed I should attend the funeral out of respect for my sister and brother. There was a part of me who knew I should show up to support them in their loss, but a much stronger force was screaming that I *not* be present. In a word, I was torn. I couldn't picture myself with Marie's relatives. I have no idea what she may have told them about me, I never associated with them in the past and I saw no common ground to share. I felt my showing would somehow be hypocritical. Marie and I did not get along to put it mildly. In my gut I honestly believed she hated me. I didn't have any kind words to share on her behalf. Susan and Dick had to shoulder through without me. I took no time off from work and treated the day as any other. Oddly, I felt sorry for her and the choices she made relative to me. In hindsight, Gisele was right, I should have been there for my siblings, and I regret my selfish decision to dismiss her passing with such little regard as I did. There are no "re-dos" in life, so I have to live with my self-centered choice. All I can say is I'm sorry I wasn't there.

On February 7th of 2017 Noah was born. Belle spent the night with us when Kirsten was in labor. I now needed two hands to count my relatives! The grandkids were so much fun to be around. This was my family, and it gave me tremendous joy. We have a lot of birthdays in February! Looking in the rearview mirror, it was obvious the emotions I craved were all right in front of me. Life was good. A dream came true.

You dream of a house
Where you would live
A place to share
A place you could live

Parties for your friends
And have people stay
A house with a garden
With children to play

Oh am I in that dream
Tell me am I in that dream

You long for a day
When you can relax
And read a good book
Stretch out on a bed

And soak up the sun
While kids ride the waves
I reach out and touch
Those beautiful days

Oh am I in that dream

Oh am I in that dream

Out there in a shade
Two drinks barely touched
Nothing seems as urgent
Nothing seems as good
There will be a day
When all my doubts are hunched
When I'll stop and pray
All my fears are crushed

Am I in that dream
Oh am I in that dream baby

Children will climb
All over our lives
Just be the potion
And that's how love survives

Am I in that dream
Am I in that dream baby
I said am I in that dream
I want to be in that dream
Oh every night

..... Paul Carrack

June 5, 2017: Gisele's dad passed away. We were there with him at the end. I spoke at the church, and it saddened me to think he wasn't a phone call away anymore. We spoke before and after every Patriots game and at times during them. When we were together, we talked family and politics. He loved a good laugh and we had many of those too. Roger's first wife filled the void of a mother for me. Roger filled a void left when my dad died. Now both those voids went unfilled. Such is life. His funeral was moving. I recall the casket exiting the church and into the hearse with the American Flag draped over it. Across the street a stranger stopped, removed his cap, and placed his hand over his heart in respect. It was so touching. We sat at the gravesite as buglers blew "Taps" then watched as the flag was removed and carefully folded into a triangle, then presented to Gisele "...on behalf of a grateful nation ...." I cried. I miss that white haired man.

OUT OF THE BLUE

March of 2018: Rhi and Mike wanted to know if they could stop by one night if we had no plans. The moment we told them we weren't available, they wanted to know about the next available day we could get together at our house. Something was definitely "up," and we speculated she was pregnant again. She was eager and determined to get us at home for some news to share. We finally found a day that worked, and when she arrived with Mike, we could tell by the look on her face they had important news to share.

She had a bag with her and asked me to sit down at the kitchen table. From out of the bag came a binder, and suddenly I'm not thinking she's pregnant. Mike bought Rhi an Ancestry DNA kit for Christmas and her results had recently come in. She had hoped to define her nationality a little more but found much more than that. Rhi and Mike explained all the steps they took leading up to making the binder. All our kids had a copy of my non-identifying information and birth name for years. The first pages were very generic and contained a lot of what I knew from my first brush with Ancestry.

A new detail caught their attention, and now mine. They were able to trace a second or third cousin with a surname "Decker," and another they didn't recognize, to the same surname. "Decker," this cousin's mother's maiden name was "Decker." My mind began to drift. Where was this going? Decker? What had they found?

They used deductive reasoning and hunches to gather more information. This mysterious cousin's mother had two sisters and one of them was the right age to be my biological mother!

Holy Shit! The woman who might be my mother had lived in western Massachusetts, so it wasn't hard to imagine her going to Hartford, Connecticut to have me. Rhi and Mike spent a few late nights going over all the facts they could find. Facebook was another tool in Rhi's bag of tricks, along with the internet and Newspapers.com. She scrolled through friend lists for common names on Facebook and found more probable relatives.

Rhi made it clear the binder was to keep her focused on a chronology which led her to each discovery. She was worried if I stopped to ask questions, they would deviate too far afield and get lost in the details, which would be answered later in her presentation. She had pictures and screen captures of what she found. Her cousin Cathy's mother was one of three Decker girls, two of which went to college (*her* cousin was also *my* cousin!). The one who didn't attend college was the same age as my biological mother (like my non-identifying info stated). Rhi turned a page in her book and said, "***I think this is your Mother***."

Her words rushed over me with all the force of a tsunami. I had to have missed something she said leading up to this. Oh my God, my Mother! My eyes filled with tears of joy, and I struggled getting my next words out. "Is she still alive?" Rhi gently broke the news she had recently passed away just 10 months prior. I cried. I found her and lost her in a matter of moments. Rhi continued, showing me pictures she believed were my two brothers and a sister. I was back in the world of wonder and amazement. Siblings! Really?

She and Mike had done a lot of homework. I wanted her to go back and walk me through the steps again and again just to convince myself this was all real, truly real. I have wanted to know who she was for my entire life and now it was right in front of me. It was an emotional night. The binder was left for me to go over and plan what steps were next. DNA had finally pointed the way. I was such a fool for not buying another kit when they improved the technology. What an impressive job these two had done!

Rhi ordered additional DNA kits for Gisele and me. As soon as they arrived, I provided my sample, and it was in the mail the next day. Now that I was a member of Ancestry again, I looked carefully at the tree Rhi, and Mike had built. I still needed to convince myself there was no other possibility it could be someone else. The Decker girls' father, my grandfather, was one of eleven children. Could one of them also have had three daughters around the age of my mother etc? I had to vet each person thoroughly for any other possibility before I approached anyone with what I believed/hoped was the truth. It would take time and digging but what else could I do? I also wanted to see my own results. They should be stronger than Rhi's to this cousin and maybe it would provide even more information. We had to debunk every possibility before we could make any contact.

I started a Word document to record any facts as I received them for a timeline. This would make it easier to find info quickly when we needed to cross reference new information. We also used this to note theories and hunches, as well as questions we needed answers to. A plan formed and a path followed. The news was shared with Kirsten and Aaron, and they too joined in the search for additional facts. When this family is mobilized, nothing can stop them.

ANCESTRY

I n addition to the massive reference library housed within Ancestry, we constructed our own database of newspapers serving the Dalton/Pittsfield, Massachusetts area where we searched for articles. The woman we believed was my mother grew up in Dalton. We noted the location of churches in these same towns. We read through high school yearbooks. We looked at area maps. We were detectives on the hunt for clues.

3/29/18: Ancestry began processing my kit. Loved the updated status they provide.

4/9/18: My DNA results were revealed. I saw the matches Rhiannon had seen but obviously with stronger connections.

Cathy, the cousin Rhi found as a match, may be my 1st cousin. This was getting REAL!

4/26/18: I contacted the Adoption Agency again to see if there was anything new they could provide. I figured with so many laws changing, maybe there was something withheld which could be released now. What's the worst that could happen? They could say no. It's what I expected based on my experience to date. I was told I could petition the court for a copy of my original birth certificate if I was adopted *prior* to 1983! Huh? A quick internet search confirmed this was bogus. It was only possible if my adoption was on or *after* October 1, 1983. I was given some options on what was available to me: A) If I wanted a copy of my non-identifying information, I would have to pay a fee of $200.00 now. This was free back in 1979. Now in order to get the simplest of information, things everyone else is entitled to, I would have to pay for it! B) I could be added to a reunion registry for a fee of $100.00. I did this decades ago and it too was free back then. C) The Agency would conduct a "full search" with no guarantees. They have a high track record of finding birthmothers, but if she is uncomfortable with contact, it would come to a screeching halt, and I would still be out $600.00 for this service. This was about the same as it was in "79. I think the fee then was $300.00 or $350.00, so with inflation, it's gone up, like everything else. None of these "options" were particularly appealing to me.

I made it known I was considering a petition of the court and was then told their role if granted, would allow me to request the birth certificate from Vital Records. I would have to petition the court to ask "permission" for my certificate! Just thinking about this drives me crazy. They don't have to say yes to my request. Think about this, the information I want is stored with "Vital" Records … Vital! Meaning "crucial," "important," "essential," "necessary," or "critical." Does the irony here resonate? Important information is being kept from me with the other important information the rest of America is entitled to. This is America for God's sake, but it sure rings of 1984… "All animals are equal, but some animals are more equal than others." I said I didn't have high expectations when I contacted the Agency, but I didn't expect to get so worked up yet again.

In a subsequent email I was also told "adoptees don't have much luck petitioning the court." So, what is the point of going through all this paperwork and wasting the time? I explained I was in possession of my non-identifying information from 1979 and merely wanted to know if there was anything else that could be released. Eventually I was told they would pull my file and take another look. I had to provide a notarized letter asking for my file, which I did the following day.

May 20th. After over three weeks of waiting, I had to follow-up on my request. They told me they were still waiting for my file to be pulled. On 5/29 I received an email with exciting news. My file had been pulled and reviewed. They found additional family information which could be shared with me! My file was turned over to another colleague who would manage it from there. I thanked them and waited, but no news materialized. No email, no letter came. I sent another email out to the person I started with; it was now June 7th. I was told they would send me something the following week. June 12^{th,} I heard from the assistant who was assigned to my file. She informed me they normally send this out via regular mail, but she would review the file this week and prepare something which could be emailed directly to me.

This was fantastic news. I wondered what was going to be revealed. I knew this was a long shot, but it was all worth it to find any shred of new information. They were extremely slow moving, but there was light at the end of the tunnel now, so it was worth every minute and every email exchange.

The next day I saw something in my IN box from the agency, which I pounced on immediately. I was stunned to read there was nothing new to be shared from my file! How could this be? Once again, my hopes were elevated and abruptly crushed by this ridiculous system. They ended the exchange with a pitch for their "search service," again. I made my disappointment known and asked what kind of information they had but could not share, as well as some specific curiosities I had. I went on to disclose my mother's name and address as well as my grandparents. I think I did that just because I could. I wanted to prove I had my stuff together and was methodical in my quest for relevant facts. They offered me a clean copy of my 1979 info since my old one was in tough shape... there would be no charge for it either. I accepted, thinking maybe they would slip something else in that might be helpful. I had nothing to lose, but I was also ticked off at these people for leading me on and wasting my time.

I didn't get my new copy until June 27th; more than two weeks after being told there was nothing new to share. I opened the file and noticed one thing which was different right away. It was the only thing not on the original copy I had from almost 40 years ago. On the first page there is some very general information regarding both parents. For my mother where it asks "Nationality (citizenship):" they had typed "American," but directly above that was a handwritten "Northern European." This handwritten note was not on my other copy! This meant someone accessed my file after 1979 for some reason. Why? What were they referencing? What other info did they possess? I know this is trivial, but it's the idea someone pulled my file, a file that should have remained dormant for decades. Did my mother make contact for some reason after 1979? The new information was accurate according to my Ancestry DNA results, but who else would know that, and why record it? Another mystery that will not be solved. While I dealt with the Adoption Agency, I continued investigating the path clearly provided by my DNA. The only answers for me would be through following the genetic results science unearthed.

5/6/18: Our research over the past couple of months did not provide any realistic alternatives to what Rhiannon believed pointed to my biological family. I tried every way I could think of to debunk her theory, but the bottom line remained where it had been from the beginning. I was convinced there were no other avenues left to explore. This gave me the confidence I needed to do what I had only dreamed of for decades; compose a short letter to a member of my family. It was surreal and my mind was still flooded with negative thoughts along with the positive: What if we missed something and Cathy is really a second cousin? What if she doesn't want to talk to me? What if she knows about me? What if she knows someone who knows about me? What if she never checks her email? Should I call instead of write? What would I do if I were her? It was endless.

245

I reached out to my first cousin Cathy, through Ancestry's email system, but she had not been active on Ancestry for about a year. I provided multiple ways she could respond if she was so inclined.

May 06, 2018

Hi Cathy,

My name is Dan Stedfast. I recently took a DNA test and the results pointed to you and Leigh Stinson as very strong matches (first cousins). I have several other matches but none closer than either of you. I have been digging for clues through Ancestry.com, while building a tree showing various connections and can see we have similar branches to our trees. If you log into Ancestry, you will see me listed as "stdfst." I am older than you; born in Hartford Connecticut in 1953. My tree is constructed using a fair amount of speculation and as a result, have not made it public until I confirm some of these theories. I was hoping you or Leigh might have some time to discuss the specifics as to how I fit in the tree.

My contact information is:

Daniel Stedfast
180 Mast Road
Epping, NH 03042
dstedfast@gmail.com
Home Phone: XXX-XXX-XXXX
Cell: XXX-XXX-XXXX

I would be remiss if I didn't tell you I was adopted as a child and my birth name was Martin Clarke Decker. I'm married (43 years this August), have three healthy children, and three energetic grandkids.

Please contact me by whichever means you are most comfortable. I am still working, so the home phone would be best in the evening after 6 PM or anytime on the weekend. The cell can also be used any time, but I may not pick up immediately, if I'm in a meeting.

Looking forward to hearing from you.

Your Cousin,
Dan

After a week of waiting without a response I tried another cousin, Cathy's brother Leigh. On 5/12/18 I sent him the same information and told him I had reached out to Cathy already but hadn't heard back. The next day was a Sunday; Gisele and I went for a drive to Gloucester. I received a reply from Leigh that afternoon and he would be open to talk. I explained I wasn't home but could have our errands finished in a few hours and be back home to talk later. We agreed on 6 PM. We made it home with about ten minutes to spare. Leigh and I talked for about an hour. He was very open and gave me info for the family tree, but he really didn't have any information about me specifically. He did give me David Fitzgerald's email address (which I already had) and I thanked him for it. I think the last thing he said was I had nothing to lose by contacting Dave. He was right and I knew it.

Daniel Stedfast **<dstedfast@gmail.com>**	May 14, 2018, 6:11 PM

Hello David,

My name is Daniel Stedfast. Earlier this year I took a DNA test and with the results, began building a family tree. I have been in touch with Leigh Stinson as it turns out he is my first cousin. I was adopted as a child; my birth name was Martin Clarke Decker. I have some non-identifying information from the agency that placed me, and when combined with the DNA, makes a very strong case for whom my biological mother is. I was born in Hartford Connecticut on February 27, 1953. My mother was 22 years old according to the records. She was a high school graduate and had two sisters, both college graduates. Her religion is listed as Protestant. It is highly likely that Leigh and I have common grandparents.

My contact information is:

Daniel Stedfast

180 Mast Road

Epping, NH 03042

dstedfast@gmail.com

Home Phone: XXX-XXX-XXXX

Cell: XXX-XXX-XXXX

I'm married (43 years this August), have three healthy children, and three energetic grandkids.

Please contact me by whichever means you are most comfortable. I am still working, so the home phone would be best in the evening after 6 PM or anytime on the weekend. The cell can also be used anytime but I may not pick up immediately if I'm in a meeting.

Looking forward to hearing from you.

Dan

I have been searching for my family for a very long time.

The next day I received a reply, but it wasn't from David. His/my brother Brian got back to me, and things started rolling! There was some anticipated skepticism, but not too much.

Brian Fitzgerald	May 15, 2018, 12:37 PM
to **Dave**, me	

Hello Dan!

My brother Dave passed along your message. We're intrigued!

My natural inclination is to doubt my mom would have kept a secret like this, but I'm approaching it with an open mind. The constellation of facts you've got all line up: she would have been 22 in 1953, two college educated sisters and high school for herself, protestant religion. Most Deckers in the region would have come from Dutch protestant stock though, and realistically the sister facts, while compelling, could have applied to other 22-year-old Decker women, and there were a lot of Decker lines throughout the Hudson valley and into Connecticut and Massachusetts.

Hartford is interesting as a possible link. While my mom was from Springfield, Massachusetts (my birthplace) my dad and mom's first home together was in Hartford. They married in 1956.

I don't know how much you've researched Joyce, our mom. She passed away last year (penniless after long illness). She had cat allergies, (which all of us, my brother Dave and sister Anne, inherited), and suffered from pernicious anemia and diabetes -- which none of us ended up with. I throw them out there as possible genetic markers. My mom went into a diabetic coma in 2001 which left her blind. She was an avid reader and prided herself on that in particular since she didn't go to college as her sisters, Jean and Lois, did.

Between myself and Carli Drake, a first cousin once removed, we've put together a family tree that's fairly exhaustive on the Decker side back to my Great-grandfather John Decker. About his father, James Decker, we know very little except that he was born out of wedlock (and so records are hard to find). You're more than welcome to have a look at what's there and see if anything rings any genetic bells. There's a few pictures of us there along with my mom and her parents which you can scrutinize for resemblances, and a couple recordings of my mom late in her years talking about her youth.

As to genetic testing I've done only the 25 Y-Chromosome marker test, which I just realized will tell us nothing about whether we're related via my mom as it's strictly paternal genetics. You've done a mitochondrial DNA test I'm presuming -- do you know how many matches you had with Leigh, and what the likely percentage match within one generation was?

Would you be willing to share the results? I'm not averse to getting my mitochondrial markers mapped to see if there's a match there.

Do you have any information or clues about your biological father? Or know where that "Clarke" in your birth name came from?

I'm living in Amsterdam in the Netherlands (part of the reason I'm fascinated with the Dutch lineage) with my wife and two sons, 18 and 14. Please do get back and let's see if we can figure out this puzzle together.

Best,

Brian

Daniel Stedfast	May 15, 2018, 1:17 PM
to Brian, Dave	

Wow, where do I begin?
I took the basic DNA test provided by Ancestry. My match with Leigh is very strong:
Amount of Shared DNA: 449 centimorgans shared across 19 DNA segments.

I also match with Cathy (even stronger): 633 centimorgans shared across 33 DNA segments.

Jon Decker too: 523 centimorgans shared across 25 DNA segments.

I kind of think this is my family..... I have been scrounging for clues, playing detective along with my daughters once we started to get some traction. The name Decker I've known about for a long time, but without the DNA testing, it was hard to do much with it. There are other strong matches too, but the names are coded and there are no trees linked.... I'm suspicious about one being Julie Hopper and have asked Leigh to contact her.

Oh, there is so much to say, and I don't want to come across as a blithering idiot or creep. I have been reading up on the family and have bits and pieces. I was crushed to learn of Joyce's passing; I've wanted to meet her my whole life. My oldest daughter, Rhiannon resembles her high school yearbook picture from 1950.

Our tree is big considering we have literally just started it maybe 6 or 7 weeks ago. Almost 1200 people. As for the "Clarke" ... my non-identifying information states my mother was seeing a married man who was 33 years old. She was a friend of his wife. He was a pilot in WWII, was described as friendly, witty, and well liked. There was a man in Dalton (a small town) at that time who meets that description, but I don't have any factual evidence to support my suspicion. I will share it with you (I will share any and all) but I could be wrong. We think it is Steve Clarke. He worked for Crane as did our Grandfather Clarence. He was also active with the church and coached kids' athletic teams, played golf etc.

I'm at work right now and just want to focus on my response to you more.... Believe it or not I'm shaking as I type. I can send copies of these documents to you. I want to explore the link to the tree you sent. I really want to just keep going with this, but I have a meeting coming up very soon.

Brian, thank-you so much for contacting me and having an open mind.... That was a huge concern for me. Pictures.... Can't wait to see pictures. My Wife Gisele says you and I look alike. I've heard things like that my whole life "you look like so and so" but seldom do I agree ... I do see you in my younger pictures.

Okay I'm rambling and I have to get back to work. Hard to focus right now. Want to share this with my wife and kids. There is so much I want to know!
Best Back at You,

Dan

I provided a short summary of who I was, so they had a rough idea of what I might be like. I was very excited and highly charged. My whole world was exploding with new information... real information... facts... pictures! Brian was not as convinced as we were, I had to respect that and provide him as much space as he needed. He was willing to take another DNA test with Ancestry which would tell us everything we needed to know, but the waiting would be agony.

Brian Fitzgerald	May 16, 2018, 4:02 PM
to me, David	

Dear Dan,

Well, add knee problems to the list of possible Decker family traits - I had a torn meniscus scraped 15 years ago and was told I had the knees of a 65-year-old, and my mom suffered from knee problems her whole life. And boats - Dave and Annie and I all grew up on Cayuga Lake and boats are in our blood.

Clarke doesn't mean anything to me. But my mom *was* engaged to a pilot, a fellow named Bob Burke, whom she dated in High School. Last night I went through what old letters and postcards I have, it looks like she broke off her engagement with Bob sometime in the late summer - autumn of 1952, while he was stationed in Germany. There's a letter in October anyway from Bob lamenting that she had stopped writing and pleading for her to take him back. Circumstantial, but a storyline that makes sense if she was pregnant with someone else's child - or his? He wasn't married, wasn't 33, so that contradicts the information from your agency, but I suppose it's not impossible that he was the father and she decided not to tell him of the pregnancy, and even to obfuscate some of the facts. She spoke openly and fondly about Bob Burke throughout her life, and I don't ever remember hearing the reason for the breakup.

Yesterday I ordered the Ancestry.com Autosomal DNA kit. It'll probably be 10 weeks or so before the kit arrives, goes back, and we get results. But if you and I share Cms in the 1700 matches range that'd be definitive. I do want to raise a note of caution though -- I know you've wanted to know the real story for a long time, and thinking you've found it can be really seductive. I know there's an accumulation of circumstantial evidence, but if we take a really hard look so far it's actually fairly flimsy. I've been down this genealogical sleuthing route with theories about individuals in my dad's timeline, and I knitted together compelling fragments of facts that fit a theory that I held on to only to find they were just smoke. As far as I can tell the DNA match numbers even with Cathy are in the low range for a first cousin. There's a real possibility that she's a second or third cousin, and we can expect a lot of genetic similarity among all the Deckers of New England as it's likely many will have come from a single Hudson Valley line from the 1600s.

So while we keep an open mind to the possibility, let's also keep an open mind that your mom might have been a different Decker. As I reflect back on things I remember about my mom's attitudes toward secrecy and reactions to possible triggers for a child she gave up, I can't quite reconcile it with this information. While I can't discount the rational possibility, there's not an emotional ring of truth to match - it doesn't explain unexplained behavior or connect any dots that were disconnected. It doesn't raise an "AHA!" in me that clicks any mysteries in place. Maybe that's a false expectation, who knows? If the test comes back positive, I suppose there's quite a bit of reconsideration we'll have to do.

In the meantime, thanks for sharing your story. You've had an interesting life, and it'd be great to swap more stories. I'm attaching a few pictures of Joyce over the years. If you have a link to the family tree you've constructed or want to be in touch on Ancestry.com, I'm brianfit58 there.

Best,

Brian

At this point my head was spinning faster than a disc drive. Emails between me, Annie, Brian, Rhi, Kirsten, and Gisele were constant, continuous, and overlapping. I would send something out and three more would pop up within minutes. Folders were set up and shared on internet drives, pictures, photocopies, files of various things were exchanged. Ideas, suspicions, hunches, theories along with facts were digested. Brian asked me if it was okay to share this new info with a mutual cousin named Carli who had invested significant time over the years with Brian on the Decker family history. Of course, I said yes.

05/19/2018 was an emotional Saturday. Brian shared three audio recordings he made with our mother. He was obviously coming around to the conclusion we probably shared the same mother. I was never able to meet her, but hearing her voice was so special, so unexpected. I've listened to them several times now. These are cherished treasures to me.

On 5/20/18 we heard from Carli. She had stories to share as she recalled her time with my grandparents in Dalton, MA when she was young.

Just to make things crazier, I sent out an email through Ancestry to several cousins representing my paternal side:

5/25/18: Sent via Ancestry.com to my strongest DNA matches *not* related to the Decker family. We used Cathy, Leigh, and Jon as "screens" to filter one side of the family from the other.

Hello. My DNA results through Ancestry.com show us as a

match (family). I took the test to determine my roots. I was adopted and DNA is my best chance at discovering my family. Since I don't know where I would reside in any tree, I was hoping you could share a few things that might lead me to my tree. I'm looking for relatives who have a connection to Dalton or Pittsfield MA (anywhere in that general area). I was born in 1953 as Martin Clarke Decker. Ancestry suggests we may share a grandparent, great-grandparent, or great-great-grandparent. If you could provide any information or especially names, I might be able to piece this together. Thank-you for anything you can provide.

Sincerely,

Stdfst

Responses appeared in my email quickly and information flowed back and forth. Oddly, the strongest DNA match did not answer, but rather suddenly disappeared from view on the Ancestry site. Very peculiar timing. I wondered if that was a clue? Did he know something? I had no way of contacting him anymore, so I asked other cousins if they knew who he was. Only one did but they weren't close, and he hadn't spoken to him in a long while. He agreed to try to find him.

I was constantly checking my email and responding to everything I saw. It was getting too difficult to keep Rhi, Kirsten, Gisele, and Aaron in the loop on everything, so I had to pick and choose which things to share and how often. I still had my job to keep up with, we were buying new windows for the house, so we had companies stopping by for estimates and sales pitches to deal with as well. We were also looking at a new roof... a metal one this time.

I would wake first thing in the morning to read email that

came in while I slept. I checked again as soon as I got to work and throughout the day. As soon as I got home, I was back on the computer. We had a couple of family trees going now and they were growing. I had notes and screen captures of sections from family trees floating around everywhere. My briefcase was full of loose ends I hoped to connect at some point. Mike put together a list of relatives from my paternal side with his thoughts as to who my father might be. It was interesting but I couldn't accept it without doing the research myself. I had to be certain nothing was overlooked. I created my own spreadsheet where I noted the facts associated with each person I was investigating. This proved invaluable as time went on. It prevented me from going over the same information multiple times. (For the record, Mike 's assumptions were excellent).

THE EUREKA MOMENT

6/22/18: Brian's Ancestry DNA results were in.

It was a Friday and after work, I found myself sitting on the front steps waiting for Gisele to come home from Gloucester, eating a slice of cold pizza with a glass of beer. I was killing time and decided to check in with the mobile Ancestry app on my phone. Immediately, I saw a picture of Brian and thought "that's odd", how could ..... Whoa! Really?! Then I saw the cM numbers and recalled the "magic" range and average from one of his first emails that would have to be present for us to be brothers and quickly knew we were a match! I was hooting and jumping outside the house like a crazy person. With no one home to share the news, I went straight to the computer and in this highly charged, emotional state, promptly sent out a textless email to Brian. After realizing I failed to say anything, I corrected the omission and sent word to my kids. I wanted to share this news with Gisele in the worst way and couldn't believe she wasn't home yet. Gisele has been with me the entire time I have actively searched. She is the one who encouraged me to keep at it after every agonizing setback. She, more than anyone, knew how much this mattered to me.

I needed to share what was going on with everyone before I burst. I typed away.....and sent a broadcast email:

I have some news to share, and I apologize if I jump around a bit. There is a lot to say, but I don't think I can sum it all up in a single message. I'm sure there will be many questions after you read this. The conflict between too few and too many facts will likely come into play. Don't worry, this is not bad news. Please take a deep breath, and maybe one more....some of this you know, and some you don't.

The DNA results are in (1775 centimorgans across 61 strands of DNA) and now I feel free to say a great many things I've been reluctant to voice. This letter is going out to those who known me, as well as those who are just getting to know me. I have never felt so whole as I do right now. I have never really wanted for anything in my life, with one significant exception. I have always wanted to know about my biological family; who are they, where are they, what were the circumstances that led my mother to place me for adoption? I have always known I was adopted so that was never a secret. I grew up with twin sisters who were adopted from a different family two years after me. As a child, adoption seemed "normal" to me. My adoptive parents did not get along and as a result the family I started with split apart. My sisters went with their mother and I with my dad.

For many years I visited my mother and sisters every third weekend and for a month in the summers. This made me different than the kids I grew up with. I wasn't always around to hangout. I couldn't play Little League because I would be gone for a month during the season. I left my friends behind when it was "that weekend." When I visited, I had different friends but would have to leave them too when it was time to return home. I was always bouncing between homes and never felt like I was in one place. I was different.

I would see family resemblances when I went to a

friend's house. There were traits and tendencies that were obvious too. These things were the subjects of family jokes or stories and are often taken for granted, but not by me. Just seeing these and knowing they didn't apply to me was obvious. There was nothing that could be done to change it, so I just pushed it aside and tried to concentrate on just being a kid, a different kid. I just wanted to fit in somewhere, anywhere. My dad was always my best friend, and we shared a very strong bond. I wanted to be just like him, and he treated me like a son, the way it should be. I miss him every day. My Grandmother was a particularly important person in my life. She was loving and always doing something special with me or for me. I cherished every moment I spent with her and always looked forward to every opportunity to be with her. She taught me manners and the importance of going to church and being honest. I miss her every day too. My Aunt Joyce was also special to me as she was the rebel of her generation and on that level, I had a strong connection with her as well. We did not see each other often, but when we did It was always fun and interesting. Toward the end of her life, we would email each other, and I always marveled at how she took on new challenges. She was quite an artist with a keen sense for detail and could she tell a story! I miss her too.

My dad remarried and we moved to Magnolia. Probably the best thing that could have happened to me at that young age. I fell in love with the ocean and all things relating to it. Magnolia was a small town; everyone's phone number was the same except for the last three digits. We left our doors unlocked; everyone knew each other. Families looked out for one another's kids. It was a magical place to grow up. My dad and his new wife had children. My dad's first blood children. I was the older brother again and really enjoyed watching Susan and Dick grow up. Family resemblances were there! These were definitely my dad's kids. My dad's wife changed and suddenly I felt like I was on the outside looking in. She made comments that weren't pleasant and drove wedges between me and "her" kids (suddenly the blood mattered). Finally, I couldn't take it anymore and at the ripe age of sixteen I left home. I waited until my dad was on a business trip because I didn't know how to tell him what had been going on. I had a job at a country club in the next town and could live there if I had my parents' permission. This forced me to call my dad and spill the beans about leaving home. His reaction was not what I expected; he laughed. He hadn't actually gone on a business trip. He decided to leave home too and was staying in Boston. We both bailed at the same time.

I worked the summer at the country club and my dad found an apartment for us in this new town just before school began. We started over again, just the two of us. By the end of my junior year of high school I had the urge to be on my own and ended up with a bunch of guys sharing a place in Magnolia. My dad was dating a woman who was married. He had known her many years ago from Maine. They would eventually marry and be together until he passed away. He finally found the woman he needed and loved. I moved to Ohio for the second half of my senior year. Didn't have a job and completed high school at night. My long hair prevented me from attending day school. I returned to Magnolia for the summer. This was my rebellious time, and I made some choices that could have gone very wrong for me, but I was lucky enough not to get in any trouble. I thank my upbringing for keeping me safe. Another group of friends was heading to California, and I went with them. One by one each headed back east but I stayed on by myself for two years. I visited my Aunt Joyce a few times and got to know my cousins a little better. I had a steady job and a little money in my pocket.

I returned to Magnolia and worked on a sailboat for the summer. When fall came, I was offered a job where I met the woman I love, we married and then came a child of our own. Suddenly I'm thinking about medical history again. What am I passing on to our child? I thought of how many times I've been asked for my medical history over the years and could only shrug in response and say, "I don't know. I was adopted." This was the statement that always brought me back to that unknown vague place I kept buried.

My mother was in poor health just before she died but managed to pass on some information, which led me to the agency that placed me for adoption. I attended adoptee meetings in Boston with Gisele. I listened to reunion stories and wanted to have one of my own. I met with the state legislature to help change the laws governing adoption in Massachusetts (I was so nervous my dad might see me on TV). Eventually I wrote the agency for my non-identifying information. I learned a few things but couldn't do much with it. I managed to learn my birth name and figured this would lead me to my mother. This proved more difficult than I could have imagined. Gisele and I went to Hartford to attempt getting my birth certificate. That failed. We went to the agency, but they could not provide any more than they had given me already. I was on the reunion registry in case my mother was ever looking for me. Rhiannon was born and with that I met the first blood relative I'd ever known - and she kind of looked like me! Aaron was born followed by Kirsten. Everyone seemed healthy. Years went by.

I took a DNA test when they became available to the public at a reasonable cost. I didn't match anyone. When Ancestry changed their testing technology, they asked for more money to redo the test and it was then I looked at the program as a scam.... I didn't want to get excited yet again only to find nothing to lead me to my family. I declined to take the new test.

By now I had developed high blood pressure, survived cancer, and experienced rickety knees from dancing. Whatever hereditary health issues I had were already passed on to our kids. The goal had shifted from learning my history to keeping them informed of my health so they could take the proper precautions to ensure theirs. Years go by.

Rhiannon becomes pregnant and develops a diabetic condition. Kirsten is pregnant. We have grandchildren! The family (my family) is growing. Now I need more than one hand to count the number of blood relatives I have. I am alive to see all of this and very grateful. Just a few years later brings us to 2018.

Rhiannon takes a DNA test and suddenly things are happening. She finds matches linking directly to Decker, my birth name, and we are off on another mission to fill in the voids. It is bittersweet because if all of this research is right, my mother just passed away before I could meet her. The contact with cousins led to contact with siblings (half siblings if you want to get technical). There is this hypothetical family coin. On one side is a family with no knowledge of me whatsoever. On the other is me who has always believed there was a family out there. Suddenly each side is aware of the other. Shock on one side; joy on the other. How do you process this kind of information? I could not have hoped for a better reaction from my siblings and cousins. What a long ride this has been.

Susan and Dick are sister and brother to me. Always have been and always will be, nothing will ever change that. My excitement has been so hard to control while waiting for Brian's DNA test results to come in.... This is the proof that validates all of the speculation and deductive reasoning we have been working with on the maternal side. I think it is fair to say we realized these facts would be very hard to explain away even before Brian volunteered to take the DNA test. As this realization settled in, it became more acceptable every day that we really were family. Still, I chose not to share this news with anyone just in case history found a way of disappointing me again. Since we first established contact, we are exchanging email almost every day and oftentimes multiple exchanges in a day. Pictures and voice recordings were shared along with newspaper clippings and postcards from the past. I have hundreds of emails since we started down this path. I have hundreds of biological connections through Ancestry now .... hundreds! I am in contact with other DNA matches trying to see how I fit in with them too. On the maternal side we have a name and DNA matches. On the paternal side I *may* have a match but no name. Everything there is still pure speculation based on theory and nothing yet has emerged to give us clear direction. We continue using educated guesswork as our guide.

With the DNA confirmation now established (again, thank-you Brian), we can definitively say we are close family! Leigh, Carli, Laurie, Brian, Annie, and Cathy have been fantastic..... David, I know you're out there too. I can't wait to meet you all. We have so much to talk about. In the short time we've been acquainted, I know you are all good people who anyone would be proud to call "family." The childhood memories you've shared with me are priceless.

My quest is not over though. I'm still looking for my biological father and the Fitzgeralds (Brian, Annie, and David) have been instrumental in helping build a timeline for Joyce (my mother .... Can I really say that now?) that may lead us to him. If that proves unsuccessful, we still have DNA; look what it has done so far!

I want everyone to know about these developments in my life and share with me, this most exciting time. I am a positive person and I see a very bright road ahead. Who knows how long we have to walk this road or where it will take us. I love the view and want to enjoy every step of the journey.

Much more to come....*stay tuned*!

Dan

6/23/18: The next morning there was an email from my brother! My brother!!!!! Tears of joy filled my eyes as I read each word.

Dear Dan,

Welcome to the family, big brother.

I got the results late, late last night and went to bed joyful for you and the resolution of your journey, and a bit sad and curious as well. First, that you never got that reunion story

COLORED THREADS

with Mom (yes, you can call her that now) and that she went to her grave with this secret. Of all the things I wished I'd asked her about before her passing, suddenly there's an entirely new and unexpected chapter.

I woke up this morning from a wonderful dream. I was at our grandparents' house in Dalton, Massachusetts. I was a kid again. Deck and Nana were doing Deck and Nana things, in the garden and the kitchen. I was bored, and I took a walk around the front left corner of the house to discover a secret cove, a bit of seashore, right there next to the house. I was confused, and amazed, wondering why we never spent time there or played there with the sea so close to the house, right around the front left corner, which was the corner we never walked around. But there was another feeling too, of plain joy, that this beautiful shore was there.

I'm glad Rhiannon took that test. I'm glad the Stinsons took one too. I'm glad you wrote to Dave. I'm glad Dave passed along your email. I'm grateful for all the little clues the adoption agency and my mom's correspondence provided. The chain could have broken at any one of those steps.

I look forward to getting to know you and your family and exploring this new ocean that just popped up out of nowhere.

Love,

Brian

I have a family of flesh and blood, the real deal and I know who they are and best of all, they accept me! The biggest fear you bear in silence is rejection. From birth until this moment, I have had more than my share of rejection. It is a horrible feeling; one I couldn't bring myself to share with anyone. Some people retreat into a shell, some follow a destructive path of self-loathing, others lash out at the world or delve into drugs or alcohol to numb the pain. I skirted around the fringes of these feelings but somehow deep down remained positive and hopeful. Despite making some very bad choices along the way, I managed to avoid any major trouble. I look back and realize how lucky I am to be alive to experience this miraculous moment.

Brian followed this email with another stating he had added me to his extensive family tree! I have a hard time expressing how honored this seemingly simple act made me feel. Unless you've put the mileage on that I have, it's hard to fully fathom the totality of what being a part of a family tree means. I was a branch for the first time! Emotions were literally pouring out of me. Gisele was back in Gloucester with her sister, getting her dad's condo ready for sale; he passed away a year ago this month. I'm sure she would rather have been home sharing all the joy surrounding me. I never experienced so many varied emotional feelings. I so wanted to meet my mother. I've thought about her my entire life ... so many years, and to miss the opportunity .... to be so close to getting these answers and not ever seeing her was a heartbreak. Then there is Brian, Annie, and David and their families and so on to explore and learn about. I am a very lucky guy.

―――――――――――――――――――――――――――――――――

―――――――――――――――――

Email from Annie came in:

I am so glad I made extra coffee this morning! Welcome Daniel! One of my favorite songs when I was a teen was Elton John's "Daniel." I played it over and over...
Daniel my brother, you are older than me, do you still feel the pain, or the scars that won't heal. Your eyes have died, but you see more than I, Daniel you're a star.....

I didn't know then how prophetic that could be! From your biography I am guessing that you, Dave, Brian, and I all share a love of late 60's music. When we were teens disco
was big, but we were listening to Jefferson Airplane, Crosby Stills, Nash & Young, Grassroots, The Who, Cat Stevens and Brian even played the part of Ringo in a Beatles play as a child. (I think it was Ringo...) Although the three of us are different in many ways, we always agreed upon and liked the same music!

Brian, loved the secret cove dream story. Your creative brain never stops working.

I am surprised Mom didn't seem to get nervous or ask a lot when you did the DNA on the Fitzgerald side of the family. You would think she would have suspected at that
time that we may have been able to find Daniel. Oh well, I guess many things will still remain a mystery.

Daniel, I was trying to figure out why the thought of a new brother made me so happy. Oh, that didn't come out right: Sorry Dave & Brian.
What I mean is...an additional brother...

Annie

_____

I cried when I read Annie's email. I felt the connection growing weeks earlier, but now it just hit me full force. Annie, my new sister, would later refer to me as her "bonus brother" which sounded absolutely perfect to me.

_____

Email from Dave came in:
Daniel,

I chose not to participate in the earlier discussions only in that I did not want to expend the emotional energy until the results were in. I have spent much time in life going down a path only to find no end. Well, this one is different. I am kind of in shock at the moment and can only think of " Welcome Aboard". I think you will find your siblings very diverse, but all share a Loving and Honest Core value that Mom instilled in all of us every day. Many stories to tell...Talk soon

Dave

_____

And at long last I heard from Dave! The silence was broken and would reveal a heart of gold in short order. I was brimming with euphoric excitement at knowing all my siblings were with me. I was not alone anymore. This may sound odd but do not confuse it with being lonely. There is a deep-rooted space in your heart which is meant for your family. That space was occupied by Gisele and the kids but there remained room for those who were missing. It is an emptiness which can only be filled by siblings and parents. I felt this warmth as my heart filled as never before. This is something most people take for granted. **To say it was a busy day was downplaying it to the Nth degree.**

A few weeks after Brian and I matched, I made a point of talking with Susan and Dick:

To my sister Susan (Boopa) and brother Dick (the Holy Terror),

It has been almost a month since I broke the news of finding (proof positive) my biological family. We had been talking via email often leading up to the DNA evidence confirming the facts Rhiannon and I had already concluded were in fact true. It was obvious they could not deny the overwhelming evidence we put forth, but no one wanted to say it out loud or in writing. Our conversations are a little deeper, a little more personal and continue to strengthen the newly formed bond we all share.

Things could have gone very differently than they have, and this is a testament to the kind of people they are. They are good people... I think very different from one another but sharing a similar core. Brian Fitzgerald is the oldest (turns 60 this month) followed by Annie 58 or 9 and today is David's birthday (he is 57). Brian was very involved in Greenpeace for many years and lives in Amsterdam. Annie works in a claims office in NY and David is politically active in his town (Seneca Falls, NY) and is a CCO of an auto paint company. We share a love of reading, writing and music. Annie is not a fan of social media, David has a presence but doesn't use it much, Brian is everywhere (Google him). They are all sincere people who have welcomed me, Gisele, and our kids into their lives.

Brian will be visiting the USA very soon and David has a special surprise planned for him. He has rented a limo bus for the better part of a day. It holds 18 people and David has set aside 4 seats for me ... he wants us to attend this surprise! We are all going to NY to meet the family. Prior to that, I have a cousin coming up here two weekends from now to say hi. It is all overwhelming, and so good. I've been saving emails (well over 1000 now) connected to the search process and conversations in general. I don't know what I plan to do with them but I'm sure something will pop in my head.

They are also interested in who my biological father is/was. The man we thought was the most likely candidate doesn't seem so promising of late. My DNA matches that don't include Brian probably represent my paternal side. Brian knows a lot about genealogy and is doing a great deal of research on my behalf. We get closer to solving this mystery every day.

Rhiannon has been incredible with her energy and enthusiasm. We've been in contact with many cousins too. It is amazing. The emotional rollercoaster never stops. What I hear and see is processed through all new filters. I feel different in a very good way. Emotions I didn't even know I had, are coming out. Some of the things they have said just really get to me. I can't wait to meet them. Oh, there are physical resemblances too!

Dick called me out of the blue today and as we talked, I reminded myself I wanted to bring you both up to speed with the events that have taken over my life... even my dreams. Oh, and they have vivid dreams in color like I do. My heart has an enormous capacity for love. The two of you are deeply situated in prime locations which will never be vacated. You may not be blood, but to me you will always be my family. We have memories that only we share and that's the way I always want it, just ours. I'm not leaving you, I'm learning about my heritage, my roots, why I'm me. It's more than just the environment you are raised in. There are things about me I don't think I admitted to myself. I surrounded myself with some strong walls and only a few people ever really got inside. You two for sure, Dad, Gisele, Grandma... very few. I never wanted to be hurt or disappointed and I chose wisely, you guys never let me down. So, my adventure continues.

I go to bed exhausted every night, but the sense of accomplishment is always there. I have been at this for a long time but never experienced the success that DNA provided... It was Rhiannon who put this machine in motion. Gisele and I talk more than ever, she's been great too. Most of the conversations are about me, which in time will weigh heavy, I'm sure, but for now there is so much to talk about. Every day is another chance to solve a puzzle and there are so many people sharing the load and contributing. What an experience. I was saying just the other day to someone, we all have important moments in our lives that rise to the top of our memories... experiences which are profound or deep or exciting. We can talk about them with others, and they will resonate because we've had similar experiences. Your first romance, marriage, birth of a child, loss of a loved one... the list goes on and on, but this is unlike anything else to me. You don't strike up a conversation with "Oh, I just met my family for the first time in 65 years" and expect a similar response. This is really out there.

Anyway, there will be lots more to tell after we finally get together next month. Until then please know how very much I love you and how strongly I know this will never change. Think of me and wonder "what the heck is he up to today?" .... Then just smile because that's what I'm doing.

July 28, 2018: We (Gisele, Kirsten's family and Rhi's) met Cathy Rohrs and her daughter Elizabeth. They drove up to Rhi's house from Connecticut to give me a very nice PowerPoint presentation with photos and captions to help acclimate me to the family a little better. There were pictures of my mom and her sisters all together. Cathy also gave me several letters Joyce wrote to her mother Lois! Also, a letter from Annie to Lois informing her when Mom lost her sight. Seeing her handwriting, the way she wrote and how she expressed herself meant a great deal to me. There were also a couple of golf tees, pencils and ball spot/dot that were from Deck. Speaking of whom, I saw my first really clear pictures of him, and Gisele picked up on some resemblance right away. What a great thing Cathy did by driving all this way just to meet us.

Wednesday 8/8/18: The previous Friday I requested a few days off from work with no notice and I wasn't sure how many days I'd need either. My boss wasn't the slightest bit curious as to what was going on with me. Either he was too busy to ask, or he simply didn't care (hint: He never asked me about the trip even after I told him I met my family for the first time. What does that tell you about him?). All I could think about was meeting my new family in New York. The few close friends I had at work were excited for me.

I was very busy at work leaving instructions on what needed attention while I was gone. I raced home to finish packing, knowing the time had finally come... countdown to departure on a trip unlike any other. All the detective work put in by so many of us, for so long, would culminate in the next few days. Pinch me, I'm dreaming! Thousands of e-mails, image files shared via cloud-based folders, a PowerPoint slide presentation and personal letters written decades back, hand delivered to me (thank-you Cousin Cathy), non-identifying information from my past, family trees and all those conversations contributed to a full-blown information overload. All I could say was bring it on!

August 9, 2018: The dream grew closer to reality with each mile dropped and hour that passed. We stopped in Dalton to see the house on Central Avenue where my mother grew up. There was a "For Sale" sign in front of it; we drove by several times. From there we found Steven Clarke's home just a couple of blocks away. On to the cemetery just down the street where we found the stones marking the graves of my grandparents and great-grandparents. Relatives I never knew, stones I could now touch. I felt something very deep inside, it was a connection, real and tangible. I realized the significance of crossed clubs on "Deck's" stone, it meant something to me because I knew how much he loved golf. It was all sinking in now. We drove on to Pittsfield to meet Cousin Carli and chat for a bit. I've met another cousin. It felt great.

Our daughters' families left their homes after us but were closer to Seneca Falls than we. Gisele received steady updates on what they were doing and where they were. Kirsten was at a rest area letting the kids run around for a while just as I realized we were coming up on their location. We stopped and spent some time with them, then played car tag on the thruway for the rest of the trip.

We passed right by the diner where we are going to meet in the morning for breakfast. It was on the same road as our hotel. Once we settled in our room it (the big "it") really began to take hold. I'm going to meet my family in the morning; Annie's going to be there with my brothers.... Wow!.. Gisele and I went into Seneca Falls for dinner but basically settled on a quick bite. Somewhere not too far away was my family; they could walk by us at any minute. I don't want to wait but I was too tired to do much anyway. I knew it's best to just stick with the plan Dave suggested. The morning would get here, but patience needs to be exercised. Gisele was steady as a rock and did her best to divert my attention. I tried reading for a while, then drifted off to sleep.

A RECOUNTING OF WHEN
I MET MY SIBLINGS:

F riday morning arrives just like it was supposed to. Scattered clouds under a blue sky; now the waiting is toughest. Do we want to arrive first or last? Does it really matter? We parked at Magee's Diner and walked to a picnic table. As I lean against it, I see a face through the windshield of the car parked directly in front of me. I know it's Annie's husband, Steve. We greet and he tells us Annie is inside. I see another car pull in and recognize Brian riding shotgun; Dave must be driving. I see my brothers .... My Brothers, walking toward me. What a feeling! We lock eyes, scan faces, smile .... Hugs all around. Contact!

We head inside and there is Annie. Another hug, God this feels so good. We settle at a table and break the ice. Conversation, with family... again, wow! We marvel at the circumstances which brought us together. Me, out of the blue, into their world; they on the other hand were the family I always believed was out there somewhere. I can't explain it any other way. It wasn't based on factual evidence of any kind; it was a feeling comprised equally of both hope and faith. Together at last after a lifetime of waiting.

Gisele captured the first picture of us, which is now the first thing I see when I turn on my PC or phone. We already knew we had some things in common from the numerous email exchanges, and those were strengthened as we talked. When the subject shifted to music, the pace picked up. We all had stories to tell, and, in the excitement, I think I said I was almost a roadie for Alice Cooper, I misspoke ... it was Brownsville Station (the opening act for Alice) – just had to get that out there. We finally got around to ordering breakfast (very good by the way – nice choice Dave). After a couple of hours, we parted to get ready for our next meeting later in the afternoon.

What a way to start a day. We pulled alongside Dave and Brian at the first traffic light. They were turning left while we headed straight. I was waving my arms and rolling down the window as the light changed and they turned; they never saw me. I wonder what they were talking about (laughing out loud).

Gisele brought the girls up to speed on our meeting while I went over the pictures she took with her phone, over and over again. My brothers and sister. It really happened, really.... Time passed slowly as we got ready for round two. The GPS showed this multi-road mess of a map which would probably take twice as long as it should, but the path was leading to Dave and Lisa's house where there would be even more family, so who cares. Three generations of Stedfasts were about to converge with three generations of Fitzgeralds.

Dave met us at the door (after we turned our three-car parade around on the access road). We arrived in our best "beachy" attire. Somehow, we had similar colors... a well-balanced and blended group for sure. A card and frame for Brian to celebrate a "very merry unbirthday" and a small book of photos for my siblings. I received my, correction, our mother's baby book, which was such a thoughtful gift. Thank-you so very much for parting with it. In addition, I received a copy of Joyce's medical history. This is something I have wanted for a very long time. My doctor has wanted this too! Why adoption agencies were not instructed to maintain this information for the benefit of the adoptee is a conversation for another day; now I have it and can pass it on to my children. Introductions were happening in several places at the same time, inside and out as people associated faces with the names. Lots of smiles and questions and comparisons and more smiles. What a blessing this is.

We moved outside for picture taking. Such a beautiful home and location on the lake. The photographer was very good and arranged us just so... and so ... and so until we got it right. Noah and Pete managed to make it just in time to be included (thank-you Noah). It took a while to capture all the families, but this allowed for more mingling. Dave readied the

Miss Fitz for a ride on the lake. Dave and Brian, Kirsten, Belle, Pete, Noah, Rhi, Nolan, Gisele, me, and Teddy headed out. Captain Dave pointed out various points of interest. We slowed to look at our mother's house … this was where she lost her sight. I could see Dave was a little choked up as he told us. Mom liked to feed the ducks, and the duck hunter neighbors thought that was just fine. Teddy fell asleep against me a few times but woke to the boat pounding through a wake. That little man (as Belle called him) made me feel very comfortable too. He was fascinated by the birds he saw… called them "mommy birds." We spent the rest of the trip looking for more "mommy birds." Brian showed me where his wedding reception was held and told me about the Frisbees at his wedding and the burned dock from a campfire. It felt good to be on the water again.

Back at the house we talked and watched our kids, they were running back and forth on the lawn. They did a little "fishing" too. Annie, Dave, and Brian received music boxes from me just before Jake arrived with dinner. Little pockets of conversations merged and separated like they would in any family. All three generations were connecting on their own. This was amazing. I had to chuckle inside as I watched Julia ask her dad about what was going to happen on Saturday. Brian was just a few feet away and didn't know what was planned. Dave's face turned a deep red as he tried to get Julia to stop. Too funny. Enjoyed hearing Doon tell us about diabolo (I kept hearing "diablo") and his adventures. Dylan's rosy cheeks reminded us of our son Aaron when he was younger; he unfortunately couldn't make the trip. Martha seemed to generate a spiritual calm all around her. Nicole has the gift of gab and kept the pace of the conversation moving forward. Jake was cerebral and confident with a great sense of humor. Rhiannon, Kirsten, Pete, and Mike had conversations of their own going with the new family members and it all seemed so natural..... this is really happening, right? Lisa set up a group on Facebook for all of us to post pictures to …. I'll need some help with that for sure. Eventually the girls went back to their hotel. Gisele and I stayed a little longer. I brought the very last bottle of strawberry mead I made sixteen years ago and figured there would be no better way of finishing off this day than with a toast. Here's to FAMILY. Gisele and I called it a day and headed to our hotel.

Saturday afternoon we picked up our daughters and headed for the Fitzgerald's house; it was time for the big birthday adventure. The mystery trip to celebrate Brian turning 60. Jake and Nicole spotted Kirsten and Pete on the sidewalk in Geneva earlier in the day (how cool was that!) As soon as we arrived, we were introduced to lifelong friends of the family... more faces! They all wanted to know how this joining of the family came to be, and I will never tire of telling the story.

Annie and Brian had already started going through the thumb drives of music I gave them, and I learned Dave wanted to have that music playing outside when we arrived in the afternoon (very thoughtful ... but the drive was too big to cast through a cell phone). Dave announced we all had to sign a release form before we could board the bus and out came the clipboard. We would see this a few more times as it was used for roll call each time we got on the bus.

We met Zoe Ritter who had lived in both Epping and Brentwood for many years and her sister Mary. There were David and Janet Kelleher, Jeffrey Flynn (Best man at Brian and Martha's wedding), and Margaret Cook. Dave got us on the bus (clipboard in hand), and we were on our way. Brian tried to get the thumb drive to play on the stereo but again, I think it was too big for the system to read – nice try Brian, but we have Margret! "99 bottles of beer on the wall – oh no!" Julia and Margaret did the "Ann Margret" in the aisle. Eventually we gained some traction with "Jeremiah was a Bullfrog." Lots of laughing and reminiscing .... Just what was on tap was still a mystery.

Steve pointed out many significant sites along the way including where Margaret and Martha lived. The cousin connection was going strong toward the back of the bus while, Brian was catching up with friends. The radio drifted in and out of clarity and the volume was all over the place, beer and wine were flowing and everyone was happy to be part of this merry band going to ... somewhere.

Lake Ontario came into view, and we learned we were going to the Port of Rochester. The bus emptied and we headed for the docks. Most of us boarded a peddle/paddle boat ... Dave gave up his seat so one of our daughters could take part. Gisele didn't want to see them separated as this was a chance for them to escape Mommy-hood for one day. She would not have wanted to be confined on a boat not knowing what lay ahead and not having a bathroom to go to, and I'm sure she would not be too enthusiastic about all the peddling either. She volunteered to stay behind, as did Nicole, who was pregnant.

Captain Brian and his first mate, whose name escapes me now, gave us the dos and don'ts and off we went up the Genesee River. We passed docked boats; boats at anchor, fishing; families walking the shore; relics, wildlife etc. We peddled on in the sun, had some good music playing and the beer and wine were always close by. We peddled some more and eventually made a 180 turn then headed back.... Still peddling away when Rhiannon leaned in and said," If you peddle backwards, there is no resistance" .... Okay enough peddling. Lisa was Captain for a while (Captain Brian and Lisa have the same hat size!) ... what is your favorite shot? fuzzy nipples, slippery navels ... Get it straight! Pickle juice and Jameson-Doon! Brian? Say that again?...lemon drop, Jägermeister, Basil Hayden, ... Doone's bottle opener ring was cool until Margaret opened a **GLASS** bottle in front of the 1st mate (you've been ratted out Margret!). No glass on board, we had been warned!

We definitely had an appetite after all the peddling. We pulled up to the ROC Harbor Clam Company... and reunited with those we left on the shore. Waiting for us in the restaurant were littleneck clams steamed in personal sized net-bags, butter so hot it would melt a cup! (yikes, Jake!) ... lobster mac and cheese... fried pickles... salads, beer and wine on ice, an open bar and Doon has an "X" on his hand, not bad Doon! ... Two surprise guests were waiting for Brian (Chris and Jay?). We all ate our fill, more picture taking, more laughs.... So, what is the best motion picture soundtrack? Forrest Gump? Baby

Driver? The Commitments wasn't too shabby in my opinion. It was just so much fun engaging.

Back on the bus and there was Dave's clipboard again -- roll call! The merry band of unbirthdayers was moving again. Conversations fueled by alcohol and joy continued, the radio blared as we made our way back to Seneca Falls. Once again at the Fitzgeralds, we looked up and saw a few shooting stars. Said our "good nights" and parted company.... What a day. Dave and Lisa, thank-you so much for including us on this adventure. You have wonderful friends and friendships.

We drove back to the Hotel with shooting stars overhead reliving the experiences of the day. The past two days exceeded my very optimistic expectations. I know there are words to express my feelings, it is finding just the right ones that slows me down. I know they are all superlatives, and there must be a bunch of adjectives to go along with them. For now, I'm still processing all of this and will be for quite a while.

Sunday was yet another plan to boat to a location for a late breakfast/early lunch. Dave and Lisa, I don't know where you get the energy from to keep this pace up. I really didn't need anything more.... My new family was enough for me, and I needed down time. Kirsten and her family were on their way back to NH. Gisele and I met Rhi, Mike, and Nolan in Geneva where we had lunch and walked the boardwalk to get some ice cream. I left them to return to Dave and Lisa's and found a slow-moving group outside on the deck by the water, drinking water. We were all a little less lively, than the day before. The sky threatened rain and we moved up to the house and talked a little more. There was a deep quiet eventually and I knew I should be saying goodbye, but those words weren't coming easily. The last thing I wanted to say was goodbye. We just started on this new chapter. Brian reassured me we had already established a bond and that it wasn't going away. A brotherly hug and I knew he was right. Martha's hug was so comforting, Lisa's so kind and caring.... Dave said he was just glad he didn't delete me! That was perfect timing and you just had to laugh. Thank-you all so much......

I drove back to Geneva to find everyone, and we got ready for dinner in Dundee. Glenora Winery was just great (Lisa, you are so right about the view). The food and service were outstanding. As we got in the car, I saw a very bright shooting star. No one else saw it and it was the only one witnessed that evening, was that you Mom? Back at Rhi and Mike's hotel, Gisele and I said goodnight and were very surprised to see a gift bag in our backseat with a card from Dave and Lisa. The magic just never ends. You guys are fantastic.

Much love to all our new family and friends from the kinfolk in New Hampshire.

LIFE IN NEW HAMPSHIRE
AND MORE SEARCHING

Back at work I was beaming, and I shared my family story with several people... then several more. There was no way I could contain myself. I wanted to share it with my boss, but the opportunity never materialized.

I was compelled to learn as much as I could about my still mysterious paternal side. I speculated Ancestry was not going to be enough. Rather than working with one DNA database, why not add another?

8/26/18: I Joined 23&Me. I added another column to my spreadsheet for which database a username was linked to. I found a few which appeared in both Ancestry and 23&Me. My results showed a different paternal haplogroup from the one I received via my Y-chromosome test provided by Ancestry nine years prior. I belong to the R-Z326 group. 23&Me makes it easy to look at Y-DNA results from your autosomal testing (for a small fee) if you are so inclined. I sent out more emails to cousins in hopes of connecting the dots. What I learned from 23&Me was added to our family tree on Ancestry as their software was more robust. I quickly established new paternal matches I could use to determine which side of the tree other matches belonged to. I had a number of relatives offer to help me trace down leads or do research for me. It was amazing the amount of support I had.

September 15, 2018: Was a beautiful day for an outdoor wedding. We had a rehearsal in our backyard a couple of days prior, followed by an excellent Italian meal at a restaurant in Barrington, then spent 9/14/22 setting up for the big day at Camp Jewel in Kingston, NH. Jared and Aaron were finally getting married. We strung Edison lights everywhere (supplied by Jared's parents) and stacked more cases of wine than I could have imagined (also supplied by Jared's parents). When the day came, the guys were dressed in suits and looked stunningly handsome. Their joy was shared by everyone attending. We walked out to the edge of a pond under a canopy of pines for the ceremony. The party after was wonderful. The guys danced with their moms and then their first dance together as a married couple. The music they chose was Fleetwood Mac's "Need Your Love Some Bad":

Need someone's hand to lead me through the night
I need someone's arms to hold and squeeze me tight
Now, when the night begins, I'm at an end
Because I need your love so bad

I need some lips to feel next to mine
I need someone to stand up and tell me when I'm lyin'
And when the lights are low, and it's time to go
That's when I need your love so bad

So why don't you give it up, and bring it home to me
Or write it on a piece of paper, baby, so it can be read to me

Tell me that you love me, and stop drivin' me mad
Ooh, because I, I need your love so bad

Need your soft voice, that talked to me at night
I don't want you to worry, baby
I know we can make everything alright
Listen to my plea, baby, bring it to me
Because I need your love so bad

The night was in full swing thereafter. The food was great. The DJ played from a list the guys put together which got everyone dancing. Neckties were loosened and buttons unbuttoned, a few shoes were tossed off as the dancing took over. There were cocktails served and did I mention there were close to a million bottles of wine? I think there was more than one bottle for each person in attendance. The photographer was phenomenal and also helped keep everyone on schedule leading up to the exchange of vows. She joined in the festivities eventually. A campfire was lit as a few exhausted people settled into wooden Adirondack chairs.

The next day was a low energy event as we cleaned up the tables and took down the decorations. We loaded unopened cases of wine back into the vehicles they arrived in (how much wine did the Martins buy?). All our kids were now happily married and as parents, Gisele and I could not have been happier. Jared was now part of our family, and we were thrilled. I don't think I had ever seen Aaron so happy as he was on his wedding day.

HOLLY

November 16th, 2018: Gisele received a very unusual message through Facebook:

My name is Holly McNulty Williams. I may be way off base and if I am, I am so very sorry to bother you. I'm sorry if you feel offended or angered by my questions. Causing pain or discomfort is not now or ever one of my intentions. I am wondering if you gave birth to a child and then gave her up for adoption on Sept 1,1974 in Boston. If I have reached the correct person, rest assured I do not intend to cause chaos to you or your family. If I am correct, I first and foremost have questions about medical history for you and if you know, for my biological father. This is truly where my curiosity has ended until a few weeks ago. For Mother's Day this year I gave myself the gift of MyHeritage.com DNA. In September, a new match was found. Aaron Stedfast. He is listed as my nephew or half-brother. After a suggestion from a coworker, I looked at his Facebook page and noticed a recent wedding and a family picture. When I saw your picture, my stomach flipped over with some kind of familiarity. I did not want to contact him, in case I am completely wrong or he is not aware of a child that would have been an older sibling given up. I don't want to blow up his life. My intention is not to hurt or harm anyone. I am purely interested in information. Again, if I am wrong, I'm sorry to have wasted your time. If I am correct, any information you would be willing to share would be so greatly appreciated. Thank you. Holly Williams

My head and my heart told me Holly was my daughter, and I immediately composed a letter stating why I felt that way. Gisele thought I should wait on sending it just to let the facts settle before rushing to any conclusion. I chose to explore various scenarios with Holly but made it clear there was a likely outcome that would point to me as her father.

November 18, 2018, I sent an email to Holly:

Hi Holly, I'm Gisele's husband Dan. Ever since Gisele opened your message on Friday, she has shared your conversations with me. Like you, I was adopted shortly after birth. I have been giving a lot of thought to your situation (we both have) and want to help you unravel this mystery. It is obvious by the strength of your DNA match you are a close member of our family, regardless as to exactly how, and we will figure it out ... together. It is interesting you see physical similarities between yourself and Gisele.

There are several possibilities to consider. MyHeritage suggests you are an aunt or half-sister to our son Aaron.

- To be an aunt would mean Gisele's mother had a child we didn't know about who gave birth to you in 1974. Given the closeness of her side of the family, I don't think that secret could have remained buried all these years, so to me, that is not a possibility; however, Gisele believes her very Catholic family *could* keep something like this quiet. Gisele's mom married when she was 26 or 27 years old. This possibility has to remain viable.
- I was engaged to Gisele in 1974 and know she was not pregnant at that time, so that is out. She is not your mom. We both agree on this.
- A very strong DNA match is possible between 1st cousins: Gisele has a cousin where they share over 1,300 centimorgans. Your match is even stronger than that, so I'm not sure if you could still be a cousin to Aaron with numbers that high. The only possibility I see would be 2nd cousin, which would diminish the number of centimorgans significantly, so I don't see this as possible either.

As you know, I was adopted too. This opens up additional and unusual possibilities.

- If my mother gave up a child before she gave me up, and that child was your mother or father (half sibling to me), you would be an aunt to Aaron. I've seen pictures of my mother after high school and before I was likely conceived; she did not look pregnant. I think this scenario is also unlikely.
- If one of my siblings had a child, you could be a strong cousin to Aaron. On my maternal side, I am the oldest sibling so it is unlikely that any of them would be a parent to you. On my paternal side, it is a black hole. I don't know who my father is/was. If he happens to be your father too, you could be an aunt to Aaron (and a half-sister to me). Given our difference in age (21 years) I would think this unlikely, but possible.
- If I were your father, you would be a half-sister to Aaron. When Gisele and I were engaged in 1974, we received a call from a social worker stating a woman claimed I was a father to her child (I believe she said girl – Gisele believes it was a boy). I thought it was highly unlikely (but not impossible) because I had been with her but one time. We never heard anything after that. I know you feel there is a resemblance or familiarity you see in Gisele, which confuses things a little, but this is a possibility. If this turns out to be true, I will certainly share additional details with you.

The Ancestry DNA results should provide a very clear path for you to follow. Both of our daughters, Gisele and I are all in that database. You will see instantly if you are related to either Gisele or me and that should give you a direction for more answers to the questions you have. You will definitely have a strong match with our daughters, and we will be interested to see just how strong that is. I share 1,775 centimorgans with my half-brother. As an adoptee, I know how exciting this is for you to be so close to answers you've had inside for so long. I have been stunned at the number of adopted cousins I have discovered on my paternal side as I've looked for my biological father. So far, I've found six in the last few months.

We appreciate you contacting Gisele rather than Aaron; your discretion says a lot about the quality of your character. He may see the match at any time and ask us about it (he may already have seen it and is wondering how to bring the subject up). Again, the DNA will provide the answers and lead us via facts to an outcome. Regardless of where the DNA evidence takes you, we will help you with your search, after all, you are family!

Gisele had first seen the Facebook message from Holly in October, while we were vacationing in, of all places, Cape Cod! She didn't recognize the sender and thought it might be a scam of some type. We ate dinner one night at a restaurant that was a short walking distance from Holly's home in Harwich Port, MA. How odd was it, for the first time in decades, we were on Cape Cod, while Holly was busily putting some of the pieces together as to her lineage? I'm not sure if Holly sent multiple messages to Gisele or if she eventually answered one that had been sitting unopened for some time. Regardless, a whole new chapter in our lives was now open.

11/26/2018 I joined MyHeritage while Holly did the same with Ancestry. A month later, on 12/25/2018, my results were in, and I immediately wrote Holly:

Hello Holly. I'm Dan, your biological father. Words I'm sure you have wanted to hear for a very long time. Hopefully, this finds you in good health. I would like to talk with you via whatever means you are most comfortable and answer any questions I can. Like you, I was adopted shortly after birth. This year I have learned who my mother (your grandmother) was and have met two brothers and a sister (your uncles and aunt). I now have family medical history and that too can be shared with you. I have a fairly good idea who your mother likely is and can give you a few names to check. You also have two sisters and a brother. They are still processing all of this. When Gisele showed me your first message, we thought about your birthdate, and I knew I should take the DNA test through MyHeritage. It was kind of a race between Ancestry and MyHeritage as to who would provide the results first. This has been quite a year. I have pictures of family members to show you too. Please let me know how you would like to move forward from here. We are home alone today (Christmas Day), as we had the family over on the Eve. Tomorrow I am back to work and have plans afterwards. Thursday evening and on would be fine also.

Holly's response:

Hi Dan, this is such a crazy experience. Nice to make your acquaintance. This is nuts to be discovering my roots during the holidays. A bit overwhelming. I would love to hear any information you can provide. Possibilities of mother is my first question. Then the natural, I think, questions follow. Did you know of my existence? Was it a mutual decision to look at adoption? The health questions come next... I realize this will be an evolving discovery as we find more family members. What kind of adoption experience did you have? What was it like getting in touch with your biological family? I can't wait to hear anything and everything. My husband and I are up visiting my sister and her family—my niece turns 5 today. Talk about a great Christmas gift!! I think written word is my communication venue of choice at the moment. Digesting all this new info is definitely taking a moment for me. Thank you so very much to you for reaching out. I have very much enjoyed chatting with Gisele and look forward to it more. Hope Christmas was wonderful for all of you. It sure will be the most memorable for me. Talk soon. Holly

Gisele and Holly corresponded often as did Holly and me. I informed my family and Gisele's as there was no point in holding back anything. In order to share documents and pictures I set up a shared folder online where I dropped things in as I found them. Holly now knew who her biological parents were and had medical history. She hit the jackpot for information.

A note on MyHeritage: They have a very powerful tool called AutoCluster Analysis which sorts relatives by common ancestor. If you know certain people are on one side of your tree and a couple show that you were never sure of within a specific cluster, you can logically assume they all come from the same ancestor. I found this quite useful.

January 17, 2019: Holly's results appeared on Ancestry confirming what we already knew from MyHeritage.

Over the next several months Holly and I shared many long emails and got to know each other a little better. Facebook made it easy to share pictures of what we were doing too. Finally in October of 2019 Gisele and I met Holly and her husband John at a restaurant near their house on the Cape. The same one we visited the year prior, just a short walk from their home. It was an amazing experience seeing a full-grown woman who is your daughter for the first time. There was a lot of staring, smiling and pleasant conversation. Questions went back and forth as you would expect. It struck me as so unbelievable that I was meeting someone I had not known existed right after doing the same with my siblings the previous summer. How many people can say something like that? We saw Holly a second time before we left the Cape. Our signals were crossed when we couldn't figure out which Dunkin' Donuts to meet at but when we finally got on the same page (insert laughter), we had a longer and more in depth talk about our pasts and how we arrived at this point in our lives. We connected at a deeper level, and it felt good. Holly, it turns out, is an excellent hugger!

TIME FOR A CHANGE

By the end of the year, I knew I had reached the conclusion of my tenure at Advance Reproductions. As soon as 2019 rolled around on the new calendars, I made my intension to retire known to management. I gave them ample time to find a replacement, and a date was set for the end of May. Had they demonstrated they wanted to keep me with a raise in pay or bit of recognition for the effort I put in, I would have stayed longer. Instead, I was met with second guesses and unnecessary questions and unfounded implications. This wasn't the same company I joined all those years ago... or was it? I think there was a real need for the company to cut costs even further and my salary was one of their largest. It sure felt like they wanted me out. I'm not one to work where I'm not wanted, and they must have known that. I didn't get the help I needed, nor the resources I requested to improve our capabilities. I was blamed for a failing system that lacked sufficient personnel and tools to manage it. Even a customer quality problem which defied logic, was blamed on me... never mind the facts which exonerated me!

The last straw was a written warning in my personnel file. I prepared a five-page rebuttal disputing every statement leveled against me, but it didn't matter. They wanted my salary back. They believed one of the young engineers I hired could do the same job for less money. Good luck. He didn't last long before the pressure and frustration got to him. He quit. My boss was one cold fish. None of the owners came to me when news I was retiring came out. No thanks for the years of service. No acknowledgement of any kind. That hurt. I never want to see any of the owners or my ex-boss again. I would like to go back and visit with my coworkers, but I don't want to risk seeing those who let me down. What was once my best job ever, now left a sour taste in my mouth that just wouldn't go away. I try not to think about it at all, but there are moments when the injustice briefly returns. My last day was May 31. My boss gave a speech in the cafeteria and rather than expanding on my accomplishments, it sounded like he was patting himself on the back for his ability to recognize the skill set I had when he hired me. He had such an ego and it needed constant feeding. Time to move on.

MEDICAL CONCERNS

1 2/12/19: My lab results came in from a routine bloodwork check and the numbers finally crossed the line into the official zone of diabetes (just barely). After years hovering in a "prediabetic" status, I finally slipped over the edge into the legitimate "diabetic" category (again, just barely). Now there is so much to learn about nutrition and reading labels in the supermarket. Dreaded, but reality. I have to pay more attention ...who am I kidding, I have to *start* paying attention to what I consume. This disease is also hereditary. Rhiannon developed the gestational form while carrying Nolan and it never went away. Now I have it. There is a family history with diabetes. My mother had a far more severe condition which eventually robbed her of her vision after falling into a coma while she lived alone. I'm told losing 10% of your body weight might reverse things enough to get me off the now prescribed Metformin. I don't need to take any more pills!

Prostate Cancer also runs in families. In the summer of 2019, my PSA numbers jumped after being steady and low for years. I was referred to a specialist and after a thorough (ugh!) exam, he noted an enlarged prostate. The plan was to retest, but his "oh–so- pleasant" exam resulted in an infection which left me sick as a dog. The retest was performed before I was diagnosed with the infection, so the numbers spiked wildly high. Once the antibiotics kicked in, I felt better but it would take a long time for the PSA to drop to normal lows for me. We waited a couple months and retested. The numbers were coming down dramatically but nowhere near where he wanted to see them. We would wait some more and retest. Numbers were still higher than we wanted but down again. A biopsy would now be necessary.

I didn't sleep well the night before the procedure. I had weird dreams when I dozed off about how the samples would be taken. When I woke in the morning (February 6th, 2020) it was snowing with a gradual change over to sleet then rain. A sloppy drive to the doctor's office that morning. What an unpleasant experience. I've had a dozen or more colonoscopies, but this was different. I had taken a dose of antibiotics on the drive to the office and received a shot in the butt just before we began the sampling process. I spoke to a nurse who administered the shot, but never saw her face. The doctor was talking to me and eventually leaned over, so I managed a glimpse of him at one point. The guy who did the prep work did take the time to explain what was going to happen, and he did his best to reassure me I was in good hands and that he would be there throughout the procedure and after. He would answer any questions I might have. I dropped my pants and underwear down past my knees (my snow boots were still on). I laid on a bed with my face to the wall and knees to my chest. My ass is hanging off the bed waiting for the inevitable to begin.

Once they have the arsenal inserted, they numb the prostate in four separate locations going through the rectum wall in the process each time. Now numb, they extract a dozen samples of prostate tissue, again through the rectum wall. I hear a distinct loud snap each time they remove a bit of tissue. When it was over, I was told my prostate was twice the size it should be, but there was nothing obvious to worry about. The tissue samples would be checked for microscopic traces of cancer, and it would take a week before we knew anything. The drive home was uneventful. The roads were better until I was almost home. I didn't feel like myself though. I had this anxious feeling coupled with nervous energy and a lack of concentration. I needed a distraction but had no idea what was going to hold my interest. I was also tired from the lack of sleep the previous night. Gisele suggested we watch a concert dvd and that was just the thing for me. I felt better right away and when it was over a couple of hours later, I turned on some old music from the 60s and sat in a comfortable chair for hours, dozing from time to time. The sun was going down when I finally got up from the chair, I felt like my normal self again. Now I would have to wait patiently for my results. Feb 13th I got the news. I had tested positive for prostate cancer.

February of 2020 Aaron and Jared were vacationing in Italy as we all heard the news about the spread of Covid-19 in Europe, with Italy being a major hot spot. Our concern grew more anxious with each day they were out there. Fortunately, they were spared catching the virus and returned home to immediately start their quarantine. No one knew then just how much chaos would ensue over this virus in the coming years!

March 5, 2020, I sent an email out to the kids and close family:

With the cluster of birthdays now behind us and Aaron is back from Italy, the time has come to share some news. I must emphasize there is no need to be overly concerned, which is the justification I used to hold off until now to let you know I have a trace amount of prostate cancer. When I say "trace," I mean just that. Twelve samples were taken, and a biopsy performed on each one. Only one tested positive and that sample only contained 10% cancer. What this translates to is the least aggressive category there is for prostate cancer, which is not that uncommon in men my age. It could remain at this level for many years without getting any worse and at this stage, the treatment to get rid of it would be worse than the disease itself. I am not concerned, and neither should any of you. Truth be told, I'm more concerned with diabetes than I am with this. This was caught at a very early stage through routine testing as part of my annual physical exam. My PSA numbers over the years have been very steady and low but suddenly they jumped. My primary care doctor wanted me to see a specialist who gave me an exam and in the process of poking around caused a urinary infection. This infection caused my PSA to spike extremely high and required antibiotics to eradicate. The PSA numbers came down eventually over the next several months but never returned to my normal low levels. Since I didn't feel sick the next step was to perform a biopsy on the prostate. This was done on February 6th. In all honesty I expected the results to be positive for cancer based on the information I read. I didn't require a doctor's diagnosis to determine where the information available to me was headed. I did my research and was hoping for the result I heard on the 13th. It was the best possible news given the possibilities. We know people who have had this and are doing fine today. Some do absolutely nothing and have not suffered any ill effects. Some will have surgery and or radiation and be okay. I am nowhere near that point. Right now, we will watch where the PSA numbers go over time. Every four months I will be checked. Next year I will likely have another biopsy performed and possibly an MRI. We will see what the data will show before we take any significant action. I can't downplay this enough to all of you. I'm okay, physically, and mentally. Aaron, you need to know this as prostate cancer can be hereditary. Make sure your doctor checks PSA as part of your physical exam. I have done a lot of reading on what my options are and what courses of action I should consider. These have been discussed with my doctor and he is willing to do anything I decide, but he feels it is best to look at this over time also. The protocol he has in place will let us know when and if this changes (becomes aggressive). I am very comfortable with waiting right now.

Love to each of you. In the immortal words of Ford Perfect (look him up), "Don't Panic!"

August 2020: Everyone was quarantining due to Covid. Gisele and I spent a lot of time working in the yard, taking long walks on newly discovered trails close to the house, and gardening.

My weight was slowly dropping, and I was getting in good shape. We were isolated but making the most of it. "15 days to stop the spread" was a joke. We had no idea how long this was going to go on for.

Back in the spring, we ordered a screen house, and it was due to arrive soon. I cut down several trees and stacked the logs near our campfire area. There were piles of small branches left behind which had to be dragged over to the berm at the edge of the property. When I grabbed one and pulled, I felt something "go" in my back. It felt different than what I have experienced many other times over the years. I stopped at once and figured I was done for the day. It would probably take a few days of rest to get back to normal... done this 100 times in the past.

It didn't get better. I had trouble walking, even standing for short periods of time bothered me. I was prescribed muscle relaxers ... then anti-inflammatory drugs...then physical therapy followed by cortisone shots next to my spine. My ankles felt like they were sprained, my right leg was numb, I had shooting pain running from my ass down my legs. Muscle spasms, and what felt like burning electrical shocks ripped through my legs and feet. It was horrible. Finally, an MRI was scheduled. I met with a spinal surgeon who explained my situation very clearly.

My epidural space is narrow and has been since birth (congenital). Over the years I have put my back through a lot and as a result, have several bulging discs to show for it. In early August, the disc between L4 and L5 herniated, which is pinching my spinal cord. Throw in several bone spurs on various vertebrae and you have a good idea what my lower back is like. Cortisone injections are not going to resolve this, nor will physical therapy. Surgeries (laminectomy and discectomy) will be required. A section of bone will be removed as well as any loose disc fragments. No guarantee the leg numbness will go away but they were hopeful. Pain and the other sensations should go away, and I should return to normal without restrictions once fully healed.

12/6/2020: I drove all the way to Beth Israel in Boston for my pre-surgery Covid screening. Massachusetts is canceling all elective surgeries in anticipation of a covid surge that would require more beds. My surgery was considered elective! No way could I function like that indefinitely. I needed to have this done.

12/8/2020: Surgery at Beth Israel Deaconess Medical Center... Time moved from 9 AM to 6:30 AM due to the anticipated need for covid beds. Originally planned for at least one night in the hospital after surgery. Massachusetts was canceling elective surgery that requires an overnight stay. Goal now was to perform the surgery and get me home the same day. I was the only patient scheduled with my doctor that day. My son in law, Mike, drove me in that morning and picked me up later the same afternoon. We wore masks in the car and rolled the windows down to draw in fresh frigid winter air.

The surgery went well. The recovery was painful, and the numbness improved but never went away. I have nerve damage. I don't see me dancing again which really sucks. I can walk okay but my balance is iffy at times. I've gained weight instead of losing it.

Once the pandemic slowed, I followed up on nagging medical issues I hadn't be able to tend to:

- Routine physicals are back on track.
- I had an MRI on my prostate and there was nothing of significance to see.
- Through diet, I've lowered my A1c to more normal levels.
- I've had veins ablated in both legs to reduce the swelling (unrelated to my back issues) but unfortunately they are still swollen.
- I had surgery on my right hand to restore movement

due to trigger fingers.

- My wisdom teeth have been extracted.
- Biopsies on my back and a spot on the inside of my lip were both negative.
- I've had another colonoscopy (think it was my 11th), and all looks good.

Life was slowly returning to normal.

MY ORIGINAL BIRTH CERTIFICATE

For years, a group called Access Connecticut Now petitioned the Connecticut legislature on behalf of adoptees and birth parents to have the law preventing people like me from learning the truth about themselves.

Under current state law, only people whose adoptions were finalized on or after Oct. 1, 1983, or before 1944, can access their original birth certificates.

This law went into effect in 1975 without any public hearing. Had I started my search earlier, I could have obtained my original birth certificate without any problem. Why in 1975 did the law change? Why did it affect only those born after 1944? Doesn't it seem odd? Was someone trying to seal records to prevent a truth from coming to light? A scandal perhaps? Regardless, I was a victim of this change.

Access Connecticut put forth a bill to fix things ... And I was delighted to see their efforts victorious. Their bill below:

Restore Access to Original Birth Certificates

Access Connecticut **supports House Bill 6105, An Act Concerning Access to Original Birth Records By Adult Adopted Persons**, which would restore the right of every adopted adult citizen in Connecticut to obtain a copy of her original, true birth certificate. The bill would build on a law passed in 2014 that has worked **successfully and as intended**.

What the bill does

House Bill 6105 allows all adoptees, including persons

adopted before October 1, 1983, and their adult children or grandchildren, to obtain uncertified copies of their own original birth certificate from the registrar of the town where they were born.

Why the bill is necessary

The legislature should **approve House Bill 6105** for the following reasons:

- **Provides equal protection under the law and ends discrimination**. Adopted persons should be treated fairly and consistently and rules should be applied to them uniformly, like any other ordinary person who can obtain his original birth certificate. Currently, state law *discriminates* between adopted persons and non-adopted persons and *between* older and younger adoptees. Under current law, pre-1983 adult adoptees cannot obtain their original birth certificate until their biological parents are deceased. Why should a state official be able to view the birth certificate but the adoptee cannot? On what basis does the state rely for an agency to possess a document containing information about a citizen that he cannot access?

- **Affirms a human and civil right.** It is a basic human and civil right for every person to know his biological origins. Birth mothers were not promised confidentiality and were advised that their identity could be obtained by their adult son/daughter but would not be available to the public.

- **Evolving change in policy to update the law and improve efficiency**. State policy has shifted gradually over the years as society's understanding of adoption and its impact has changed. The bill merely implements the natural evolution of the law, reflecting our modern, enlightened understanding of adoption policies, changes in society and technology and their impact over time. It would streamline government efficiency, provide transparency and enhance regulatory consistency.

- **Protects the health of adoptees and their children.** House Bill 6105 would facilitate adoptees' access to medical health history information, which they cannot readily access like non-adoptees.

- **Recent experience and authority**. House Bill 6105 would restore a right that existed until 1975 for all adult adoptees in Connecticut, when a floor amendment approved without notice or hearing sealed birth records for adoptees. *Access was once the law.*

- **Allows birth parents to privately communicate with adoptees**. The law requires the Department of Children and Families to provide birth parents with a contact preference form allowing them to privately express their preference for contact.

- **Protects privacy more than consumer DNA testing or social media.** A private, confidential communication between an adoptee and a birth parent is better than possible public disclosure by consumer DNA testing or social media.

- **Widespread support.** Data and surveys show that the vast majority of birth mothers, adoptive parents, adult adoptees and Connecticut residents support access.

Please contact Karen Caffrey, co-President of Access Connecticut Now, Inc., at (860) 306-0900, or Cindy Wolfe Boynton, co-President of Access Connecticut Now, Inc., at (203) 214-7554 with any questions or for additional information about the bill.

January 29, 2021

July 1, 2021

I was one of many who supported this bill and watched with great anticipation as it progressed from committee, through the house and senate, and ultimately to the Governor's office where it was signed into law and then went into effect on July 1, 2021. I filled out my request form, mailed it in along with a $65.00 money order, then did what I always do ... waited. Note: A regular copy of a birth certificate costs $15.00 to $20.00.

I wondered who might be listed on the certificate as father. It could be blank which meant I learned nothing new. If Steven Clarke was listed, it would suggest my mother believed he was the father or wished he was the father. If the man I believe to be my father was listed, it would put all my speculation to rest.

July 31, 2021: My original birth certificate arrived in the mail. Unfortunately, the father was left blank. It would have been nice to see the name who I believe is my father .... I would have loved to remove all speculation, but the DNA really points to one person. I will believe Wallace Pinney is my father until I see something to dispute that. This was Rhiannon's suspicion from early on.

The birth certificate however did provide me some new information and new questions too. My first and middle name were typed but my surname was handwritten. I found that odd. Almost like adding "Decker" was an afterthought... "Martin Clarke" could have stood alone as a complete name. The other thing I saw was the address where my mother lived when I was born. 319 Barbour Street Hartford, CT. My suspicions were confirmed when I did some research using Newspapers.com. She stayed at a home for unwed mothers. I can only imagine the shame placed on young women and girls back then who "were in trouble." It breaks my heart to think about what she went through to bring me into this world and then keep the secret to herself. The home was 12 minutes from the hospital where I was born. I don't know how long she lived there. It seems like she had good support, but the feeling of guilt had to be horrible. It was a different world back then.

.... AND WHO IS MY BIOLOGICAL FATHER?

My daughter Rhiannon and I built a public tree representing my paternal side and expanded it to include just shy of 7,000 people. I discovered a number of paternal side DNA matches and vetted these as best I could from the three DNA testing sites I belong to. I preferred Ancestry's tree building tools, so this is where the tree resides. I have well over 100 confirmed DNA matches in that one tree! These are all specific and important pieces of a complicated puzzle. I had a lot of help scrutinizing ideas, chasing leads, visiting libraries, and listening to stories. So many of my newfound cousins have been there for me, offering support and assistance wherever they can help.

My DNA family has grown exponentially, and I am flooded with email and Facebook postings from my new cousins – I love it. With so many connections you'd think I could have figured out the mystery of who my father was. I kept waiting for that one big match, a proof positive match that would leave no doubt... like the match I had with Brian on my mother's side. It never came and is not likely to ever come. This left me following whatever logic trails existed as best I could. Based on the strength of matches and a hunch from Rhiannon, we "*selected*" Wallace Pinney as my likely father. This allowed Ancestry to show associations using Thrulines. Their software scours trees for likely matches where there is shared DNA between me and someone else. Those DNA matches not found through the Ancestry database were added to our Ancestry tree manually over time. I couldn't believe how easy some of these matches could be located in our tree....and they all went through Wallace Pinney's family.

I kept seeing the same surnames repeating. I saw strong DNA relationships to strings of siblings in the same family. I knew I had the right family but who could it be, exactly? I ruled out all but Wallace Pinney (there is a very weak case to be made for his brother, but I don't think it is likely). Wallace lived close to my mother, and his wife worked for the same company as my mother. His age matches that noted on my non identifying information from the adoption agency. Much of this info can be stretched loosely to connect Wallace. Wallace wanted children, but his wife could not conceive. He fathered a child with another woman and later adopted this boy (and his half-brother) who was born a year or so after me (unfortunately, he died as a young teenager). Had this young man lived, his DNA would answer any speculation on Wallace being my biological father. Wallace died in 1966 as a result of a tractor accident.

My brother Brian uploaded my raw DNA file and the tree we built to GEDmatch which crawls through other like submissions (dna +tree). He found I had dna matches with all four of Wallace's grandparents! I wasn't surprised by this, as I had seen so many matches to so many close relatives of his already. What I hadn't done, was look at them from the perspective of grandparents. Using Thrulines, I was able to confirm the same thing as GEDmatch. I also took things one step further back and found I had DNA matches with seven out of eight of Wallace's great-grandparents! Based on all the evidence and facts available, I have to conclude Wallace Pinney was my father. The only thing which could change that would have to be some overwhelming evidence to the contrary, and I can't see that happening.

The secret my mother and Wallace shared was well kept and leaves me the freedom to wonder and fantasize for the rest of my life.

Rhi and I have both had the opportunity to speak with Jean (Tina) Pinney who was married to Wallace's adopted son Gregory (no DNA relation to me) who has since passed away himself. She painted a compelling story in support of Wallace being my father. It is also likely I had a half-brother named Gordon who died as a teenager. Her story to us goes as follows: Wallace's wife Janet lived in New Lebanon, NY (note: Showboat Club was in the same town) and worked with my mother at the Rice Silk Mill. Wallace wanted children but Janet could not conceive. She was, however, willing to allow Wallace the freedom to have a child with another woman who lived with them in their home. This would have been my brother Gordon. How my mother and Wallace got together to have me is a mystery we will probably never unravel.

There are some more colorful details not included here as they cannot be substantiated, though, I must confess, serve to satisfy several gaps in the picture.

All evidence points to Wallace Pinney.

THE FIRST HOLLY-DAY

10/2/21 or as it is now known by my family is "Holly-day". Gisele and I met Holly and her husband John before the pandemic altered everyone's life. We emailed, texted, and shared comments on Facebook often. Over time Rhiannon, Kirsten, and Aaron joined in via social media too. Covid kept everyone separated until the adults were all vaccinated, and a mutually free calendar date agreed on. Planning began in earnest as the day neared, and the anticipation grew.

Aaron flew in from Michigan just for the event. A gift basket was assembled, a meal planned, and outdoor games and activities arranged. Another basket filled with old photos was neatly prepared. Holly and John pulled into Rhiannon's driveway, and I saw them through the windows as they approached the front door. I was reminded immediately of when I first saw Holly through the restaurant windows on Cape Cod. I stood back and watched the reactions of "the siblings" as they hugged for the first time. The irony of what was happening very much alive in my brain.

Everyone looked so happy! Hugs and smiles and looks made for a joyful union. I was the last one in on the hugs as I felt this was more about the "kids" getting to know each other. I was content to stand back and watch. Coffee was poured and we took seats around the large dining room table and enjoyed some muffins. Holly came prepared with an album filled with documentation (far more than I ever had) detailing her parents' interaction with the adoption agency, foster parents' notes, and non-identifying information. Holly read the contents out loud, and we all contributed thoughts and observations about the process. Aaron, and his husband Jared, were in the process of adopting a child of their own. He said a lot of what we were hearing was still going on today. My description of record received quite a few laughs, as the facts were somewhat less than factual, but hey, it was a long time ago.

With the turn of a page, we saw the first of many pictures and the obvious comparisons began in full. The physical similarities became apparent immediately. We all saw Rhiannon right away in Holly's baby pictures. Rhiannon pulled a high school picture of my mother (their grandmother) from the wall and matched it with her own high school photo for Holly to see. It wasn't long before Kirsten was rifling through her baby pictures to compare with one of Holly's! They looked like the same child! This went on page after page as the time flew by. The last pictures were of Holly's biological mother's family. She met them just a couple of weeks prior. Nancy's (her bio mom) version of the circumstances leading to Holly's conception matched mine and we learned she carried Holly for forty-two weeks; two weeks later than typical.

The conversation veered into how it was we all found each other. Who learned what, when, and how. Missed and unopened messages. Which DNA test kits were used and what was discovered and just how we all got to be sitting around this table today. Everyone had something to contribute as we listed the sequence of events as they unfolded and recognized how easy it would have been to have seen this whole thing collapse at various points.

We switched from coffee to mimosas and wandered outside with the grandkids for a while. It all seemed so comfortable and quite natural. Then Nolan, Belle and Noah all wanted Holly's attention at the jungle gym, kids camp, and other climbing/swinging toys. Noah dug for gems in the sandbox and had to show Holly the orange one he found.

Kirsten and Rhi presented Holly with a basket of goodies, and

I was impressed with the handwritten recipe book containing many of our family holiday favorites. Holly had surprises for us too! Customized key chains with "found you" prominently displayed on the center of a ring with our names and today's date. Each family had a Christmas ornament. Holly wanted us to pick which one we wanted to see if we picked what she guessed we would.... And we did! We each received matching Cape Cod tee shirts (even the grandkids) and some homemade rub for grilling (Aaron's was almost confiscated by airport security on his way home).

The siblings formed teams for a game of cornhole. There was action, drama, clutch points both missed and gained, lead changes and above all laughter. Watching them all play a game together was amazing to me. How did I get this lucky? Gisele and I talked about how much we knew they all had in common and now they were all discovering it for themselves.

Lunch was ready on the back porch, and we dug into platters of sandwiches and finger rolls, veggie dips and beans and wieners followed by picture albums Gisele made for our kids many years ago. Holly scrutinized every picture and the "kids" delivered context and commentary. I enjoyed the show. More stories and laughs. The grandkids were driving toy cars around the yard and once the albums had concluded, we joined them. Holly and John set up a tripod for some family pictures and we got in various poses. Once this was done there were several isolated conversations as we watched the kids roaming around us. John got his metal detector out and Noah followed him everywhere. Mike set up a deep fryer for the turkey, while Rhi and Kirsten placed other dishes in the oven. A few of us had a small bourbon toast before Rhi reappeared with some mead and shot glasses. We toasted to our union then watched Mike submerge the turkey ever so slowly. Only in New Hampshire would we sit around a bubbling turkey in the driveway talking and drinking and laughing.

Dinner was on the front porch at one long table. It was a

mock Thanksgiving meal and once again we were all eating. The weather had been overcast with a chance of rain all day, but it never came. Everything was working out. As we finished eating and clearing, we congregated around the campfire Mike had started. Holly brought cookies she made and Rhi set out the "Auntie Gloria bars" while the kids got ready for toasting marshmallows... gotta have 'smores!

Once we had our fill of dessert it was time to call it a day .... A fantastic day. It was decided earlier, the first Saturday in October would be Holly-day going forward. Calendars were to be marked for 2022 and ideas for sooner get togethers discussed. The day could not have gone any better, aside from Gisele twisting her knee toward the end of the night. The goodbye hugs had to come. Noah came running down the hall with his arms open yelling "Holly" and gave her a huge hug goodbye .... Just perfect!

Aaron set up a shared folder online for all of us to dump pictures in the next morning. It filled rapidly. Everyone made it home safely with new memories that will last forever.

Holly left blank pages at the back of her album because she knew there was more to our story. I just think that is so profound. Spot on Holly!

The story of my life is unique, just like yours. Is it that different than so many other adoptees? The answer lies in the details. If you boil it all down, my story is repeated, throughout time, and in every country. Children are placed for adoption every day. My son and his husband are looking to adopt as I write this book. I have corresponded with a number of cousins who are adopted, or one of their parents was adopted, or a grandparent was orphaned etc. When I was young, I had questions that went unanswered (actually, unasked). I struggled with who I was and turned to alcohol, drugs, and music to escape. I quit searching for my truth, got married and had a family before giving in to the nagging voice driving me toward learning what I had always wanted to know. The joy of learning my truth is difficult to convey, but I sincerely hope you, my dear reader, have some idea after reading all of this, what I experienced. I have to thank Gisele for keeping the flame alive when I was frustrated, angry, and disappointed. Her strength when I was losing mine, helped lead me to the greatest joy I have ever known. I would be remiss if I didn't include Rhi and Mike in all of this. They were the ones who assembled facts that put me on the path to finally find my truth. My family helped me find my family.

RANDOM THOUGHTS IN NO PARTICULAR ORDER

My biological mother's name was "Joyce." My dad's last wife (a stepmother to me) was named "Joyce." Gisele's stepmother was named "Joyce." My favorite aunt was named "Joyce." Gisele had a cousin, Joyce. Friends we met on PEI were Gary and Joyce. Joyce kept appearing throughout my life.

It's odd when someone references my mother because the first thing I would think was "which one?" I had a mental list. Did this person know I was adopted? If not, skip ahead to Nancy or Marie or Joyce. Did they know Nancy? If not …etc. It was worse when someone said I looked like my mother because *that* was impossible!

Now when I refer to my brother, people will ask "which one?" Up until recently, I only had one brother. I always refer to Dick as my brother though we share no DNA. Brian and Dave are half-brothers as we share our mother's DNA, and I am getting used to calling them brothers and they in turn refer to me as brother (wow does that feel good to say). Same is true for sisters! When it comes to sisters, I've always had to be specific because there were six of them from three different families…. Now there are seven. I wonder if I have siblings on my paternal side. Oh, the confusion!

When I am with Brian, Dave or Annie I hesitate to say "Mom," though I want to. I have no problem with "our mother" … so odd.

My adoptive mother was Nancy. Holly's biological mother was also a Nancy.

An article from Feb 7, 1951, stated the home on 319 Barbour Street run by the Woman's Aid Society, was the only Protestant Home for unwed mothers in the state. Approximately 30 to 40 girls would reside there each year. Women lived there as they brought new life into the world. Years later it became a funeral home where you paid respects to those who had passed on. Such irony.

I reached out to Dave one year, almost to the day, after our mother passed away.

I had two birthdays each year for a while. That was unusual. Maybe the first unusual thing I remember about myself which set me apart from everyone else. I didn't know why I had another birthday in July, since I knew I was born in February. My friends didn't come to the summer birthday, only my family. It was a birthday though... I remember the cake and candles. ... I was very happy.

Magnolia is and always will be, home to me. I didn't move there until I was eight years old and moved out of the house when I was sixteen. Not a long time when you think about it. I would come back there to live for only short periods after that. I was always "coming back" to Magnolia from somewhere.

After the hospital I was entrusted to foster care until I was 4 ½ months old. At that time, I was placed with Monty and Nancy because it represented a stable, safe, and nurturing environment for me to grow in. Wow, did they miss the mark on that one!

Leaving home at 16 was unusual ... I didn't know anyone who had done that before or since.

Staying in California long after all my "Magnolia West "friends returned home was something I had to do for me. I had to prove to myself I could survive on my own with help from no one. Where does that come from?

I think about the bond between my dad and me and how the

love triumphed over the times when we viewed the world from such different perspectives. He was right about so many things I got wrong.

My brother Brian followed a path that ultimately led him to Greenpeace. As a teen I was on a similar path and had I not settled down when I did, I might have gone in the same direction as Brian. It was all about making the world a better place for everyone. I used to get mad at my friends if they flicked a cigarette butt out the window or littered. I never littered. I have tremendous respect for nature. I wish I had known my siblings when I was younger. We all share a love of the water and so much more.

5 cents would buy all 28 pages of the Hartford Courant on 2/27/1953. Now I need to subscribe to Newspapers.com to find the info that was so inexpensive back in the day ... Not complaining! Thank God for Newspapers.com!

The friend who introduced me to the Gallery was Steve Amelia ... Steven Clarke Amelia. That's *Clarke*, with an "*e*" at the end. Steven Clarke was the guy Rhi and I believed was the man my non-identifying information from the adoption agency referenced as my father. Just another weird coincidence.

There are more concerts I attended than are documented here. On the UCSB campus it wasn't unusual to see someone, or some group appear unannounced anywhere on the campus grounds. I think I saw War (Low Rider), Al Kooper and several others. Once I went digital, I used the calendar in Microsoft for an account I no longer have, making it hard to fit anything from there into this timeline. We saw Fleetwood Mac again, Chis Isaak, Raul Malo, The Mavericks, Boz Scaggs, Grey Eye Glances, Eric Church, Vince Gill with his band and as a duo with Lyle Lovett, Alison Krauss, Toad the Wet Sprocket, Richie Havens, and on and on. Music is one of the few constants in my life.

I wonder what the reactions will be from those who read this.

I hope the effort was worth it. There is so much that isn't here. I tried not to offend anyone, and I deliberately avoided using many names. This is not a "tell all" book.

For someone like me who wanted blood relatives so badly, it is strange I never pursued the possibility that Holly was my daughter (she found us, not the other way around). Now that she found us, I'm so happy she is part of the family. Denial can be overwhelmingly powerful and blinding.

When I was in my late teens and early twenties, I never expected to live a long life given the lifestyle I chose. Once I was married, I wanted a long life, then cancer struck. I went back to thinking I wouldn't be around all that long. Now I'm looking at seventy and thinking I've been on the planet a while now. How the heck did I do it? I must have an angel or two riding shotgun. I've seen my kids get married. They are all successful. I have energetic, funny, loving, and smart grandchildren. Not too bad for a guy like me.

When I was young, I couldn't imagine living away from the ocean. Even when I moved to California, I lived on the water. We bought our home in Epping, NH and are surrounded by hundreds of acres of woodlands. I love it here, but as soon as I'm near the ocean something clicks, and I don't want to leave.

I worry I repeated some things in this book too often and maybe sound like I'm whining as a result. Those things came up repeatedly in my life and the recurring themes drove me batty. If it comes across as whining, I apologize. There are only so many ways you can complain about the same damn thing!

When I was a teen, I had very little respect for law enforcement or the "establishment" in general. Gloucester cops were corrupt, Manchester's were naive and incompetent, Santa Barbara cops were animals looking for trouble, Isla Vista's had their hearts and heads in the right place but if push came to shove, they took orders from those who would think nothing of busting a few heads open. Now I have the utmost respect for police officers and what they do every day. Ya, there are a few bad apples in the mix, like everywhere in life, but for the most part these people are heroes. Not sure if this is just the natural maturing process or the "establishment" cleaning up their act. Either way it represents a major change in how I view things. Somehow, I went from "Winter in America" by Gil Scott-Heron to "Proud to be an American" by Lee Greenwood. Maybe it was because I started a family or maybe it was because of 9-11. So many things work their way into your thought process and gain traction over time. I am happier now than I was then.

I wonder when the right time will be for this book to see the light of day. Do I share it now or wait until I pass away? I think it will feel strange to put this out there. I exposed my soul in here. Gisele didn't learn anything from reading this that she didn't already know. She is my wife after all! What will my new (bonus) siblings think when they read this? Gisele thinks I should publish it. It seems pretentious to think my story would be worthwhile reading if you didn't know me to begin with. Some might get confirmation on some things they suspected. There will be some who will simply say "so what" after reading it. My friends in Magnolia may get a kick out of a few events, but some of them have already passed away. I don't think my story is so unusual. The fact that I wrote it down may be unusual. Not everyone does that!

When daydreaming, my thoughts race through wild and impossible scenarios to the point where they almost feel real. "I don't know why I go to extremes. Too high or too low, there ain't no in between." Credit Billy Joel. That's kind of me in a nutshell. Other songs I identify with are:

- The Boxer by Simon and Garfunkel
- Younger Generation by the Lovin' Spoonful
- What About Me by Quicksilver Messenger Service
- 40,000 Headmen by Traffic
- Little Bit of Me by Melainie

- I Talk to The Wind by King Crimson
- Me by Paula Cole
- Deliver Me by Sonjia Dada
- Easy to Slip by Little Feat
- That's Not Me by the Beach Boys
- I Just Wasn't Made for These Times also by the Beach Boys
- God only Knows ....Yes, another one by the Beach Boys
- I Don't Know Why by Shawn Colvin
- Daddy's Tune by Jackson Browne
- Groovin' Is Easy by Electric Flag
- We Should be Together by Jefferson Airplane
- Sea Child by Hot Tuna
- Am I in That Dream ...Paul Carrack
- Genesis by Jorma Kaukonan

My dad loved sports and played all of them. He also loved to ski (he taught local kids the basics at Stage Fort Park in Gloucester), raced bobsleds, and flew planes. He adored all things boats and had many over the years (and helped with the restoration of the schooner Adventure). He was a talented woodworker and carver. I learned a lot from him. I played football and baseball, and he went to every game, but he never saw his beloved Patriots win any of their Super Bowls or the Red Sox a World Series.... He also came up to NH to watch our son Aaron play hockey. Couldn't ask for a better dad.

Somehow, I survived the trappings around me despite myself. Whether it was by the mercy of God or pure luck, I am still here. We all make choices in selecting the path that weaves through our lives, I'm no different. It is only with hindsight I realize how far I've come and can give name to the obstacles that steadfastly blocked my way. The psychology at work is beyond me, so I leave that to the experts. Was I happy? I'll answer with "I think so" for when I was younger... I sure appeared happy to any casual observer. I don't remember being depressed. I remember a happy home, lots of toys, a yard to explore, friends, our dog … yes, I was happy when I was young. Later in life maybe not so much. I masked any pain with my go to remedies. Music, drugs, and alcohol were all a means of escape for me. I immersed myself ("I don't know why I go to extremes!"). When I was a kid, my bike and boat offered me freedom as did hitchhiking a few years later. It seemed I was always trying to get away or escape. Now I feel found and grounded (thanks to Gisele), but I still use music and alcohol to relieve stress (I can now say I don't go to those same extremes anymore – thank God).

As an ONLY child, despite siblings, I was still a lonely child and craved acceptance wherever I could find it. Rejection hardened the wall around my emotional core. I was reluctant to openly show my deepest feelings in front of people. Compartmentalization became easier as time went on. My feelings emerge when I watch a movie, listen to music, or read a book (comics when I was a kid). I get caught up in the emotion when I'm alone. I guess I feel safer when no one is watching.

During my research for this book, I discovered my adoptive mother, Nancy, had been married before she married my dad! Newspapers.com revealed an engagement when she was sixteen followed by a wedding at seventeen. I couldn't find any record of a divorce and can only speculate why this was never made known to me. Often marriages at such a young age back then involved a pregnancy. Perhaps this is how she found out she couldn't bear children or was the reason they divorced or had the marriage annulled. I have no way of puzzling this out and wonder if the twins (my sisters) know any of this.

In 1951, my soon to be adoptive parents lived in West Hartford, CT, just fifteen minutes away from the home where my biological mother resided in the weeks leading up to my birth. They could have crossed paths at some point. How strange is that?

I had an email from Brian where he mentioned a podcast about the release of a collection of old Joni Mitchell songs. He referenced the meaning of "Little Green," a song I knew, but obviously not too well. I listened to it immediately and for the first time understood what it was about. I couldn't believe I never put the pieces together before. Anyone reading this should sit down and give it a listen. It will put tears in your eyes.

So many times, while writing this, my thoughts turned to Holly. In my mind I was never supposed to "be." I was an accident. Maybe a "whoops" or even worse. Holly was never "planned" either. We both were spared an abortion and eventually adopted, then through DNA matching, managed to meet. She has found siblings (on both sides of her biological parents) she didn't know existed, as did I. I am amazed at how similar our stories are.

Had I been raised a "Decker" would my mother have ever met Thomas Fitzgerald? Would there be a Brian, Annie, or Dave? The world is a better place with these wonderful people in it. I have a wealth of newfound family because I was given up for (or entrusted to) adoption. Thank-you Mom.

While searching for the "long lost paternal side of my family" I was stunned by the number of cousins who noted they too were adopted, or a parent or grandparent was. I highlighted these in red on the Excel spreadsheet I used to keep track of genetic matches. I plan on following up with them to see how their searches have progressed and offer any help I can.

I am eternally grateful for the efforts of my paternal cousins and their spouses in helping me unravel as much as I have on that branch of my tree. So many complete strangers offered to do research, share stories, make trips to libraries, provide pictures, or correct errors in my tree, because they cared. I joined Facebook because it was so much easier to stay in touch with them through social media. For the record, Facebook still leaves a lot to be desired.

In Closing

I enjoy writing fiction, though never good enough to publish anything. Writing this took far more effort and time than I expected it would. Well over two years to pen this far exceeded my most liberal expectation. Because it is factual, I had to validate the details as best I could. My timeline had to be as accurate as I could reconstruct it. This effort started as a list of random memories all needing to be arranged into some logical order. I had to make a choice between grouping like events regardless of time or attempt stringing things together in sequence (which is what I settled on). I found I made multiple duplicated accounts of the same event, which had to be merged and/or deleted. There were times I discovered more about something I'd already written, which required a review and rewrite to section. How much detail to include was another consideration. There were times when I was fixated on minor details and spent far too long researching a date or a place (many of the concerts fall into this category). Sometimes I couldn't find what I was looking for. I had scraps of information scattered everywhere in need of sorting then expanded upon. Often, I found writing this was more of a chore, and it brought out deep emotions I hadn't expected. I relived things I wanted to forget and took joy in remembering many special events too. I learned things I never expected (like my adoptive mother was married before she and my dad tied the knot). I reflected long on "relatives" from my past and did a little research on them just so I had some closure.

Not everything in my life is included in this book. You didn't find reference to old girlfriends or the first time I had sex, or what drugs I may have taken, but there is enough in here to give you some idea. So many of the things we did as kids in Magnolia aren't here either; I couldn't put them in any kind of order. Suffice it to say we were wild as kids. We took crazy risks, and we covered a lot of ground (and water!). Magnolia does something to me whenever I visit. Memories come flooding back, though the town has changed so much. They (my memories) bring a smile to me whenever I need one. Multimillion dollar homes and condos are everywhere now. The wealthy have discovered the jewel I grew up in. They can have the location, but they will never have the spark we shared when we were young.

There is no point in detailing my political views on anything either. Is it important to know who I voted for in any given election? It shouldn't matter what I think, that's personal. I don't like or dislike a person because they agree or disagree with me. I believe I have the capacity to listen, then analyze before taking a stand on any issue. Like most people, your politics are shaped over time then tempered by the personal experiences and circumstances which revolve around you. I don't believe in everything the same way I did when I was 20. Suffice it to say I was an active teenager. Leaving home at an early age exposed me to things I otherwise may never have experienced. I was adventurous, certainly curious, bold, often fearless, occasionally reckless, at times rebellious, and a touch mischievous. I was always searching for something I couldn't quite explain, much less grasp. I had things to prove to myself and others, and I did them.

Looking back, I have few regrets as these are the things that shaped me. I was fortunate enough to have been given a solid foundation to build from when I was a child. I owe this to my father and grandmother primarily, but it was reinforced by the families of my friends as they had similar values. Living in a small town like Magnolia also made a difference. I truly wonder how many places still exist that could ever compare with that experience.

I never wish for things to have been different. If they had, I would have missed out on so much. I do wish I had met my mother and known the circumstances she and my father shared which ultimately led to my birth. I'm sure that is quite a story. I can't help but think of Holly as I'm writing this. She and I share a similar narrative and I'm saddened by the fact I didn't know her while she was growing up. I'm so thankful we have finally connected and become a part of each other's life. Seems like I've come full circle.

I made a lot of friends along the way. Some are now gone. Some are out of touch. Others come and go at various times. New friends continue to emerge as do my newfound cousins! I have so many! Susan and Dick have surprised me throughout this journey. I feared letting them know how I felt about searching for nothing. They had figured me out long before I did. I believe Gisele is in the same category. She intuitively knew I was a little broken at my core. She was always there to encourage me to learn more or try again whenever I hit a wall. She went to adoptee meetings with me and was there when I went to Hartford looking for more answers. She experienced the ups and downs of searching and I probably wouldn't have stuck with it had it not been for her support. I love her so very much!

The time has come for us to pause
And think of living as it was
Into the future we must cross (must cross)
And I'd like to go with you
And I'd like to go with you

You say I'm harder than a wall
A marble shaft about to fall
I love you dearer than them all (them all)
So let me stay with you
So let me stay with you

And as we walked into the day
Skies of blue had turned to grey

I might have not been clear to say (to say)
I never looked away
I never looked away

And though I'm feeling you inside
My life is rolling with the tide
I'd like to see it be an open ride
Along with you
Going along with you

The time we borrowed from ourselves
Can't stay within a vaulted well
And living turns into a lender's will
So let me come with you
And let me come with you

And when we came out into view
And there I found myself with you
And breathing felt like something new
Along with you
Going along with you

.... Jorma Kaukonan

If I had to sum everything up, I'd say I had a good life. There certainly was an element of intense longing which lingered throughout my childhood and well beyond. I think this served to magnify the overwhelming feeling of happiness connecting with my biological family. Seeing my own children born was huge to me as they were my first blood relatives. Seeing another generation in my grandkids is so heartwarming and amazing. I'm scared to think what my life would have been like without Gisele. The best things for me happened after I met her. Connecting with Brian, Annie, and Dave was something I never dreamed would happen and through them I have learned so much about where I come from. There isn't enough time left in my life to learn it all. The physical similarities and interests we share are pleasantly astounding. I have been blessed many times over.

After experiencing so many setbacks firsthand in my search, I remember being guarded to some extent as to how much of me I would let show. There was a fear deep down the tides could turn and suddenly I would be odd man out again. Specifically, I was concerned over my perception of my mother and the potential for conflict due to my political views. Families have been ripped apart by opposing perspectives on far more trivial things. It took me a couple of years to broach the subject with Brian. I told him I had been worried I might cross a line at some point and lose the acceptance I have come to know and value so much. He told me flat out we were brothers and there was no line I could cross that would ever change that. This put me into a place I had never been before. Pent up fears instantly melted away like butter on a hot skillet.

I have written emails with tears of joy in my eyes and read others with different tears blurring my vision. I had shaky hands while typing, which required numerous spell-check corrections, not to mention sending emails without the attachments noted in the text. The excitement I've felt is so powerful and satisfying it is difficult to articulate. I may have never known my biological father, but I certainly knew who my dad was. He was the greatest man I knew, and I have such a splendid library of colorful memories. We were close, as close as a son could be to his dad.

If you read through all of this, I guess you were my target audience. I find it more than a little ironic on the morning of February 28, 1953 (the day after I came into this world) Cambridge University scientists Watson and Crick determined the structure of DNA was a double-helix polymer, or a spiral of two DNA strands, each containing a long chain of monomer nucleotides, wound around each other. According to their findings, DNA replicated itself by separating into individual strands, each of which became the template for a new double helix, the molecule containing human genes (Credit: History.com). It was their discovery that ultimately allowed me to unite with my biological family after decades of blind alleys, misinformation, stonewalling and outright lies. DNA is a wonderous thing. I have roots going back to the Mayflower and a host of interesting family members who are eager to share their histories with me. This has literally been the journey of a lifetime. It's not over yet, but this book has to come to a close at some point.

I hope you learned something that made you pause to think or consider the reason behind the things I hold dearest. Books and covers do not always go together. I think back to what I know about my dad growing up and realize it's mostly little bits and pieces of stories I heard around dinner tables with my relatives. What I know of my biological mother is a combination of research (newspapers etc.) and stories conveyed from my siblings. What I would be fascinated to learn isn't recorded anywhere. As for my biological father, it is again research, speculation, and hearsay. There is so much I don't know. Hopefully, this book will give my children a better understanding of who I am, a sense of the things that matter to me, and why.

I've visited New York twice so far to spend time with my siblings. I am at peace knowing where I belong now. I see joy on Gisele's face for me too. The kids all have a connection to a family they grew up never knowing. There are faces and names and stories to tell filled with laughter and hugs. There is blood connecting everyone. We keep discovering things we do the same way or interests we have in common. One thing that runs deep is our shared connection to music from my mother on through the generations. I love looking at the stars at night and recall as a kid, knowing the names of the constellations and where they were in the sky. I learned from Annie and Brian that our mother was also fascinated with the night sky. We all share a love of the water and being outdoors. Something my siblings shared which I found stunning was the comparison between the information we dug up during our search about our mother and the woman who raised them. It seemed like they were two different people to them.

Whatever scars I carried from my youth, were healed when I met my family. If you are reading this and have considered searching, I cheer you on. It is getting easier now. You may or may not have an experience like mine, but you will understand more about yourself by going through the process and you will find answers to questions you kept secreted away for so long. It is worth it. Never give up!

I wish there was a summary like this for the life of my dad, and naturally, my biological parents. Writing is a great outlet. You don't have to be grammatically correct or possess impeccable punctuational prowess to get your point across. You do need time and it does take effort and commitment. In the end you just might have something your kids will enjoy reading. This is dedicated to them.... I love you all so much.

Now, when it is all over
And I become a seed
They'll plant me in the universe
Where the balance gotta be
Now, I don't mind the dyin', no
It's the way it's gotta be
But I hope I leave behind
Just a little bit of me
A little bit of me

.... Melanie

From colored threads is a tapestry made.

DANIEL STEDFAST

The End

Made in United States
North Haven, CT
27 March 2023

34584774R00183